AFTER THE HURRICANE

AFTER THE HURRICANE

LINKING RECOVERY TO SUSTAINABLE DEVELOPMENT IN THE CARIBBEAN

Philip R. Berke and Timothy Beatley

THE JOHNS HOPKINS UNIVERSITY PRESS
BALTIMORE AND LONDON

Published in cooperation with the Center for American Places, Harrisonburg, Virginia

06 05 04 03 02 01 00 99 98 97   5 4 3 2 1

The Johns Hopkins University Press
2715 North Charles Street
Baltimore, Maryland 21218-4319
The Johns Hopkins University Press Ltd., London

Library of Congress Cataloging-in-Publication Data
will be found at the end of this book.

A catalog record for this book is available from the British Library.

ISBN 0-8018-5624-8

FRONTISPIECE: Satellite view of Hurricane Diana taken three days before it struck the North Carolina Coast in 1984 (Advisory Committee on the International Decade for Natural Disaster Reduction 1989).

CONTENTS

FIGURES AND MAPS

MAPS

TABLES

PREFACE AND ACKNOWLEDGMENTS

DURING THE 1980S, THE CARIBBEAN WAS HIT WITH DEVASTATING NATural disasters: hurricanes, volcanic eruptions, violent floods. These catastrophic events made attention-grabbing headlines on the evening news, but what happened after the cameras left? What was the impact of the vast amount of aid distributed to these disaster-stricken people and their communities? What was the effect of international and domestic aid from governments and private, nonprofit organizations that rushed representatives to the scene?

This book is about events that unfold beyond the scrutiny of press and television cameras. It is about the struggle of ordinary Caribbean people who act together to deal with natural disasters and with the massive infusion of postdisaster aid that is too frequently imposed on them. In an era of earth summits, declarations of international natural disaster reduction, and increasing global environmental awareness, these Caribbean people are vital to understanding how to make a link between disaster recovery and sustainable development.

This research originates in our prior studies on natural hazard avoidance strategies through land use planning and environmental design. Our focus is to improve the theoretical understanding of collective response through planning for potentially catastrophic disasters. Another motivation is to improve the understanding of how to build the capacity of local governments to undertake predisaster mitigation. Throughout the world, areas of high natural hazard are experiencing intense urbanization, and the need to safeguard people and property is crucial.

Our focus is postdisaster recovery, which has received the least attention of the four phases of the disaster policy cycle: predisaster mitigation, emergency preparedness, emergency response, and recovery. While the understanding of how and why communities recover from disasters is of crucial importance, we also explore the opportunities offered by the disaster recovery period to strengthen the capacity of local institutions to facilitate long-term social, economic, and physical development. We are most interested in how the massive amounts of aid brought into devastated areas can be used to build and support local capacity to carry out long-term development initiatives that go beyond immediate recovery needs. Can aid and recovery programs be redirected away from short-term relief, which has little linkage to local roles and capacity, toward sustainable development?

Jamaica was struck by Hurricane Gilbert in 1988. Antigua, Montserrat, and St. Kitts and Nevis were devastated by Hurricane Hugo in 1989. Our field research in these four Caribbean islands states took place over a three-year period, 1989 through 1991. Our research also included a survey of 240 households in disaster-stricken areas of St. James Parish and St. Thomas Parish in Jamaica. The survey allowed us to evaluate the impacts of a nationwide rebuilding initiative on household recovery strategies and mitigation practices in parishes with different political and socioeconomic conditions.

We single out a few individuals who were crucial in making this research happen. Franklin McDonald, former director of the Pan Caribbean Disaster Preparedness and Prevention Project in Antigua, helped in many ways with our field research and with our general education in disaster recovery issues in the Caribbean. Jeremy Collymore, the current director, was a constant source of advice and guidance throughout this study. Steven Hodges of the Construction Resource and Development Centre was our guide and teacher in his native country of Jamaica. If we do no more than share with readers the vision and wisdom of these people, we have accomplished something worthwhile.

Jennifer Worrell, currently disaster management specialist with the U.S. Agency for International Development in Kingston, Jamaica, was our research assistant in Antigua, Montserrat, and St. Kitts. She spent countless hours during the summer of 1991 helping us arrange interviews with local people who were on the frontlines during the aftermath of Hurricane Hugo. We also thank Vasu, a Jamaican taxicab driver with an intimate knowledge of the culture and the rough terrain of his native St. Thomas Parish in Jamaica. Many other special individuals and organizations throughout the Caribbean helped us with the research for this book. We cannot possibly mention them all, but we are most grateful.

In the United States, the Hazard Reduction and Recovery Center of Texas A&M University provided institutional support for much of the writing of this book. In particular, we wish to thank Dennis Wenger, director of the center, for his intellectual stimulus and for arranging institutional support for the research and writing of this book.

This book would not have been possible without financial support. We are grateful to Phillipe Boullé, of the former United Nations Disaster Relief Organization, who helped arrange funding for investigating the recovery process in the eastern Caribbean after Hurricane Hugo. We applaud Mr. Boullé's vision of the need for evaluating and monitoring external aid programs. We are also appreciative of the support provided by the National Science Foundation, which allowed us to conduct the postdisaster household survey in Jamaica. We also thank the National Science Foundation for its funding and express special appreciation to William Anderson for his advice, patience, and administrative support. However, the opinions, findings, conclusions, and recommendations expressed in this book are those of the authors and do not necessarily reflect the views of the funding institutions.

We also thank Rutherford H. Platt, professor of geography and planning law at the University of Massachusetts, who served as the peer reviewer for Johns Hopkins University Press. He gave a thoughtful critique, and as a result, the book is a considerable improvement over that early version. Thanks, also, to George F. Thompson, president of the Center for American Places, Harrisonburg, Virginia, and to all the talented professionals at the Johns Hopkins University Press who have made possible the publication of this book.

We acknowledge two academic journals for permitting us to include here major parts of previous publications. Sage Publications permitted us to use portions of an article published in the *Journal of Planning Literature* 9:370–82 (1995) (copyright © 1995 by Sage Publications), and Taylor and Francis allowed us to publish portions of an article in *Coastal Management* 21:1–23 (1993) (copyright © 1993 by Taylor and Francis).

All of these individuals and organizations have had a major influence in the material included in this book, and we are deeply appreciative of their assistance.

At the time this book went to press, Montserrat was experiencing a catastrophic series of volcanic eruptions over an 18-month period during 1996–97. Most of the island's population had been relocated to other parts of the Caribbean. The capital city of Plymouth was buried under volcanic ash and was entirely evacuated. The long-term prospects for full or even partial recovery are bleak. Nevertheless, these traumatic events do not detract from the lessons learned from the post–Hurricane Hugo recovery experiences reported in this chapter.

AFTER THE HURRICANE

1 NATURAL DISASTERS

A GLOBAL PROBLEM

WORLDWIDE, NATURAL HAZARDS HAVE INDUCED CATASTROPHIC LOSSES. From 1960 to 1990 natural disasters in the Caribbean and Latin American regions alone have caused 180,000 fatalities, caused more than US $54 billion in property damage, and disrupted the lives or more than 100 million people by destroying their housing (OAS 1990). Reconstruction in the wake of disasters can be financially devastating, as losses consume vast amounts of the limited available capital, significantly reducing resources for new investment. The adverse effects on employment, balance of trade, and foreign indebtedness can be felt for years.

Poverty is the primary root of vulnerability to natural hazards in developing countries. Although the incidence of major hazardous events has not increased in these countries, the magnitude of losses is rising dramatically (UNDRO 1991). Underdevelopment, environmental degradation, and rapidly expanding populations severely constrain the ability of these countries to cope with natural hazards. Too often, institutional and policy changes that integrate sustainable development measures to prevent or reduce future loss and human suffering are not made during rebuilding.

Disaster specialists increasingly emphasize that the recovery period offers an opportunity to strengthen local organizational capacity to facilitate long-term social, economic, and physical development. Under this approach external aid can be used to build and support local organizations to be more effective in carrying out sustainable development initiatives that endure long after a disaster. Such initiatives not only mitigate damage and distribute aid equitably, they also reinforce local capacity to resolve such problems as deficient affordable housing for the

poor, deforestation practices that induce watershed erosion and flooding, the occupation of landslide-prone hillsides by the poor, and deteriorated or nonexistent public infrastructure (water, sewer, roads). This
approach assumes that aid recipients become active participants rather
than helpless victims. Citizens are empowered to define their goals, to
control resources, and to undertake self-directed development initiatives. However, the prevailing approach of aid and recovery programs
emphasizes short-term relief, with little linkage to sustainable development concerns, local roles and capacities, and diverse social, economic,
and cultural conditions (Harrell-Bond 1986; Oliver-Smith 1990). It pre-
sumes that communities and citizens are helpless without aid; they are
seen as having limited capacity either to cope with losses or to participate effectively in redevelopment initiatives. Every year, however, relief budgets climb and multinational humanitarian organizations pro-
liferate in response to media appeals to save yet another population of
"helpless victims."

What happens after the cameras leave? What is the impact of the vast
sums of money spent? What is the effect of the work of the aid organizations propelled into the field? To whom are they accountable? Too
often, opportunities for using emergency relief for sustainable development initiatives have been missed. While the motivations of the givers
are honorable, disaster responses in the form of emergency relief often
do not support sustainable development and, worse, sometimes subvert
it. Not until recently has it been generally recognized that disasters and
development are closely connected. The International Decade for Natural Disaster Reduction, which is sponsored by the United Nations,
does place a high priority on hazard disaster relief and recovery in the
context of development. Development agencies of national governments,
multinational organizations like the World Bank, and private business
groups like the International Chamber of Commerce are increasingly
treating development as a continuum that incorporates short-term disaster relief and long-term recovery strategies.

This book is concerned with local disaster recovery efforts, how such
efforts influence prospects for enhancing sustainable development, and
the way external donor organizations provide aid to developing countries. The focus is on the four island states of Antigua, Jamaica, Montserrat, and St. Kitts and Nevis in the Caribbean region. These four states
experience widespread poverty, and the people and the governments are
engaged in a sustainable development process. More specifically, using
data from in-depth local case studies and a household survey from two

particularly destructive natural disasters, Hurricane Gilbert in 1988 and Hurricane Hugo in 1989, we seek to answer the following questions.

1. How can disaster recovery strategies achieve natural hazard mitigation, while at the same time promoting economic development?
2. How can all people, particularly the poor, be assured fair access to the benefits of mitigation and economic development?
3. How can local people meaningfully participate in formulating policies for aid distribution, disaster mitigation, and economic development?
4. How can external aid organizations (government and nongovernment) support local participatory initiatives? These and related questions constitute the substance of the research reported here.

LOSSES TO NATURAL HAZARDS

Systematic record keeping on disaster loss in developed countries is sketchy at best, but it is almost nonexistent in developing countries. Nevertheless, several studies have attempted to assess global losses by making use of a wide variety of sources from government compilations, scientific publications, and media accounts (e.g., Glickman and Golding 1992; Havlick 1986; Mitchell 1989; OAS 1990; Tomblin 1982). The consensus of these studies is that every year millions of people suffer from disasters that exact increasingly high tolls in loss of life and damage to the built environment. The annual rate of deaths from natural disasters rose sharply in the 1970s compared to the previous decade and continued to increase during the 1980s.[1] By the late 1980s the average annual global death rate exceeded 130,000 (Mitchell 1989). However, while the worldwide death toll is growing, it is falling in developed countries: between the 1960s and 1980s the mean annual death toll due to natural hazards declined by 75 percent in developed countries like Japan and the United States but increased by more than 400 percent in developing countries like India and Kenya (Mitchell 1992; Nanjira 1991).

There is also consensus that economic loss is increasing in both developed and developing countries, though it is disproportionately greater for developing countries. Mitchell (1989), for example, examined selected

---

1. Deaths are the best indicator of loss, particularly when comparing disaster losses between developed and developing countries. Mitchell's (1989) detailed study of global losses to natural disasters finds that, historically, deaths are the most consistently recorded type of loss throughout the world, and information about deaths often constitutes the only loss data available after disasters.

Asian Pacific Rim countries and found that mean annual economic losses due to floods and hurricanes (or cyclones) increased by 26 percent in Japan and 69 percent in South Korea between the 1960s and the 1980s but by 157 percent in India and 1,200 percent in the Philippines. Estimated annual losses from floods and hurricanes in the United States are expected to rise by 63 percent between 1970 and 2000 (Petak and Atkisson 1982), but such losses are expected to rise by more than 200 percent in Latin America and the Caribbean over the same period (OAS 1990).

Moreover, the proportion of loss is far more important than absolute numbers in examining distinctions among countries. For example, the economic costs of disasters in poor countries often exceeds 3–4 percent of the gross national product (ESCAP 1983; Mitchell 1989). In economically vulnerable East African countries, including Ethiopia, Mozambique, Sudan, Tanzania, and Uganda, the costs exceeded 20 percent of GNP at various times during the 1980s (Nanjira 1991). In contrast, the US$24 billion loss from the 1992 Hurricane Andrew disaster in southern Florida, which was at the time the costliest disaster in the history of the

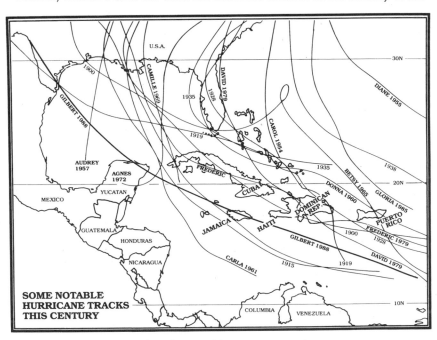

MAP 1. Hurricane tracks, the Caribbean, twentieth century (courtesy of Froglets Publications).

United States, represents an almost undetectable proportion of the nation's $6 trillion economy. The loss thus has less to do with the scope of the physical impact than with its relative proportion to the population and economy involved. A likely explanation for the upward trend in loss levels in developing countries is the substantial rise in world population and the increasing vulnerability of economically impoverished people. In its first annual *World Disasters Report* the International Federation of Red Cross and Red Crescent Societies (1993) indicated that in 1980 about 100 million people were affected by major disasters. By 1990, this figure reached 311 million, and by the year 2000 half a billion people—or 8 percent of the world's population by then—will be affected.[2]

Population growth, increasing urbanization, shortages of low-cost, low-risk land, and economic hardships mean that people in developing countries are often forced to migrate to marginal land, such as hazardous floodplains, steep ravines, or overcrowded, hazard-prone sites. Government proposals for relocation, building codes, or other risk-reducing measures could be politically explosive. Moreover, during the aftermath of a disaster there is an urgent need to replace damaged structures at the lowest possible cost. Spending sums to prevent a possible future disaster is less compelling, especially in the face of bleak economic conditions and the high cost of borrowing money, even from international development institutions. Further exacerbating the problem is the common misperception about who bears the greater financial burden of disaster losses. Representatives of international aid organizations usually believe that outside aid covers the greater portion of the costs. Cuny's (1983) assessment of who pays shows that the financial outlays of disaster-stricken developing countries almost always far exceed outside donations. Indeed, Cuny contends that the already fragile social services of host countries typically cover 60–70 percent of the costs, with aid defraying the remainder.

The Caribbean region is particularly vulnerable to natural disasters: hurricanes, earthquakes, landslides, floods, and volcanoes. Indeed, one of the deadliest volcano tragedies ever recorded occurred on the island of Martinique in 1902, leaving forty-thousand dead. Hurricanes, however, have been the most destructive natural disaster in recent history (see map 1). Table 1.1 indicates that between 1983 and 1989 the Carib-

---

2. The study includes in its definition of *disaster* droughts and civil strife as well as the more traditional hazards such as floods, hurricanes or cyclones, and earthquakes.

TABLE I.I. Selected Natural Hazard Events, the Caribbean

Country or Area	Year	Event Type	Number of Fatalities	Population Left Homeless (thousands)	Economic Losses (millions/$US)	International Assistance (millions/$US)
Antigua & Barbuda	1983	Drought	0	75		0.4
Eastern Caribbean	1989	Hurricane Hugo	21	50		11.7
Haiti	1988	Hurricane Gilbert	54	870	91	3.3
Jamaica	1986	Floods	54	40	76	3.4
	1988	Hurricane Gilbert	49	810	1,000	102.4
Nicaragua	1988	Hurricane	120	300	400	

Source: Adapted from OAS (1990).

bean region sustained more losses from hurricanes than from any other natural hazard, with approximately two million people left homeless and $1.5 billion in economic losses. In terms of value of damages from hurricanes and tropical storms, the Caribbean region ranks among the highest in the world (OAS 1990).

Thus a key concern for this book is the link between poverty and vulnerability to a disaster. The issue of reducing poverty and placing disaster recovery in the context of sustainable development must be addressed if loss of life and property is to be reduced and the capacity to recover from devastating events is to be improved. The underlying assumptions about disaster recovery, about how disaster-stricken people react, and about the role that aid plays in recovery (and by implication, in development itself) are examined.

SUSTAINABLE DEVELOPMENT AND NATURAL HAZARDS
What Is Sustainable Development?

The concept of sustainable development has evolved to focus attention on the role of resource consumption and environmental protection in economic development. Geographer Kenneth Mitchell, a leading scholar in hazards research, argues that sustainable development is potentially an important concept for the natural hazard field. He maintains that if the concept is properly implemented, losses can be dramatically reduced and considerable long-term community development benefits can be achieved. The following is an elaboration of this point of view.

Although there are many definitions, the report of the United Nations World Commission on Environment and Development (often called the Brundtland Commission, after its organizer, Gro Harlem Brundtland, the former prime minister of Norway) provides the most widely used definition by indicating that sustainable development is "development that meets the needs of the present without compromising the ability of future generations to meet their own needs" (WCED 1987, 1). To ensure that present and future needs are met requires a comprehensive strategy that recognizes economic development and environmental protection as interdependent activities. While environmental degradation from the exploitation of natural resources severely limits long-term development, wise use of resources and safeguarding the benefits provided by healthy ecosystems (e.g., wetland and sand dune systems that mitigate flooding) can spur long-term development. Sustainable development thus legitimizes the rationale for a comprehensive conservation and disaster management strategy.

Since the mid-1980s, the sustainable development concept has increasingly been embraced by the worldwide environmental movement, consisting of thousands of government and nongovernment organizations (NGOs, in United Nations parlance).[3] These groups represent many diverse interests, who do not necessarily agree about the meaning of sustainable development. As Mitchell Redclift suggests, "sustainable development has been a rallying cry for different groups: environmental scientists, economists, and Greens, in support of quite different intellectual paradigms and political ideologies. Although sustainable development is a goal that everybody considers desirable, the absence of agreement about what exactly sustainable development means has led to contradictory expectations from policy" (cited in Mitchell 1992, 2).

Although sustainable development is clearly an imprecise concept, it is becoming popular among opinion leaders and decisionmakers around the world. Many analysts recognize it as a powerful vehicle for change (Ascher and Healy 1990; Young 1990). The world's attention, for example, was focused on sustainable development as the foundation concept

3. For a detailed discussion of the evolution of the sustainable development concept and the political dynamics behind it, see Young (1990).

at the recent United Nations Conference on Environment and Development in Brazil (June 1992), otherwise known as the Earth Summit. *Agenda 21*, the action agenda for the twenty-first century adopted at the summit (Sitarz 1993), made evident that sustainable development has become widely accepted as a general policy by many national governments, by multinational organizations like the World Bank and the Organization of American States, and by an increasing number of large private corporations and business interest groups. National conservation strategies have been adopted by developed countries like Canada, Germany, Japan, and New Zealand plus developing countries like Costa Rica, Nepal, and Zambia. The International Chamber of Commerce has prepared a Sustainable Development Charter, which several multinational corporations have signed. Companies like AT&T, Dutch Shell, McDonalds, and 3M have begun to modify some of their operations in accordance with the sustainable development concept. The head of the Overseas Development Council recently endorsed the "current thinking" that "environmental preservation does not have to be a tradeoff for the elimination of poverty in the Third World. Instead, integration of these twin issues will be central to the global agenda of the 1990s" (Sewell 1989).

Moreover, the focus of many sustainable development advocates goes beyond the maintenance and preservation of the natural resource base and ecological systems. Citizens and organizations in developed and developing countries have increasingly called for the alleviation of poverty, small-scale and locally controlled development projects, and sustained increases in per capita income necessary for social progress and long-term stability of ecological systems (Ascher and Healy 1990). A position statement issued by a group of NGOs during the 1989 World Bank Group annual meeting in Washington, D.C., reflects this multiple agenda. The statement indicates that the current state of global affairs, which "threatens the well-being of not just people, but all life" reflects not only the "lack of proper maintenance of life-giving ecological systems" but also "lack of equal distribution of the world resources—both among and within nations." The statement expresses concern with the "nature of the economic development process that is directly responsible for a deepening poverty, severe environmental degradation, the further marginalization of women, children, indigenous people, and other vulnerable groups, and in many instances the deterioration of basic political, economic, cultural, and social rights" (Anonymous 1989, 9).

Commenting on this underlying environmental movement, Mitchell notes that, "Obviously something important is afoot here. It is more than just good management and wise administration. It also involves the desire for fundamental changes in the way our institutions operate and the way we conduct our individual lives. Sustainable development is both a moral concept and a managerial one" (Mitchell 1992, 2). Indeed, an effort is under way to operationalize the broad sustainable development concept into practical management tools that are tailored to the needs of different economic sectors and institutions. It is increasingly guiding agricultural policy and, to a lesser extent, urban infrastructure and national housing policies.

Sustainable Development and Natural Disaster Reduction

It is easy to understand how several underlying principles of sustainable development, as stipulated in *Agenda 21*, can be applied to natural hazard issues, particularly issues associated with disaster recovery.[4] One principle is *balancing needs and limits*. All members of society have certain minimal rights to basic health and safety needs essential to human development. Postdisaster construction and land use policies must recognize that natural disasters are recurrent events and are part of natural ecological cycles. For example, earthquakes occur periodically as a result of plate tectonic movements, and hurricanes are spawned by atmospheric heat buildups. Without recognition of natural forces as limiting factors to redevelopment, catastrophic and unnecessary loss of life and property can take place. A second principle is that of *precautionary action*. Where there are potential threats to development from natural hazards, scientific uncertainty concerning prediction of occurrence and degree of vulnerability should not postpone cost-effective structural strengthening and hazard avoidance measures during rebuilding (see figure 1.1). If all sectors of society and the economy were to practice this principle, the stimulus for improved hazard management that now comes disproportionately from the public sector or government would be fundamentally changed. Companies and other institutions would take many of the appropriate risk reduction measures themselves.

A third sustainable development principle is *intergenerational equity*. Postdisaster reconstruction that does not account for future natural disasters represents an inefficient investment of recovery aid that

4. This discussion on how principles of sustainable devlopment can be applied to natural hazards is adapted from Mitchell (1992, 2).

FIGURE I.I. Devastation along the Mexican Caribbean Coast, typical of high-income resort development throughout the Caribbean Islands (courtesy of the National Research Council).

might otherwise have been available for development investments. Future generations would thus have less available capital to invest. For example, housing investments in hazardous locations might be permitted when there is reasonable assurance that rebuilt structures could survive for several generations. The commonly followed alternative is to inefficiently use recovery aid funds to rebuild devastated areas to predisaster conditions in the face of recurrent natural disasters. A corollary principle is *reduction of poverty*. Disaster recovery efforts must strive for equity within generations, which leads to improved living conditions of the poor. Public rebuilding policies should provide for sufficient low-cost, low-risk land for high-density residential use, and recovery aid should lead to reconstructed communities that have sufficient affordable housing stocks to meet minimum building safety standards.

Two other sustainable development principles are *responsible regionalism* and *the polluter (or the culpable) pays*. Sustainable development can involve attempts to prevent rebuilding incompatible with surrounding or adjacent individual properties or with the interests of the region as a whole. Poor rebuilding practices that do not incorporate structural strengthening and that thus might cause damage to other nearby structures from windblown debris during future storms exemplifies an absence of responsible regionalism. All harm, however, is not avoidable. For example, needed upstream agriculture improvements for food or timber production might cause some additional downstream flooding. The casual actor (community or individual) must then bear the responsibility (financial and otherwise) for the harm and must assume corrective or compensatory actions.

A final principle is *participation*. Sustainable development involves the basic assumption of political equality of all concerned citizens and groups during disaster recovery. Each individual or group in a community must be provided with a morally equal opportunity in shaping disaster recovery. In particular, the full participation of the poor and other underrepresented groups is essential to achieve sustainable development. The creativity, ideals, and knowledge of local people who do not have strong formal ties with business and political authorities are essential to integrating sustainability into the recovery process.

The importance of considering the potential impact of natural disasters in devising strategies dealing with sustainable development has been recognized by the United Nations General Assembly in adopting a resolution declaring the 1990s the International Decade for Natural Disaster Reduction (IDNDR). The resolution stipulates that each member nation is to establish a national program for a decade of hazard reduction. It also emphasizes that the greatest challenge is to take advantage of the recent scientific and engineering advances to reduce the growing toll of natural disasters throughout the world. As stated in a recent report on Great Britain's role in the IDNDR, "while knowledge of ways whereby the impact of hazards can be mitigated is available in the developed world . . . the aim of the IDNDR is to foster systematic transfer to, and application of the relevant knowledge in, those countries and communities recognizably most at risk" (Royal Academy of Engineering 1993, 4).

Commenting on the relationship between natural hazards and sustainable development, the United Nations Scientific and Technical Committee urged adoption of the following text for the Earth Charter: "Repeatedly, hard-won development is set back years by natural environmental hazards which through inadequate planning, prevention, and preparedness become tragic disasters. Yet, the scientific, technical, and planning means exist to reduce losses substantially. To achieve these reductions, disaster prevention and preparedness must be recognized as an essential part of planning for sustainable development" (Hamilton 1992, 3). *Agenda 21* also gives attention to natural hazard reduction—and to disaster recovery, in particular. Postdisaster recovery policy statements, which are set forth in chapter 7 of the report, include: "redirecting inappropriate new development and human settlements to areas not prone to hazards" and supporting efforts at "contingency planning, with participation of affected communities, for postdisaster reconstruction and rehabilitation" (Sitarz 1993, 61–62).

In summary, the term *sustainable development* is so inclusive that it is possible to define it from the perspectives of a broad range of groups, including those concerned not only with environment but also with human progress, poverty alleviation, and the empowerment of excluded groups. Reflecting this multifaceted concern, sustainable development can be defined in the context of long-term disaster recovery as a process of development that achieves five interrelated and complementary goals:

1. Long-term economic development
2. Health and safety through recognizing that natural hazards pose an ecological limit to development
3. Distributional equity for current and future generations
4. The accountability of individuals (and communities) that harm others
5. The participation of all interest groups effected by recovery and development policies.

Sustainable development will be most successful if, during the recovery process, development initiatives are undertaken that recognize ecological limits, improve distributional equity, prevent or minimize harm to others, and promote participation. This book examines the extent to which these interrelated goals were achieved in several disaster recovery experiences in developing countries and identifies the key activities that local and external aid organizations undertook during the recovery process that explain this achievement. Such activities include assessment of damage and aid distribution by neighborhood associations and church groups, the support of small-scale recovery projects, and the use of field staff trained in community development by external organizations.

While the disasters offer opportunities to integrate long-term recovery with sustainable development initiatives, there are considerable political and institutional constraints to achieving such integration. One constraint is the limited, even nonexistent, influence that natural hazard issues exert on the shaping of sustainable development policies. Another constraint is the exclusion of sustainable development concerns by the international humanitarian aid delivery system, a vast network of emergency relief and development organizations. Further exacerbating matters is that these organizations have historically not acknowledged the need to become involved in long-term disaster recovery efforts.

THE EXCLUSION OF NATURAL HAZARDS FROM SUSTAINABLE DEVELOPMENT POLICYMAKING

Sustainable development is potentially important to the natural hazard field, and practitioners and researchers in the field should be involved in formulating and implementing sustainable development policies. Such involvement requires addressing problems like deforestation, soil erosion, famine, the loss of gene pools, and climate change as well as the more conventional natural hazards like inland floods, hurricanes, and earthquakes. Unfortunately, natural hazard issues currently have low visibility in the sustainable development debate. An examination by Mitchell (1992) of the documents in support of the Earth Summit revealed that only a few organizations—including a consortium of Pacific island countries, the United Nations High Commission for Refugees, the World Forum, the International Chamber of Commerce, and the Inter-American Development Bank—incorporate hazard reduction as a component of sustainable development. These organizations, however, are only a fraction of the hundreds of organizations involved in applying sustainable development principles.

Further, *Agenda 21* includes only a limited discussion of the role of sustainable development in natural hazard reduction (Sitarz 1993). *Agenda 21* is an eight-hundred-page, forty-chapter document and contains detailed discussions of how sustainable development principles are applied to a variety of issues (e.g., deforestation, biodiversity, and agriculture), but no chapter reviews the relationship between sustainable development and comprehensive hazard reduction and recovery efforts. Instead, the discussion is limited to specific hazards, such as drought and desertification. The most severe types of natural hazards, like earthquakes and hurricanes, are given limited, if any, attention. Natural hazards are often used only as indicators of nonsustainable development, as "proof that existing development practices are not sustainable and specters that menace our future if we don't mend our ways (e.g., greenhouse gases and global warming)" (Mitchell 1992, 4). Thus the role of hazard issues in the sustainable development debate is largely symbolic and has only limited impact on the shaping of sustainable development policies.

As a result of such low visibility, current characterizations of the need for natural hazard risk reduction are flawed. The rising incidence of natural disasters worldwide is commonly cited as an indicator of nonsustainable development—and the connection between disasters and development is too overwhelming to be ignored—but that does not mean that most or all natural disasters will disappear if we adopt sustainable development policies. Indeed, sustainable development is not necessarily safe development. In contemporary societies it is doubtful that improved development practices can completely prevent catastrophic events. Mitchell (1992) contends that some land uses and structures are too valuable and culturally significant to be abandoned or relocated. The capital cities of Mexico City and Wellington, New Zealand, are situated astride active seismic fault zones, and New Orleans and Venice will remain susceptible to flooding. These urban investments will require considerable protection in the foreseeable future.

Some observers contend that natural hazards should be considered not as a subset of sustainable development problems but as a separate set of problems that often overlap with sustainable development problems (Kriemer and Munasinghe 1991). In some cases, the tasks and interests of sustainable development advocates coincide with those concerned with natural hazards. The interests of those natural hazard groups involved both in mitigation through land use and development controls and in long-range disaster recovery are likely to be closely associated with the interests of sustainable development advocates: the actions of both groups are likely to reduce risk and enhance sustainable development. However, for interest groups concerned with emergency preparedness and response issues (e.g., disaster warning, search and rescue, evacuation, and sheltering), the relationship to sustainable development is less salient.

Thus even if sustainable development is successful, it will always be necessary to support institutions that deal with natural disasters, since they will continue to occur, even though with less frequency. Some of these institutions will be in concert with sustainable development, but others will not. Most of the attention of hazard management institutions is directed at coping with "routine disasters" (those that are recurrent and somewhat predictable), and since these disasters are likely to diminish if sustainable development is achieved, resources for sustainable development initiatives would be freed up (Mitchell 1992).

THE EXCLUSION OF SUSTAINABLE DEVELOPMENT
FROM THE HUMANITARIAN AID DELIVERY SYSTEM

The worldwide humanitarian aid delivery system has evolved since World War II into a vast network of donors that collect and channel resources to intervenor field organizations. The network can be broadly divided into two types of organizations: emergency relief organizations and development organizations. Harrell-Bond (1986, 16) appropriately characterizes these organizations as having assumed the role of the "conscience of the world." Their primary task is to work in the poorest reaches of the world and bring international attention to the plight of human suffering. These organizations have historically not acknowledged sustainable development in shaping their aid programs. Emergency relief organizations, most notably the International Red Cross or Red Crescent, consider disasters as isolated events that require unique, crisis-oriented, societal responses. Activities involving search and rescue for survivors, medical assistance, and provision of basic household goods (clothing, food, and blankets) and temporary sheltering are the dominant mode of response. Because disaster-stricken people are viewed as helpless victims, aid is distributed free, as a form charity.

Even though this aid may meet short-term needs, it does not address the underlying problem of disaster vulnerability in poor countries, which is caused by poverty and economic underdevelopment. In fact, there is considerable documentation that the influence of aid from emergency relief organizations can be counterproductive (Oliver-Smith and Goldman 1988; Oliver-Smith 1990; Woodrow and Anderson 1989). Aid recipients often adopt attitudes and behavior that impede their progress toward self-sufficiency. These negative responses—usually referred to as the dependency syndrome—are thought to develop when aid recipients are considered helpless, needing outsiders to plan for them and to take care of them. This assumption is the cornerstone of what Harrell-Bond (1986, 11) calls "starving child" appeals for funds by relief organizations (see figure 1.2). For example, a 1992 mailing of UNICEF letters, marked "urgent," was sent to homes (including the author's) throughout the United States stating that, "reports indicate that this is the worst drought of the century. Many countries in southern and eastern Africa are affected. The lives of 14 million children and women are at risk. Crops have been devastated, and the situation is expected to worsen. UNICEF has been providing assistance, but as the situation be-

FIGURE 1.2. Small child, wreckage of a building in background, after Hurricane Hugo (UNDRO 1989).

comes critical, more must be done. . . . Please make as generous a contribution as you can. Your help is urgently needed."

The primary objective of development organizations is economic growth and the alleviation of poverty. Historically, they have regarded disasters as nuisances and try to avoid becoming involved. Like sustainable development advocates, many development practitioners and researchers believe that development efforts spontaneously provide solutions to problems of natural hazards (Hagman 1984). The rationale is that as societies develop more resources will be available for detecting and delineating hazards, conducting potential loss assessments, and strengthening vulnerable structures. Development agencies are thus most concerned with improving the ability of poor countries to cope with the immediate and pressing challenges of poverty and underdevelopment. The argument has been made that to plan for an "unknown" disaster is a luxury that the poor countries of the world can ill afford (Havilick 1986). A request to protect residents from a fifty-year, or even a hundred-year, flood typically is given low priority on development organizations' agendas.

In the late 1970s, however, some disturbing trends began to emerge. Countries experiencing rapid development suddenly lost momentum when disasters struck. Resources for development often became scarce when they were siphoned off for recovery and reconstruction. At first, it was assumed that more disaster relief from developed countries was needed. In response, annual worldwide relief appropriations grew dramatically through the 1980s (World Bank 1990). Nevertheless, human and economic losses expanded dramatically during the same period. Why? The basic problem was the conceptual failure of both emergency and development organizations to link disasters and sustainable development. Emergency relief organizations do not address the underlying problem of disaster vulnerability in poor countries, nor do they deal with resolving problems of underdevelopment. Development agencies do not account for hazards in project investment decisions (World Bank 1990). Thus unrealistic estimates of project life expectancies and cost-benefit ratios are commonly made. The result is inefficient uses of development funds, which significantly reduce already scarce resources available for new investment.

Even worse, development projects often exacerbate the severity of disasters by inducing environmental degradation and a corresponding reduction in the capacity of ecosystems to mitigate potential disaster losses (UNDRO 1991; World Bank 1990). For example, during a heavy rain in the Dominican Republic, runoff caused by erosion from deforestation filled more than half the storage capacity of a newly built reservoir overnight (OAS 1990). The erosion was caused by a timber product extraction project that was backed by development funds from the World Bank and USAID (U.S. Agency for International Development). Throughout the 1970s and 1980s many similar projects were initiated in developing countries in Asia, Latin America, and the Caribbean to generate exports to help repay massive foreign debts. While these projects were designed to exploit the natural resource bases, they generally failed to account for the impacts of environmental degradation on potential disaster losses (World Bank 1990).

Assumptions about Humanitarian Aid

Foreign governments and aid contributors make assumptions about how emergency relief and development organizations should operate in the field. These assumptions are premised on the general perception that these organizations are not politicized and are neutral in their aid distribution. Indeed, the fundamental reason for the existence of these organizations is humanitarian. These assumptions exert significant influence on how aid programs are designed and carried out. They also have considerable impact on the prospects for incorporating the sustainable development concept into such programs. The following is an elaboration of the four assumptions, observed by Harrell-Bond (1986), that humanitarian organizations make about the people and countries they help and the responsibilities their organizations bear toward them.

One assumption is that disaster-stricken people and their communities constitute a problem, a burden, rather than an economic opportunity. Outsiders view these people as incapable of helping themselves, as needing outsiders to plan for them and to take care of them. Observing media portrayals of Ugandan refugees, Harrell-Bond (1986, 11) quotes Martin Barber's (director of the British Refugee Council) comments on posters produced by the United Nations High Commission for Refugees that depict refugees with "attitudes of submission or helplessness. They are waiting for something to happen. They are holding out their hands. The photographer was standing up and they were sitting down." Harrell-Bond further observes that, although some aid organizations are concerned about the public getting an overdose of these stark images that appeal for funds, "the nature of the contemporary . . . problem suggests that this form of marketing of refugees will continue."

A second assumption is that host government organizations are too weak, and that their personnel are insufficiently trained, to manage relief, recovery, and development projects. It follows from this assumption that outside field staff and administrative personnel are essential. It also follows from this assumption that host governments lack the capability to contribute to the aid programs developed by external organizations for disaster recovery. Some investigators maintain that this assumption has a substantial influence on the funding policies of foreign donor organizations, such as the United Nations High Commission for Refugees and government aid agencies of developed countries (Berke, Kartez, and Wenger 1993; Harrel-Bond 1986). They further contend that a countervailing view also influences the policy and administrative decisions of field staff personnel: that host governments are not weak or incompetent but, instead, are highly efficient at oppressing and exploiting the poor within their borders and that they are essentially corrupt. Thus for two mutually exclusive reasons foreign organizational staff view themselves as the most appropriate advocates for those in need of assistance. As a result, very few donor organizations (government and nongovernment) agree to give funds unilaterally to a host government.

Most funds are directed through nongovernment aid organizations or international government organizations.

A third assumption is that foreign aid organizations do not require accountability to host governments. Unlike the development field, in which projects must be negotiated between host governments and foreign experts, organizations involved with emergency relief and disaster recovery expect host governments to approve their plans without question (Lissner 1977). In essence, the control of aid is typically delegated by foreign donor organizations to humanitarian organizations operating in the host country. Moreover, the host government bureaucracy is commonly viewed as an obstacle to the free exercise of development assistance. For many so-called foreign experts, contact with the host government officials, particularly at the local level, is required only when there is a need for official approval in the form of a signature or when a crisis erupts that forces these outsiders to turn to the locals for assistance. As Karadawi (1983) observes, relations between aid organizational staff and host government officials are often characterized by mutual suspicion and distrust. As a result, the views and concerns of host officials and disaster-stricken people are not considered important and are not accounted for in the recovery or development project decisionmaking. Anderson and Woodrow (1989), Berke, Beatley, and Feagin (1993), and Lissner (1977) document how this process leads to misallocation of scarce resources and misapplication of aid.

The fourth assumption is that aid programs are designed to reflect the needs, concerns, and capabilities of the disaster-stricken people. On the contrary, many aspects of aid programs tend to reflect the needs of donors. For many aid organizations success is measured by the number of "victims" reached, the number of houses rebuilt, or the number of tons of aid distributed. Cuny (1983) contends that many organizations are "rated" by the public in terms of the amounts of material distributed in the shortest period of time. Commenting on the results of a postdisaster housing study, he argues that "intervenors consistently set higher priority on the number of housing units produced than on the contribution made to the building process" (130). Indeed, the artifact (or in this case, the number of houses) is viewed as the outcome of the program. Success is based on donor needs and not on the strengthening of local organizational capacity to undertake self-directed social, economic, and physical development. Another concern with this assumption is that the staffs of emergency relief and development organizations may be led to believe they need to have a separate and identifiable program to show their donors, becoming convinced that their way of operating is the only way, and refusing to cooperate with other organizations that do not strictly adhere to their way of doing things. The result is a greater potential for duplication of effort and for poor coordination in field efforts. Human suffering can only be prolonged by such conflict.

Any one of these assumptions may not be particularly serious, but together they can add up to a disaster recovery and development aid delivery system that is so distorted that outsiders justify and perpetuate their jobs at the expense of suffering people and communities. Such distortion poses severe constraints to disaster recovery initiatives. Thus this study of the long-term recovery process not only explains the way these obstacles can be overcome but also identifies conditions that facilitate the design of programs that integrate recovery with sustainable development.

DATA AND METHODS

This study relies on case studies of disaster recovery experiences in three island states of the Caribbean and on a survey of household responses during recovery. The case studies were designed to provide an in-depth understanding of the recovery responses of government and NGOs. The survey was designed to provide an overview of how households interact with government and nongovernment organizations in seeking resources for recovery. The survey data was supplemented with findings derived from on-site, open-ended interviews with householders and with key representatives of the organizations involved in household recovery. Data collection for the case studies and survey was guided by the conceptual framework presented in chapter 2.

The Case Studies

The case studies entailed detailed investigations of organizational behavior on Antigua, Montserrat, and St. Kitts and Nevis in the eastern Caribbean. These three study sites were selected based on several criteria. First, they were all struck by a single disastrous event—Hurricane Hugo in 1989 (see map 2). Time-dependent differences across the three case were thus minimized. Further, several internationally supported, regionwide, development and disaster planning programs with similar objectives and policies had been operating in the three study sites at the time Hugo struck. These similarities permit replication of the influence of these programs and thus enhance the generalizability (or external validity) of study findings (Yin 1984). Consequently, any differences among the cases are not due to these programs but rather to the cases themselves. Second, the sites selected all experienced moderate to severe damages. The presence of significant damage levels ensured that there was a minimal level of disaster recovery activity. Sites where damage was slight were avoided.

Third, the eastern Caribbean is part of a band of high mountains that experiences seismic activity and volcanoes, and hurricanes spawned off the African coast pass through the region. These hazards, together with deforestation and floods from frequent and heavy rainfalls, continually threaten the inhabitants of the study sites. Poverty is widespread, and people are particularly vulnerable to loss because they lack the resources to protect themselves against natural disasters. Fourth, these island states offer advantages for an analysis of recovery. Due to the work throughout the 1980s of the United Nations–sponsored Pan Caribbean Disaster Preparedness and Prevention Project, the entire region has been steadily improving its record of disaster impact and recovery. A number of disaster research and information centers have also been established, such as the Construction Resource and Development Centre in Kingston, Jamaica, and at centers at branch campuses of the University of

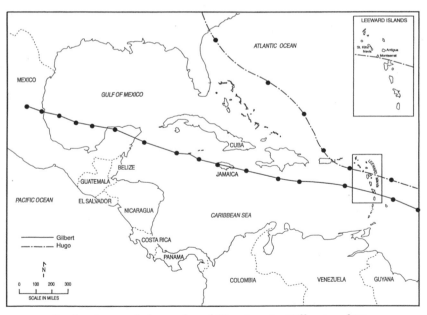

MAP 2. Study sites and the paths of Hurricanes Gilbert and Hugo.

West Indies on Barbados, Jamaica, and Trinidad. Thus this hazard-prone region, with its high number of disaster recovery initiatives, provides a valuable context for the analysis of long-term disaster recovery processes.

The case studies utilized several traditional data-gathering devices. The primary data was gathered through on-site, in-depth, face-to-face interviews with key informants involved in disaster management, recovery, and long-term development. Forty-five interviews were completed during the spring and summer of 1991—eleven on Antigua, seventeen on Montserrat, and seventeen on St. Kitts and Nevis. A snowball sampling technique was used to develop a list of informants who were key participants in the various phases of disaster recovery. The objective was to reach knowledgeable, influential people who were active participants in the disaster effort or who were in a position to objectively observe the activities of participants. Initial informants were identified based on a review of agency reports and disaster plans; these individuals were asked to identify others who should be interviewed, and thus the sample was expanded. The informants came from government agencies, foreign and domestic NGOs, and private businesses. Organizations represented national government planning, agriculture, public works, and community development and nongovernment emergency relief and development. Interviews were rich in information regarding the preimpact, postimpact, and recovery phases of disaster. They provided detailed data on the activities of government and nongovernment organizations. Interview guides were designed to identify the principal concerns about disaster recovery issues and specific recovery activities and to explore explanations of the successes and failures of the various recovery responses.

In addition to the interview data, documentary information was also gathered and analyzed. This material consisted of technical reports, disaster plans, after-action reports, newspaper coverage of the event, and published investigations.

The Survey Questionnaire

The household survey was conducted on Jamaica fifteen months after Hurricane Gilbert made landfall (December 1989). The survey was administered by the Construction Resource and Development Centre of Kingston. Two study sites were selected for the examination of disaster impacts and household responses. Parishes that were heavily damaged were first assessed, using available damage reports. Because the severe impact area covered most of the country, almost all metropolitan and rural areas were affected. The impact area also included a wide range of residential property types and socioeconomic characteristics, from squatter settlements inhabited by the poor scattered throughout the country to high-cost housing in Kingston and Montego Bay.

The two sites selected for interviewing were St. James Parish and St. Thomas Parish. No claim is made that these jurisdictions contain a representative sample of households in the disaster- stricken portion of Jamaica. However, they provide a sampling of geographic, political, and socioeconomic conditions. St. James Parish is located on the northwest coast and has a mixed agriculture- and tourism-based economy.[5] The majority of the population (157,100 in 1990) is urban (51.7 percent), as the parish contains the country's third largest city (Montego Bay, 1990 population 70,300). St. Thomas Parish is located on the southeast coast, its economy is primarily low-income agricultural, and its population (86,500 in 1990) is rural (25.8 percent urban; data from Jamaica Planning Institute 1990).The political circumstances in the two parishes are also quite different. At the time of the survey St. James was a stronghold of the political party in power (People's National Party), while St. Thomas was closely aligned with the opposition party (Jamaica Labour Party). We assumed that these contrasting conditions, as well as differences in the design of central government aid programs, affected the availability of resources for recovery, long-term responses to the disaster, and household attitudes toward government. For example, in St. James a strong economy, an urban population, and close alignments with the political party in power might have led to more resources for recovery assistance and reinforce positive attitudes toward government. On St. Thomas, a weak economy, an agricultural population, and no close alignment with the political party in power might have resulted in lower levels of resources for recovery and in negative evaluations and greater mistrust of government actions. Thus, the logic underlying the selection of these two sites was to determine the importance of these differing conditions in explaining household recovery responses.

Initially, Jamaican census estimates and maps were used to identify housing locations in accordance with the estimated socioeconomic sta-

5. St. James Parish, for example, has 6.2 percent of Jamaica's population but 41 percent of the country's motel rooms, while St. Thomas has 3.7 percent of the population with less than 1 percent of all hotel rooms. Also, St. James has only 4.7 percent of all farms in Jamaica compared to 9.1 percent for St. Thomas Parish (Jamaica Planning Unit 1990).

tus (SES) of their inhabitants. The SES estimation was then accomplished through direct observation of the extent and quality of public facilities and household facades as well as dwelling sizes, services, and type of construction. Utilizing a population breakdown scheme that reflects the national distribution of socioeconomic groups (Wint and Piersenne 1984, 79), five housing locations within each parish were then selected. For each housing location, households were chosen for the sample in proportion to socioeconomic group representation in the Jamaican population in general.[6]

Within each housing location the first household in the sample was selected randomly, and subsequent households entered the sample through use of an incremental number. Within households, respondents were selected for interviewing to satisfy the socioeconomic, gender, and age characteristics of the country. Two hundred and forty (240) households were interviewed, with 121 interviews in St. James and 119 in St. Thomas.

It was decided to use the national distribution of SES across study sites to minimize differences between the two sample household groups. While we wanted a range of household types typical of each site, there was more concern with comparability across sites. That is, it was not important that the sample be proportional across household type in each site, as long as the range of types were represented. As a result, there was some overrepresentation of the lower class in the sample for St. James and underrepresentation for St. Thomas. Our logic for maintaining comparability, however, was that because we knew social class was one of the most important theoretical variables in explaining household recovery (e.g., Bolin 1982; Bolin and Bolton 1986; Drabek and Key 1984), we wanted both parishes to have the same SES representation. Consequently, any differences between the parishes were due not to SES but rather to conditions in the parishes themselves.[7]

6. Areas surveyed in St. James Parish were Cornwall Gardens, Porto Bello, Unity Hall, Montego Hill, Bogue Heights, and Norwood. In St. Thomas Parish, the areas were Seaforth, Morant Bay, Nutts River, Lyssons, Port Morant, and Dalvey.

7. Survey results show no significant differences between parishes for six of eight household characteristics: sex, marital status, housing type, income, insurance, and level of damage. However, education and age were significantly different (chi-square p .01). A detailed discussion of these measures is included in Berke, Beatley, and Feagin (1991). Further regression analysis indicates that these two characteristics are not significant factors in explaining variables related to modes of recovery activities. Thus we are confident of the comparability between the sample groups. Berke, Beatley, and Feagin (1991) also explains in detail the results of the regression analyses.

To supplement survey data, interviews were conducted with house-holders and with representatives of organizations involved in planning, recovery, and long-term development (health, national and parish disaster planning, public works, community development, building material suppliers, lending institutions, and nongovernment relief and development). The selection of informants followed the procedure for the case studies. Six households in each parish and thirty-three representatives of organizations (eighteen in St. James and fifteen in St. Thomas) were interviewed during July 1990. The interviews followed a line of questioning similar to that of the case study interviews, with the addition of questions on household modes of recovery and household interactions with organizations involved in the recovery process.

2 RECOVERY AND SUSTAINABLE DEVELOPMENT

THIS CHAPTER PRESENTS A CONCEPTUAL FRAMEWORK FOR ANALYZING the postdisaster recovery process in the context of sustainable development. It reviews key findings and raises issues not fully addressed by the dominant disaster recovery literature. The achievement of equity, risk reduction, and long-term development through local participation in recovery planning and institutional cooperation is the central issue. Finally, a model of the postdisaster recovery and development process, and the factors that facilitate or constrain the process, is presented.

THE RECOVERY PLANNING PROCESS
Previous Research

Unfortunately, the recovery phase is the least investigated and least understood of the four phases of a disaster—predisaster mitigation, emergency preparedness, emergency response, and recovery (Drabek 1986; Rubin 1991). A few studies have examined individual and household coping behavior (Bates 1982; Bolin 1982; Bolin and Bolton 1986; Drabek and Key 1984; Pereau 1990). Some attention has been given to questioning the national economic justifications for disaster aid funds (Burby et al. 1991; Chang 1983; Friesema et al. 1979; Kunreuther 1973) and to issues of intergovernmental cooperation and to the implementation of external disaster assistance programs (Anderson and Woodrow 1989; Harrell-Bond 1986). Few studies, however, have looked at communitywide recovery (Drabek 1986).

This is particularly unfortunate, because local governments have recently been gaining experience in recovery planning. Many national governments have begun to initiate programs that assist their local jurisdictions to prepare disaster recovery and development plans (UNDRO 1991; Kreimer and Munasinghe 1991). In particular, various developing countries are attempting to integrate recovery with sustainable development initiatives. Jamaica, for example, has shifted disaster recovery responsibilities from its national emergency management agency (Office of Disaster Preparedness) to government agencies charged with environmental protection and long-term economic development and to community-based private voluntary organizations active in development initiatives such as housing, health care, watershed management, and agriculture (Brownell and Paul 1989). The enlistment of community-based organizations is to "fill the gaps" of central government recovery capabilities. In fact, since the late 1980s the Jamaican government, and other governments throughout the Caribbean, have increasingly been sharing funds, personnel, and materials with community organizations during periods of disaster recovery (ibid.).

The linkage between recovery and development was evident after the 1989 Loma Prieta earthquake in California. In this case, community-based private voluntary organizations with well-established field networks and grassroots knowledge of local conditions (e.g., the Santa Cruz County Neighborhood Survival Network) were particularly effective in integrating recovery with development (United Way 1991). These organizations used recovery funds donated after four major disasters between 1982 and 1989 to initiate programs designed to expand affordable housing units and health care facilities during rebuilding. They were also considered effective in reinforcing local government efforts in identifying and assisting affected households that were overlooked by large-scale state and federal recovery aid programs. While this evidence suggests the benefits of community involvement, it is tentative because there are few studies on the relationship between recovery and development in comparison with research on human behavior immediately before and after disaster (Drabek 1986).

Nevertheless, during the past three decades studies have begun to examine disaster recovery at the community level (e.g., Geipel 1982; Haas, Kates, and Bowden 1977; Mader 1980; Oliver-Smith 1990; Quarantelli, Dynes, and Wenger 1992; Rubin 1991; Rubin, Saperstein, and Barbee 1985). This work highlights the major impediments to the community recovery process, including such problems as staff that are unprepared to deal with aid recipients, aid that does not meet the needs of the poor, outside donor programs (government and nongovernment) that exclude local involvement, and poorly coordinated and conflicting demands from national government agencies. In sum, while this literature is still limited, it has advanced enough to provide a conceptual framework for understanding different recovery responses and the factors that might account for them.

Assumptions about the Recovery Process

In a notable study on disaster recovery, Haas, Kates, and Bowden (1977) examined the reconstruction process in four cities in the United States and Latin America. The study concludes that "disaster recovery is ordered, knowable, and predictable" (xxvi). Recovery is defined based on a descriptive conceptual model that approximates a "value added" approach, which specifies that a recovering community must undertake four stages of activities:

1. Take emergency measures for the removal of debris, the provision of temporary housing, and search and rescue.
2. Restore public services (electricity, water, and telephone).
3. Replace or reconstruct capital stock to predisaster levels.
4. Initiate reconstruction that involves economic growth and development.

(A more detailed discussion of these four stages is given in a subsequent section of this chapter.)

This model is of considerable practical significance, as it provides a parsimonious description of the complex recovery process. Indeed, the study was the first major work on long-term recovery and made a significant contribution from a limited sample of events. It proved useful in interpreting the recovery processes of the three Caribbean case studies presented in chapters 4, 5, and 6.

More recently, however, criticism has developed from a widening body of studies that reveal the conceptual and empirical shortcomings of the value added approach, which views a community as going through fixed stages, each stage being a necessary development that adds value to the final product: a recovered community. Conceptually, the approach is similar to a variety of value added frameworks that have been proposed in such fields as hazard mitigation policymaking (e.g., Slovic, Kunreuther, White 1974), collective behavior, and social movements (e.g., Smelser 1962). In the case of hazard mitigation, policy would be formed by defining goals, setting objectives, collecting information on possible alternatives, and selecting the alternative that maximizes public goals at minimum costs.

There are inherent difficulties with value added approaches. The problem is that they are linear and orderly representations of uncertain decisionmaking processes. Community decisionmaking is not a technical exercise in which each stage occurs in "proper sequence" with guaranteed outcomes (Berke, Kartez, and Wenger 1993). Recovery policymaking is intensely political. In fact, a variety of patterns can be conceptually derived and empirically observed, and the process can be altered by inaccurate appraisals of the needs of disaster-stricken citizens, intense political pressure by citizens to rebuild quickly, inadequate time and resources devoted to complex recovery problems, and the multiple and conflicting preferences of affected groups.

Several studies find the four-stage, sequential model to be an inaccurate depiction of reality. In a study of fourteen disaster-stricken communities, Rubin, Saperstein, and Barbee (1985) characterize the process quite differently. The four stages are not necessarily sequential but can occur simultaneously or in different sequences. For example, a key finding in two communities was that replacement reconstruction occurred in some areas at the same time that debris clearance was under way in other areas. Sutphen's (1983) study of a single community recovering from a flood supports the findings of Rubin and her colleagues. Specifically, Stuphen supports the basic observation of stages of recovery. However, he does not reinforce the orderly sequence of redevelopment activities shown in the four-stages model. These studies attribute such deviations from this model to variations in the extent of damages and the availability of resources within a given community. Problems with aid delivery typically stemmed from poor planning and subsequent weak local organizational capacity to respond to recovery demands.

Studies of an earthquake-devastated city in Peru (Oliver-Smith 1990; Oliver-Smith and Goldman 1988) point to rigid social stratification and the resultant inequalities in community power and influence as keys to understanding the timing and outcomes of recovery. These studies find that powerful interest groups, particularly from the business community and the upper-class elite, were able to take advantage of recovery aid because of their strong predisaster control over local institutions and their ties to central authorities. These groups were able to pressure public authorities to rebuild first in areas where they had a great interest. Poorer neighbors were more likely to have weaker ties with public authorities, and thus the process of rebuilding was less equitable for them. This also meant that any plans that might change the status quo or influence the distribution of wealth would meet with strong opposition from the community's most powerful and vocal interests. These studies and others in developing countries (Anderson and Woodrow 1989; Harrell-Bond 1986) conclude that outside aid delivery systems (international and domestic) typically do not recognize the inherent conflicts of interest in existing community social structures.

Oliver-Smith (1990) also finds that the urban reconstruction plans and designs of a central government planning agency actually reinforce social class divisions and undermine the formation of community solidarity. For example, a point system for prioritizing housing used by one central government was based on land tenure and income level and gave the highest priority for housing reconstruction to upper-income landowners and the lowest priority to the landless poor (i.e., squatters). Based on this system, elites reestablished themselves in the most favorable places, near the city center, while the poor settled on the steep, unstable slopes of the surrounding mountains. Land value was considerably lower for these distant, steep landholdings. Furthermore, postdisaster installation of public services like sewer, potable water, and electricity was almost nonexistent in these lower-class areas. Paved streets in the city center became dirt roads in the outlying areas and eventually disappeared into trails in the outermost areas. Oliver-Smith concludes that too often urban planning initiatives by outside experts, especially housing reconstruction programs, have a divisive impact on class relations by reinforcing class differences in material, spatial, and symbolic terms in the rebuilt city. The rebuilding reflects, sustains, and reproduces patterns of inequality, domination, and exploitation.

> I am neither so naive as to think that such social changes are easily designed and constructed by planners and architects into the built form of a community, nor [of] such an authoritarian frame of mind as to think they can or should be imposed by fiat without regard for public conflict, disruption, and pain. I also do not favor the drab uniformity that often characterizes postdisaster reconstruction, but housing and settlement patterns which support greater equality do not necessarily have to result in greater uniformity. When houses and settlements are reconstructed in the aftermath of disaster, we need to recognize that materials and social space have profound meanings on people, meanings that divide and separate as well as unify communities (Oliver-Smith 1990, 17).

Still other investigators (Quarentelli 1989; Wilson 1991) indicate that the redevelopment process is neither as ordered nor as predictable as suggested by the Haas et al. (1977) model. These studies maintain that the redevelopment process typically deviates from the presumed institutional model expected by central governments. They also show that, during recovery, local jurisdictions rely on organizations such as public works and planning departments rather than on local emergency or civil defense offices, which are the usual centers for government-supported emergency management or civil defense programs.

Since these traditional institutions are not used at the outset of the disaster recovery process, citizens and officials commonly devise various adaptive strategies to respond to local needs. Commenting on post-disaster recovery efforts, Kartez (1984) contends that citizens and local officials most often improvise such strategies in high-pressure decisionmaking environments. This process occurs outside the institutional context for implementing recovery programs. The outcome is cooperative adaptation among citizens and institutions. Kartez further observes that the rapid learning that takes place on the local level is an important lesson in the behavior of institutions under stress. The individuals involved in this learning process realize the limitations of the institutional arrangements in place and, consequently, alter their behavior. The key is not inflexible programs formulated in accordance with central administrative procedures, as evidenced by recovery studies in developing countries (Harrell-Bond 1986; Solo 1991). Success is explained by aid delivery systems with a capacity for embracing error, learning along with the people, and building new knowledge and institutional capacity through action, not simply demanding compliance with rigid administrative controls.

The basic challenge is to specify the conditions in which adaptive learning can take place before a disaster strikes. Disaster planners typically do not confront this fundamental issue but maintain that the major obstacle to predisaster planning is in motivating elected officials and administrative staff to participate in planning before disaster strikes (Harrell-Bond 1986; Kartez 1984). There may always be apathy, however, toward planning for disaster events, given their infrequent occurrence (Drabek 1986). Moreover, some adaptation will always be necessary during disaster recovery. Of greatest concern, however, is the issue of developing institutional arrangements for disaster recovery planning that foster rather than constrain learning. Such arrangements would also be capable of integrating useful knowledge generated from previous research into recovery planning programs.

This issue is of central importance to the field of development planning in developing countries, a field that has given considerable attention to how international aid can be effective in building local capacity to undertake self-initiated and self-directed development projects (Uphoff 1986, 1991). Development planning researchers increasingly argue that preparing for sudden events, such as natural disasters, offers opportunities for devising institutional arrangements that can embrace new and changing conditions (Anderson and Woodrow 1989; Cuny 1983; Pantelic 1991). Furthermore, disasters themselves offer opportunities to develop social resources. Often, disaster-stricken people mobilize to meet the needs not addressed by aid agencies (Oliver-Smith 1990). The intention is to strengthen local capacity to recover and to undertake economic, social, and physical development projects once the recovery effort is completed. Thus the development planning field can make an important contribution by suggesting the factors that foster institutional capacity for adaptive learning. As noted, this potential contribution has begun to be recognized by the international community concerned with implementing the 1988 United Nations resolution that designates the 1990s as the International Decade for Natural Disaster Reduction (Paudey 1990).

Moreover, the lessons learned about the transformation from deprivation to self-directed revitalization appear to cut across cultural boundaries. While there are cross-cultural differences in designing effective disaster and development planning institutions, various studies observe more similarities than differences (e.g., Bolin and Bolton 1983; Perry and Hirose 1983; Quarantelli, Dynes, and Wenger 1992). Thus lessons derived from recovery experiences in differing societies can have much cross-cultural validity and practical utility.

DISASTER RECOVERY AND SUSTAINABLE DEVELOPMENT

Several studies provide a starting point for developing a conceptual framework for linking disaster recovery and sustainable development (Anderson and Woodrow 1989; Harrel-Bond 1986; Oliver-Smith and Goldman 1988; Oliver-Smith 1990). The Oliver-Smith (1990) study perhaps best represents the characteristics of this framework. This study examines the earthquake recovery process in a community in Peru to determine how to address issues of social inequality and to avoid reconstruction investments that would site buildings in the same high-risk locations. The specific conditions needed to meet this demand were identified. Oliver-Smith finds that the chances of implementing a better postdisaster reconstruction urban land use and design strategy increase when four factors are present. First, land use planning measures must be adapted to "fit" postdisaster needs and opportunities. Second, there should be reliance on internal, local capabilities rather than on solely external resources. Third, the community must have knowledge of the requirements for external assistance. Fourth, the administration of external assistance programs needs to recognize local needs, concerns, and capabilities. These characteristics are intended to overcome the predictable political and administrative obstacles to successful organizational adaptation during recovery.

Anderson and Woodrow (1989) and Harrell-Bond (1986), among others, also maintain that the process by which viable policies and collaborative institutional arrangements are developed emphasizes local participation and initiative. These observations suggest that an effective response to recovery demands cannot be achieved in disaster recovery efforts through top-down, inflexible, and standardized approaches. Success is based on bottom-up policy and organizational development. They also suggest that when intracommunity and intergovernmental ties are strong, the citizens and organizations involved in recovery are more likely to adapt to changing conditions. Moreover, interorganizational aid delivery systems are more capable of meeting the needs of disaster-stricken citizens. Researchers in the development planning field suggest that this approach, described by scattered evidence in disaster research, is an application of "local institutional development theory," as discussed by Uphoff (1986). So far, the local institutional development approach has been primarily applied to natural resource management, health care delivery, and agricultural production, under varying social, economic, and political conditions (Ascher and Healy 1990; Cernea 1991; Korten 1980; Uphoff 1986). Research is needed on how institutional arrangements act as incentives or barriers to adapting responses that meet local needs, capacities, and opportunities during disaster recovery. In particular, this approach can be applied at both the micro (intracommunity) and macro (intergovernmental) levels of analysis.

Such past studies suggest that simply seeking local compliance with and subordination to external organizational (national and international) relief and rebuilding requirements does not produce the best results and may be dysfunctional as well. These studies also maintain that external programs for aiding community rebuilding do not always match local needs or cannot be successfully implemented without in-

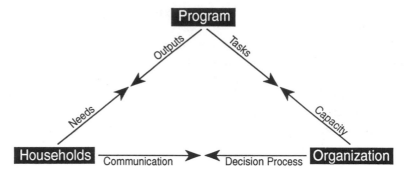

FIGURE 2.1. Requirements for successful disaster recovery planning (adapted from Korten 1980).

tralocal and intergovernmental collaboration and cooperation. The problem of achieving cooperation between communities or aid recipients and external donors has been investigated by researchers in the international development planning field, because the outcomes of such external aid have repeatedly gone awry.

Korten (1980), for example, developed an experience-based model for designing successful development aid strategies. As illustrated in figure 2.1, the strategy consists of three broad dimensions: the needs of aid recipients, the design of the aid program, and the organizational capacity of both donors and recipients. Efforts are successful when the recovery program in place is responsive to household needs and builds on strong organizations capable of achieving program goals. That is, a high degree of fit among program design, household needs, and the capacities of assisting organizations increases the chances of successful recovery efforts. The concept of fit is of central importance in the field of development planning, because research has illuminated the important relationships among needs, program, and organizational capacity, concluding that the performance of an organization is a function of fit among these dimensions (Korten 1980).

The model is helpful in describing some of the findings from disaster recovery studies. For example, Mader (1980) finds that reconstruction efforts in response to the 1968 earthquake in Santa Rosa, California, were successful due to predisaster actions that helped local authorities identify the needs for specific types of recovery aid. While this study was conducted in the United States, the findings have considerable cross-cultural validity and utility for developing countries. In this case, local planning staff persuaded federal agencies to allow the city to use aid for reconstruction to implement a preexisting downtown revitalization plan. The plan was adopted by the city in 1968 (about one year before the earthquake), after several years of consensus-building efforts by planning staff and of commissioning various economic, visual resource, and traffic circulation studies. Plan policies specified changes in permitted land uses, urban design standards, and parking provisions. City officials originally anticipated that the plan would be implemented over a ten- to fifteen-year period. The disaster, however, was viewed by local officials as a window of opportunity for rapidly implementing the plan. The downtown sustained severe damages, and substantial amounts of federal aid was available for reconstruction. Local officials were able to use the plan as a basis for specifying how aid from federal agencies should be used. The outcome of this process was that local people were able to define their own goals, to control the use of incoming resources, and to tailor the design of recovery programs to fit local needs and capacities. Moreover, this process also achieved national economic development objectives.

Other findings from investigations in developing countries (Anderson and Woodrow 1989; Harrell-Bond 1986; Oliver-Smith and Goldman 1988) indicate the difficulties that local governments have in using aid for rebuilding. These findings, however, make even more sense in light of a development planning model. Anderson and Woodrow (1989), in particular, focus on lack of local organizational capacity and a poor fit between local needs and external aid program designs. Examining these findings through a developmental planning model makes clear that either local organizational designs (as Anderson and Woodrow argue) or recovery program designs (as some California officials claimed after the Loma Prieta earthquake; see Kartez 1991) must be changed. Of course, local officials often maintain that the third component, local needs, is what external aid authorities want to change through the imposition of external program requirements, because such local needs do not fit those requirements. This issue is exactly what development models like Korten's bring to light.

In summary, the literature reveals insights for designing a conceptual framework for understanding disaster recovery and sustainable development processes. The Haas, Kates, and Bowden (1977) recovery model is useful for understanding the dynamics of recovery and development, but the four stages occur at different times and have different durations for different groups of affected residents. Thus the model can be used to

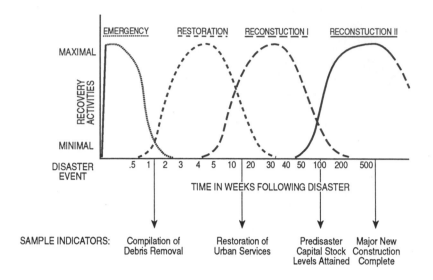

FIGURE 2.2. General model of postdisaster reconstruction and recovery (adapted from Haas, Kates, and Bowden 1977).

track variations in recovery rates and outcomes for different interest groups. Previous research has shown that variations are most pronounced when such groups are defined by social class.

Another insight considers two factors that affect variation in distributional equity, reduced risks, long-term economic development, and the safeguarding of the environment. One, local institutions should be consulted when fitting external recovery aid to local needs, since local institutions have the greatest potential to meet the needs of disaster-stricken individuals and to take advantage of their capacities. Two, external aid institutions should direct their resources to empowering local institutions, recognizing their capacity for self-directed recovery and sustainable development efforts.

THE FOUR STAGES OF THE RECOVERY PROCESS: THE HAAS, KATES, AND BOWDEN MODEL

Figure 2.2 illustrates the four stages of the recovery process and the sequence of activities in each stage. In the emergency stage, the community copes with the immediate effects of the destruction and handles the casualties and the homeless. Normal social and economic activities are disrupted. Indicators of the end of this stage are a drastic reduction in emergency distribution of food and medicine, search and rescue activities, and debris clearance efforts. In the restoration stage, the community makes temporary repairs to public utilities, housing, and business structures, and social and economic activities return to near normal. The end of this stage is marked by the return of major public utilities and transport and communication systems. The reconstruction stage is divided into two: reconstruction stage 1 is marked by the rebuilding of damaged or destroyed structures to predisaster levels. Social and economic activities also return to these levels. Indicators of the end of this period are the replacement of homes, public utilities, and structures used for businesses. The betterment and development stage (reconstruction stage 2) involves activities that lead to postdisaster improvement. These activities include (1) the strengthening of local organizational capacity to undertake long-term development projects that stem from disaster recovery work and (2) improvements to the physical character of the devastated area, such as making rebuilt structures less vulnerable to future hazardous events and creating open parks in disaster-prone areas.

INTERORGANIZATIONAL DESIGN PRINCIPLES FOR RECOVERY AND SUSTAINABLE DEVELOPMENT

A design principle is an essential factor or condition that accounts for the success of the interorganizational aid delivery system in achieving recovery and sustainable development. These principles serve to integrate the findings of research in disaster recovery and development planning in developing countries. They also reflect the broad themes set forth in *Agenda 21*, which emphasize a bottom-up approach—action through people and their communities. Recall that *Agenda 21* was produced during the 1992 Earth Summit in Rio de Janeiro to serve as a guide for nations and their communities for achieving sustainable development during the twentieth-first century. The following seven principles are considered important.

Design Principle 1: Interorganizational Coordination

Numerous organizations become involved in recovery activities after a disaster. Some organizations represent domestic or foreign governments; others are multilateral international development organizations in the nongovernment sector, including United Nations agencies; still others represent business and commercial interests. Interorganizational coordination varies tremendously across disaster settings. Some disaster recovery efforts are tightly knit and well organized and involve frequent and sustained interaction; the capacity of organizations to communicate, to adapt, and to implement coordinated and consistent recovery programs is high. Other disaster recovery settings are fragmented and unorganized, and interorganizational coordination tends to be infrequent and piecemeal. The activities of these organizations overlap, and interorganizational competition to assist those in need ensues (NGOs often want to assist more people in order to be eligible for more donor funds). Recovery aid is not likely to meet local needs, and knowledge of local capacities to undertake self-directed recovery and development work is minimal. The potential to adapt to changing local conditions in these settings is low.

When coordination is maximal, communication among participants is high. Organizations share common information, which generates common outlooks and ways of viewing the opportunities and constraints posed by different situations. Organizations become more aware of one another's activities and interests. Local people have a greater chance of communicating to external organizations their needs and capacities for recovery. There is more opportunity for mutual adaptation to changing needs and for the adoption and implementation of coordinated recovery responses. Furthermore, local organizations are more likely to enhance the work of external organizations through the use of field staff and through their knowledge of local circumstances.

The consequences of disaster recovery and development efforts without substantial interaction and coordination among participating organizations have been investigated. Oliver-Smith (1990), for one, suggests that the outcomes of urban planning during the earthquake disaster aftermath in Yungay, Peru, were similar to outcomes of traditional predisaster planning. Planning, in both instances, relies on expert knowledge and does not incorporate the values of local people. The reliance on plans developed by experts in Yungay did not induce participation because it eliminated the need for the disaster-stricken people to come together and solve their problems in a cooperative spirit. In addition, Oliver-Smith found that because Yungay's business establishment had communitywide interests and was well organized it had a disproportionate influence on postdisaster planning compared to local residents. Downtown merchants, for example, closely monitored recovery issues that affected their interests. They became involved with plan proposals at the early stages of discussion and understood the consequences of alternative proposals on their interests early in the recovery process. By comparison, disaster-stricken residents only became aware that something was afoot and were not capable of rapidly organizing and responding. Thus the traditional form of urban planning occurred during disaster recovery and, as expected, tended to favor commercial interests over those who were suffering the most and were less capable, at the outset, of self-organizing.

Pereau's (1990) study of tornado disaster recovery in the impoverished Mexican American community of Saragosa finds that interorganizational communication and coordination was low. Recovery for the most part was organized outside of the community, with little input from local people. The idea that the citizens might be given assistance to rebuild and to organize their own reconstruction was apparently never seriously considered by the external organizations involved. According to one informed local leader, "they say we received a lot from the agencies, churches, and others from the outside world . . . and they say we are spoiled kids. I really think that we could have had more input into what they were going to do . . . more choices. . . . I would like to [have] set up a committee of all agencies and find out what they could do; and then I would have input from the people. Ask the people, and then try to work out what could happen" (19).

The outcome of the recovery process was predictable. Compared to predisaster conditions, Saragosans considered themselves much worse off. Evidence from a random survey by Pereau (1990) reveals strong dissatisfaction with postdisaster housing conditions. More than half of all disaster-stricken residents surveyed indicated that the replacement housing they received was "worse" on a variety of measures, including quality, size, comfort, and "feelings" about the physical layout of the rebuilt neighborhoods.

Design Principles 2 and 3: Monitoring and Enforcement

The monitors of the distribution and impacts of aid are members of organizations that have well-established field staffs or are the aid recipients themselves. Aid recipients who attempt to receive a disproportionate amount of assistance are likely to be deterred by other disaster-stricken people, or officials from organizations with well-established field staffs, or both. In successful disaster recovery settings, the monitoring of aid distribution is not undertaken by external authorities but by organizations that have familiarity with local damage patterns, skills for rebuilding, and culturally defined building material needs. Moreover, even though it is frequently presumed that aid recipients will not spend the time and effort to monitor each other's use of aid, emerging evidence indicates that substantial monitoring does occur (Anderson and Woodrow 1989; Harrel Bond 1986).

To explain the investment in monitoring activities that occurs in recovery settings that have the active participation of local people, the term *quasi-voluntary compliance* can be useful. It has been used by Levi (1988) to describe the behavior of taxpayers in settings in which most taxpayers choose to comply. Paying taxes is voluntary in the sense that individuals choose to comply in many situations in which they are not being directly coerced. However, it is quasi-voluntary, because the noncompliant are subject to coercion (if they are caught). Taxpayers, according to Levi, will adopt a strategy of quasi-voluntary compliance when they have confidence (1) that compliance will achieve a larger collective benefit (i.e., the government is perceived to be using tax funds for its intended purposes) and (2) that other citizens will comply as well. Levi indicates that the "compliance of each depends on the compliance of others. No one prefers to be a 'sucker'" (53). That is, if one individual pays the tax but another does not pay his share, the latter will benefit from the former's compliance.

Levi views some form of enforcement or sanctioning as an essential condition to achieving quasi-voluntary compliance. From her perspective, enforcement increases the confidence of individuals that they are not suckers. As long as they are confident that others are cooperating and that the government provides collective benefits, they comply willingly to tax laws. In Levi's theory, enforcement is normally provided by the external governing organization, although enforcement can come from other sources (i.e., local field staff and aid recipients). The general presumption has been that participants (e.g., aid recipients or taxpayers) will not undertake mutual monitoring and enforcement because such actions involve relatively high personal costs and produce collective benefits that are diffuse and not of direct benefit to the individuals themselves. As Elster (1989, 41) states, "punishment almost invariably is costly to the punisher, while the benefits from punishment are diffusely distributed over the members." However, evidence suggests that individuals do monitor and that the costs of this action are not high.

In postdisaster settings, the low cost of monitoring stems from the high demand and low supply of resources needed for recovery. Harrell-Bond (1986), for example, contends that if some individuals in a community receive more than their fair share of donated building materials their disaster-stricken neighbors often surmise that they will receive less. Thus, community members are well aware of those who get more than their fair share. Harrell-Bond finds that disaster-stricken individuals within a community act as mutually reinforcing deterrents to noncompliance. Unlike an external organization, local people do not have to invest additional time and effort in monitoring: it is a by-product of their own strong motivation to ensure that each household receives assistance based on need. (This finding is clearly evident in the Jamaica case study, presented in chapter 3.)

Ostrom's (1990) study of local institutional management of renewable natural resources encountered similar local monitoring. In the appropriation of water for irrigation and for fishing-site rotation systems, cheaters can be observed at low cost by those who most want to deter them. The irrigator, for example, who nears the end of his turn would like to extend the time of his turn (and thus the amount of water obtained). The next irrigator in the rotation system, who is waiting for the other to finish, would like to start early. The presence of the first irrigator deters the second from an early start, the presence of the second irrigator deters the first from a late ending. The same sequence occurs in the rotation of fishing rights. As with recovery aid distribution, natural resource rotation systems place the key actors most concerned with cheating in direct contact with one another.

A previously unrecognized benefit of local monitoring is information gathering, which can be costly for external organizations. In postdisaster situations, participating organizations must contend with incomplete information, but the information obtained by monitors can improve the success of strategic decisions about aid delivery and program design. People who are close to the actual recovery actions have considerable knowledge of what people do and what outcomes can be expected under differing aid programs. If a monitor discovers an infraction in the use of aid, it is possible to learn about the particular circumstances surrounding the infraction and to participate in decisionmaking on appropriate enforcement measures and changes in aid program design.

The second and third interorganizational design principles—monitoring and enforcement—thus jointly operate to enhance the prospects of successful disaster recovery in the context of sustainable development. It is possible to summarize the arguments made up to this point. When local people have opportunities to participate in the design of coordinated recovery and development assistance programs (design principle 1) to be monitored by local people (design principle 2) that have input into decisions about enforcement procedures (design principle 3), the problems of achieving meaningful local participation and of obtaining information are solved at the same time. People who believe that aid delivery will be fair and equitable, that there will be a collective benefit from recovery and community development, and that monitoring will protect them from being cheated are willing to make a commitment to participate. That is, once disaster-stricken people make commitments, they are then motivated to monitor other people's behaviors, at least periodically, to assure themselves that others are not breaking the rules. Thus commitment and mutual monitoring reinforce one another, especially when local people are given opportunities to monitor (which reduces costs for external organizations) and to participate in program design and implementation.

Design Principle 4: The Recognition of Rights

The rights of local people to undertake self-directed recovery and development initiatives are not challenged by external authorities. Disaster-stricken people frequently organize on their own without creating formal government plans and programs. In many disaster recovery situations, local people have the best understanding of neighborhood damage patterns and of the types urban design, land use, and construction practices compatible with local cultural and social traditions. Provided that external organizations give at least minimal recognition to the legitimacy of local knowledge and capabilities, disaster-stricken people are often able to monitor and enforce recovery and to development initiatives themselves.

However, if external organizations presume that they know best and that they should have complete authority, it will be difficult for local people to exert control over their own their own destinies. External aid organizations tend to ignore local organizations and officials when carrying out recovery and development programs (Anderson and Woodrow 1989; Harrell-Bond 1986; Oliver-Smith 1990). The failure to recognize legitimate local concerns and rights often contributes to the problems of aid programs, because disaster-stricken people are rarely allowed the opportunity to find their own solutions. When community rights are not recognized, external aid is more likely to not fit specific community needs and capabilities. The denial of local rights encourages conflict and provides little opportunity to negotiate coordinated and appropriate interorganizational arrangements. Moreover, local people will not be able to help carry out the external initiatives and may even be a major factor in ensuring their failure.

Design Principle 5: Leadership

Local leaders have the necessary expertise, political skill, persistence, and creative and flexible styles of problem solving and decisionmaking to participate in the recovery and development process. They are willing give their time and energy, and sometimes money, to ensure that particular issues are placed on public agendas and are given priority. Leaders can direct the recovery process in strategic directions. They might be local or national government officials or field staff members of an NGO. Kingdon's (1986) study of agenda setting in public policymaking arenas suggests that successful leaders exhibit several personal characteristics: expertise in the subject area (e.g., organization building, fund raising, or knowledge of local construction practices), political skill in forming coalitions that advocate a point of view of particular interest groups, and most important, perseverance. Kingdon contends that perseverance implies a willingness to devote enormous amounts of time and energy over a considerable period of time to create a political climate receptive to the views of the interests represented by the leader.

While Kingdon's study focuses on the predisaster public policy adoption process, it is evident that these leadership characteristics also apply to the postdisaster setting. In fact, Kingdon argues that a "crisis" often provides leaders with a "window of opportunity" to put their proposals on the public agenda. During this period, leaders are "ready" to take advantage of the opportunity to advocate their points of view as solutions to the problems at hand. Leaders must use their skills to ensure that their solutions are adopted by organizations involved in the postcrisis response effort. Kingdon also argues that windows of opportunity do not stay open long. If solutions are not arrived at quickly, the window closes. The disaster that prompted the window to open soon passes from the scene. Kingdon assumes that, once the crises subsides, leaders revert to advocating issues and points of view that are low on public agendas. Evidence derived from the limited number of disaster recovery studies suggests, however, that the influence of successful leaders often grows stronger after a disaster. Harrell-Bond (1986) and Wenger (1978), in particular, maintain that, although some proposals may be successfully enacted during the immediate disaster aftermath, those individuals (and organizations) that were persistent advocates before the event will also persist during the long-term recovery. An important distinction, according to these investigators, is that because leaders are typically ready to take advantage of a crisis situation their positions of influence in public policy arenas are often elevated. Compared to the predisaster period, they thus can have greater impact on strategic public policy-making long after the event.

Oliver-Smith and Goldman (1988) further point out that it is crucial for leaders to act as advocates for groups that typically are underrepresented in postdisaster recovery planning and policymaking. These investigators find that postdisaster recovery plans are often expressions of the values of a few powerful special interests and do not meet the needs of the disaster-stricken public, particularly the poor. A key conclusion of their study is that government and NGO officials should take on leadership roles to advocate alternative proposals for underrepresented groups. The very act of advocacy clarifies assumptions and enhances communication and, thereby, promotes accurate judgments about the particular consequences of recovery and development decisions on the underrepresented. Thus, the leadership role is educational: those that are underrepresented learn about their rights, opportunities, and resources in the context of disaster recovery and development policy debates.

Design Principle 6: Linkage

External disaster recovery aid is linked to well-established local development activities. When a community adopts an externally supported development activity like reforestation or self-help housing construction, a precedent is established. Once that occurs, local reaction and the acceptance of outside projects in that arena are never quite the same. Establishing a precedent does not necessarily imply that a program has made a dramatic change in development, at least not in the short run. The step might or might not be small. The importance of such initiatives lies in their precedent-setting nature. Precedents are important because local people become accustomed to the new way of doing things and outside organizations gain an understanding of local needs and capabilities to undertake development work. While a given development project may involve just a few to hundreds of local people, inertia sets in, and it becomes easier to channel more development work in the same direction.

Once a precedent is established in one arena, it can be used to gradually open new opportunities and to promote similar change in a similar arena of development. In this sense, external disaster recovery aid can further build and support local organizations to be more effective in undertaking self-directed sustainable development initiatives. A good example of such linkage is presented in chapter 4, which discusses how an external NGO recognized the hurricane disaster on Montserrat as an opportunity to link recovery aid with several preexisting development projects.

Spillover is promoted when leaders are persistent in their efforts and use their expertise to develop linkages. For an issue to progress from one arena to another, it must be linked to an issue in the second arena. In other words, the two issues need to be placed in the same category of public concern. For example, people may easily move from one issue (e.g., environmental protection of watersheds) to the next (e.g., risk reduction by locating postdisaster redevelopment away from steep slopes) because they are linked to the common category of sustainable development. It could be argued that sustainable development is advanced during reconstruction by linking watershed protection issues to risk reduction issues. Environmentalists will support limiting redevelopment on steep slopes because deforestation, soil erosion, and excessive siltation of downstream surface waters would be reduced. Hazard specialists will be supportive because risk reduction will be achieved as loss from landslides and downstream flooding from excessive watershed development will be reduced. Thus, instead of treating the two activities as separate administrative functions they can be integrated and, in turn, become more politically feasible.

Design Principle 7: Resources

Resources should fit the recovery needs and the capabilities of the disaster-stricken community. Disaster recovery initiatives can wax or wane according to the availability of resources that fit local needs and capacities. Resources can be monetary or nonmonetary. Monetary resources can be cash payments for use in purchasing materials for rebuilding. As discussed in the Jamaican case in chapter 3, monetary resources can also be in the form of a government-issued building stamp, which is redeemed for its cash value in building materials. Nonmonetary resources include the direct provision of building materials, additional staff from humanitarian organizations, and postdisaster building construction workshops.

The key characteristic of successful aid distribution is that external aid organizations distribute resources in ways that build and support the capacity of people to meet their own needs. As articulated by Gran (1983), the resource distribution strategy should assign the individual the role not of "subject but of actor who controls the resources and directs the processes affecting his or her life" (146). The intent of this participatory strategy is less dependency on external donors and greater self-reliance by recovering communities. The chances for a successful transition from recovery to sustained development efforts will increase as well.

Harrell-Bond's (1986) study of the role of aid for Ugandan refugees in the mid-1970s finds that, while emergency aid of food and medical supplies was critical for saving lives and for getting people back on their feet, aid for long-term development was often poorly matched to the needs and capacities of local people to undertake development work. This study also finds that aid was typically given based on the assumption that the external aid program knew best about what was needed. When aid is given in this way, it is almost always sold on the black market to enable refugees to obtain cash for purchasing capital (tools for farming or cooking utensils for making food) to make goods they can sell. As is evident in the Jamaican case, the widespread practice of selling or bartering away aid is a common when aid poorly fits needs and capacities. The implication of aid being used for such unintended purposes is that people attempt to meet their own needs as defined by them.

CONCLUSIONS

The conceptual framework presented in this chapter is still speculative, of course. We hope it will generate debate and further theoretical and empirical work. Our primary concern, however, is to understand the links between sustainable development and recovery through practical application. As the Sustainable Challenge Foundation (1994), notes, sustainability is not simply a theoretical concept and is meaningless without practical application.

The conceptual framework was used to interpret the data collected for this study: the case studies of three island states recovering from Hurricane Hugo in the eastern Caribbean and the on-site survey of households in two parishes in Jamaica recovering from Hurricane Gilbert.

3 JAMAICA

INFLUENCES OF INSTITUTIONAL RESPONSE ON HOUSEHOLD RECOVERY

WHILE THE SUBSEQUENT THREE CHAPTERS FOCUS ON THE RECOVERY responses of organizations, this chapter examines the relationship between households and aid delivery organizations after the 1988 Hurricane Gilbert disaster on Jamaica. We use the institutional design principles discussed in chapter 2 to interpret household recovery and aid delivery efforts in the context of sustainable development. Recall that an institutional design principle is an essential factor or condition that accounts for the success of the interorganizational delivery system in achieving recovery and sustainable development. While subsequent chapters present findings for each principle on a case-by-case basis, findings in this chapter are presented based on a household survey and on interviews with householders and representatives of organizations involved in the recovery. The findings are then evaluated for each principle at the conclusion of this chapter.

As discussed in detail in chapter 1, two comparable samples of households were selected from St. James Parish and St. Thomas Parish on Jamaica. Economic and political conditions vary considerably between the two parishes. The St. James economy is mixed agriculture and tourism. The majority of the population is urban and has a higher median income than the national median. St. Thomas's economy is primarily low income and agriculture based, and its population is rural in character. St. James was a stronghold of the political party in power (People's National Party) in the central government at the time of this study. St. Thomas was closely aligned with the opposition party (Jamaica Labour Party). We assumed that these contrasting conditions, as well as differences in the design of external aid delivery systems, could influence the availability of resources for recovery, a household's attitude toward government, and long-term household responses to the disaster. This chapter consists of seven sections. First, an overview of Jamaica's social, political, and hazard vulnerability setting is provided. Second, demographic and socioeconomic characteristics and the damage patterns of survey households are examined. Third, recovery strategies used by households to overcome disaster-related losses are explored. The strategies consist of activities that include using government aid (the Building Stamp Programme) and rebuilding efforts that involve seeking temporary housing and acquiring building materials. Fourth, the evidence on household mitigation practices used during rebuilding is reviewed. Fifth, household evaluations of government recovery actions are discussed. Sixth, a detailed review of the government's zinc sheet distribution program is presented. Finally, the Jamaican recovery experience is evaluated based on the institutional design principles presented in chapter 2.

AN OVERVIEW OF JAMAICA

The Social and Political Setting

Jamaica, at 4,411 square miles (11,000 square kilometers), is the Caribbean's third largest island. Its terrain consists of a mountainous and highland interior (over half the island is above a thousand feet elevation), surrounded by coastal flatlands. Jamaica's rugged interior is marked dramatically by the Blue Mountains, which rise to a height of 7,400, the highest mountains in the Caribbean (Government of Jamaica 1987). Jamaica has a 550–mile-long coast, with varied shoreline features, from cliffs to mangrove swamps to white beaches.

Jamaica is a relatively young country, having gained its independence from Great Britain only in 1962. It is a parliamentary democracy, with executive governance through a prime minister and cabinet ministers (cabinet ministries address such areas as public health and construction and housing, though they are often renamed and restructured in each different government). The legislative branch consists of an appointed senate and a popularly elected house of representatives. The country is also divided into three counties and fourteen parishes. Local governance occurs through parish councils. Jamaica's governance structure is very centralized, however, and the parishes have relatively few powers and responsibilities.

Two political parties dominate Jamaica—the Jamaica Labour Party (JLP) and the People's National Party (PNP). Much of the process and interplay by which public resources are distributed on Jamaica, including posthurricane disaster assistance, can be explained in terms of competition between these two parties. As Stone (1989) notes, Jamaica is an "atypical Third World country in that it has a stable two-party system in which power has been shared by the two major political parties" (20). This peaceful sharing of power was seen dramatically in the change of government a few months following Hurricane Gilbert, from the JLP government of Edward Seaga to the PNP government of Michael Manley.

While there is much that the PNP and JPL agree upon, they are characterized by some major differences in political and economic philosophy. The PNP has been more socialist leaning, more oriented toward state ownership and state control of the economy, while the JLP has been more capitalist and free market oriented. The PNP is generally more liberal and left leaning (described as the "party of change"), and the JLP more conservative (described as the "party of stability"). Despite these policy differences, both are seen as populist parties and have a common commitment to social development and taking care of the basic needs of the population (e.g., providing health care and education). One of the realities of the Jamaican political system, and one that affects the distribution of disaster benefits, is a belief in political patronage. Stone notes that this is a shared belief between the two parties, "whereby scarce benefits that flow from government policies and expenditures (jobs, housing, contracts, etc.) are allocated to party supporters" (22).

Jamaica's economy is mainly based on its land and natural resources. Historically, agriculture has been the largest sector, with major export crops being sugarcane, bananas, citrus, cocoa, and coffee (Government of Jamaica 1987). This sector still employs the largest number of people. Since the 1950s, mining (primarily bauxite) and tourism have become major forces in the economy and especially important sources of foreign income. In recent years tourism has emerged as the largest source of foreign exchange, and extensive resort development has occurred (and continues to occur), especially along the north coast. Such coastal growth has, in turn, exposed increasing development to the threats of hurricanes and coastal storms.

Jamaica is indeed a Third World country and exhibits many of the typical problems of Third World nations. Despite steady improvements in general living conditions (e.g., high life expectancy and literacy rates), many problems persist, including high unemployment (hovering around 25 percent during the 1980s), high external debt, poverty, and sharp social and economic inequalities (Davies and Witter 1989). About one-third of the country's population is considered to be below the poverty line, and an estimated 8 percent of the population lives in squatter camps.

Jamaica's Vulnerable Population

Jamaica is subject to a variety of potentially devastating natural hazards. The most notable and serious threats are from hurricanes, coastal storms, and earthquakes. However, other serious hazards include tsunamis (several have been experienced on the north coast), inland flooding, coastal erosion, and landslides, known as landslips (Government of Jamaica 1987). The earthquake threat is a particularly serious one, given that Jamaica is in such close proximity (about ninety miles) from the Caymon fault, which separates the Caribbean and North American tectonic plates. Major seismic events have been experienced in the past (large earthquakes occurred in 1692 and 1907), and indeed the capital city of Kingston was founded as a direct result of the destruction of Port Royal from the 1692 earthquake. There seems to be considerable consensus among the seismic community that a moderately high earthquake in the Kingston area is likely to occur in the near future (Shepard 1988). In recent years, substantial development pressures have been experienced along the coast, where extensive wetlands have been filled (many areas are built on unconsolidated materials subject to seismic liquefaction) and where erosion is a problem. Coastal erosion has been exacerbated by both the location of new development (and the construction of shore armoring devices) and the mining of sand (itself driven by building and development pressures).

While Hurricane Gilbert was the first hurricane to directly strike Jamaica in more than thirty-five years (since Hurricane Carla in 1951), Jamaica lies in the center of a path of Caribbean hurricanes and coastal storms. Between 1886 and 1967, nineteen hurricanes and tropical storms directly hit Jamaica, with ninety-eight coming within 150 miles of the island.

Jamaica, then, is subject to several serious natural hazards. The fact that, by the time Gilbert struck, it had been many years since the island had experienced either a direct hurricane strike or an earthquake (1907 being the last earthquake) means that the country had been in a period of complacency about the potential for disaster. As a USAID report (1989) notes, "One might characterize Jamaica as a country at high risk to disasters, but with a low sense of preparedness or attention to mitigating measures" (1). Across this hazardous topography and landscape is spread a population of approximately 2.5 million people (about 2.4 million when Gilbert struck). The historic settlement pattern of Jamaica has further contributed to risk exposure. Less than half the country's population is urban, with many towns and villages located in remote hilly areas (see figure 3.1). Jamaica, as a result, has an extensive network (9,200 miles) of roads connecting this dispersed rural population.

Many Jamaicans, in both urban and rural areas, live in vulnerable locations. Low-income and squatter communities, especially, lie in high-hazard floodplains and gullies and areas prone to landsliding (see figure 3.2). In theory, development activities (and the location of development) are controlled through the Jamaica Town and Country Planning Act (enacted in 1957 and based on the British planning model) and the central government's Town Planning Authority. In reality, much of the building and development that occurs is not regulated and occurs through the country's large informal housing and building sector. A related problem on Jamaica has been the lack of maps that accurately delineate hazardous areas and that could be used to steer development (and squatter communities) away from high-risk locations. The Jamaican government began a floodplain mapping program in the mid-1980s, but little progress had been made prior to Hurricane Gilbert (Molina 1989).

While a national building code is also in place, there are enforcement problems. Parish councils, in charge of enforcement of the building code, are severely understaffed, as there is often only a single building inspector for an entire parish (McCarthy 1991). Again, much of the housing, particularly for lower-income Jamaicans, is constructed through the informal sector and is built with simple materials and unskilled labor. Homes are typically basic wood-frame structures, usually with zinc or aluminum roofing. These homes usually have little hurricane reinforcing and are not well connected to their foundations (see figure 3.3). USAID estimates that at least half the homes on Jamaica could be described in this way (USAID 1989). The general conditions of poverty and low income is a fundamental root cause of disaster vulnerability. Population growth may further confound these problems. Projections suggest a possible rise to a high of 2.75 million by the year 2000 (Jamaica Planning Institute 1991). Jamaica's annual growth rate of 1.4 percent places it in the "moderate" category among developing countries, yet there is a strong possibility that even this growth rate will lead to fur-

FIGURE 3.1. Small village in the Blue Mountains (photograph by Philip R. Berke).

FIGURE 3.2. Low-income squatter development located along a high-hazard floodplain of the Yallas River (photograph by Timothy Beatley).

ther environmental degradation and an increase in the numbers of people living in marginal housing in vulnerable locations.

Particularly troubling, both before and since Hurricane Gilbert, has been the gradual destruction and degradation of the country's natural environment. Deforestation and the expansion of agriculture onto high-slope and marginal areas has resulted in a substantial soil erosion problem. Destruction of trees and vegetation has also occurred as a result of small-scale production of charcoal, primarily for household cooling. A World Bank report notes that, of thirty-three watersheds on Jamaica, nineteen are "badly eroded" (World Bank 1993). This gradual degradation of the natural environment means not only that important ecological and economic resources are lost but also that the environment is less capable of buffering and mitigating the forces of hurricanes and storms.

The Impact of Hurricane Gilbert

Prior to Hurricane Gilbert, Jamaica had not experienced a direct hit from a hurricane in more than thirty-five years. Gilbert struck on September 12, 1988, and exposed the fundamental vulnerability of Jamaica to these natural forces and added substantially to the existing social

FIGURE 3.3. Typical low-income house with little, if any, hurricane reinforcement (photograph by Philip R. Berke).

FIGURE 3.4. Tents used by low-income, homeless people, several months after Hurricane Gilbert (photograph by Timothy Beatley).

FIGURE 3.5. Airplane, thrown against roadside trees leading to airport in Kingston, that became a national symbol of the destruction caused by Hurricane Gilbert (photograph by Philip R. Berke).

and economic woes of the country. When it came ashore, Gilbert was a severe storm, with sustained winds exceeding 80 miles per hour and wind gusts to nearly 140 miles per hour. Gilbert was a fast-moving storm, moving across the entire length of the island in about nine hours. The track of the storm meant that there were few areas in the country that were not impacted. Forty-five people were killed, and some 400,000 were evacuated from their homes. Several thousands had been squatters so were unable to use conventional sources of aid to re-build. These people lived in tents for a number of months after the hur-ricane (see figure 3.4).

Most of the damages resulted from the storm's high winds and from rainfall. A very high percentage of homes and buildings were damaged or destroyed. It has been estimated that some 20 percent of the island's housing stock was damaged and 2 percent was destroyed (USAID 1989). Not surprisingly, low-income residents were the hardest hit by the hur-ricane. Damages to public utilities were also substantial, especially to the Jamaica Power Company, due to the extensive toppling of electric poles. Other public buildings and infrastructure were destroyed or damaged, including airports, hospitals and clinics, roads and bridges, and schools and community centers (see figure 3.5). There were signifi-cant damages to crops (e.g., the banana crop was virtually wiped out) and to the natural environment (for a review of the ecological effects of the storm, see Caribbean Environment Programme 1989). Some sixty thousand acres of natural forests were destroyed as well as a substan-tial acreage of plantation trees (Barker and Miller 1990). Landslides and beach erosion were also experienced. Total damages have been esti-mated to exceed US$1 billion.

The erosion and flooding that followed the storm were, again, symp-tomatic of the gradual degradation of the Jamaican natural environment and its ability to adapt to and withstand hurricanes. Despite a recent spate of environmental laws and regulations, many environmentally de-structive practices, including deforestation, mangrove destruction, and mining, continue. Barker and Miller (1990) note the environmental fragility of the island: "Prior to the onslaught of Hurricane Gilbert, many of the watersheds across Jamaica, and especially in the steeply sloping, highly desertified terrain of the Blue Mountains, were in a badly degraded condition due to accelerated erosion as a consequence of both historical and contemporary agricultural practice. . . . As a re-sult, the potential damaging effects of Gilbert were maximized because the environment was already in a fragile state" (111).

HOUSEHOLD CHARACTERISTICS
AND DAMAGE PATTERNS

The characteristics used to describe the predisaster demographics of the survey households were sex, education, marital status, housing type, income, and presence of insurance. The damage to the housing of these households were measured on a four-point scale consistent with the building damage categories used for determining eligibility for the government's Building Stamp Programme. A score of 1 (the Programme's "no damage") indicated no damage, a score of 2 (the Programme's "light damage") indicated partial roof loss, a score of 3 (the Programme's "heavy damage") indicated severe damage to roof and walls, and a score of 4 (the Programme's "destroyed") indicated total loss. Table 3.1 shows that there were no significant differences between the two parishes for six of eight household characteristics: sex, marital status, housing type, income, insurance, and level of damage.[1] Even though education and age were significantly different ($p < .01$), these characteristics were not significant in explaining modes of recovery activities and mitigation and compliance decisions (Berke, Beatley, and Feagin 1991).[2] Thus, as discussed in chapter 1, we are confident of the comparability between the sample groups.

Of particular interest are the findings for housing type and damage characteristics. Using a housing market classification model developed by Lim (1987), three categories of housing types were created based on land and house tenure status of households. *Owners* refer to householders who have legal ownership title to the land and house, *renters* are householders who have legal title to rent or lease the house and land, and *squatters* are householders who own or rent the house but who have illegal and insecure land tenure status. Table 3.1 shows that a ma-

---

1. An occupation classification scheme for Jamaican residents (Wint and Persenne 1984) was used for asking householders their annual income. It is particularly difficult to determine income levels for poor households, as income is often sporadic and household members do not typically add up money earned each month or year (CRDC 1990).

2. Logistical regression analysis was used to test the effect of education, age, and other characteristics listed in table 3.1. This type of analysis was used when the dependent variable was dichotomous. Variables presented in tables 3.3 through 3.8 were dichotomized. Least-squares regression analysis was used to explain variation in an index value by summing the items listed in table 3.9.

TABLE 3.I. Characteristics of Survey Respondents, St. James and
St. Thomas

	St. James (%)	St. Thomas (%)	Chi-Square
Sex			.8[a]
Male	43.0	48.7	
Female	57.0	51.3	
Education			16.8 (<.01)[b]
Completed secondary school	50.4	63.4	
Did not complete high school	8.7	.9	
High school graduate	10.4	12.8	
Attended college	30.4	18.0	
Marital status			.93[a]
Single	26.5	28.2	
Common law marriage	19.0	23.1	
Legal marriage	54.6	48.7	
Age			15.9 (<.01)[b]
Less than 18	0.0	1.7	
18–35	32.2	16.8	
36–45	30.6	21.8	
46–55	16.5	26.9	
Over 55	20.7	32.8	
Housing category			.8[a]
Squatter	14.9	15.1	
Renter	33.9	28.6	
Owner	51.2	56.3	
Income level (as evidenced by occupation)			1.0[a]
Upper income	11.6	8.4	
Upper middle/middle	28.1	26.9	
Working class	28.1	27.7	
Poor	32.2	37.0	
Insurance coverage			.6[a]
Had insurance	56.7	52.5	
Had no insurance	43.3	48.5	
Level of housing damage[b]			4.2[a]
No damage	0.0	1.7	
Partial loss of roof	27.3	30.2	
Heavy loss of roof and walls	57.9	45.4	
House totaly destroyed	14.9	22.7	

[a] Not significant.
[b] Significant.
[c] The no-damage and partial-loss-of-roof categories were collapsed to compute the chi-square.

jority of respondents in both parishes were owners. Renters comprised the next highest proportion, with squatters the smallest proportion.[3]

Hurricane Gilbert's winds were in excess of 130 miles per hour; not since Hurricane Charlie of 1951 had Jamaica experienced such devastation. A majority of households in both parishes (72.8 percent in St. James and 68.1 percent in St. Thomas) suffered either heavy losses to walls and roofs or the total destruction of their homes, and few households (none in St. James and only 1.7 percent in St. Thomas) escaped damage. Indeed, throughout Jamaica damage to the built environment was an estimated $US1 billion (IMPERU 1989), with a death toll of forty-five and 400,000 people rendered temporarily homeless. To put these costs into perspective, the damage exceeded the country's annual foreign exchange earnings from exports (Barker and Miller 1990). Table 3.2, which presents findings on damages by housing type for each parish, shows that squatters suffered more than renters and owners.[4] A plausible explanation for this pattern is that, given the insecure land tenure status of squatters, they have little incentive to invest in building or maintaining well-constructed housing. In an islandwide survey of damages, IMPERU (1989) found that squatters, and low-income households in general, tend to build homes that are not securely anchored to foundations and that are constructed with thin wooden siding and flooring.

3. Caution should be used in interpreting these housing distribution findings. Clarke (1989) documents numerous obstacles to obtaining accurate assessments of the squatter population on Jamaica (e.g., high mobility, no formal address, and reluctance to divulge land tenure status) and the resulting wide variations in squatter population estimates. In a survey of 342 households in four parishes recovering from Hurricane Gilbert, Cuffe (1989) found that squatters were underrepresented, and renters overrepresented, in the sample. The study notes that numerous squatters misrepresented their land tenure status, indicating that they had a legal lease land tenure arrangement. This response was likely due to fear of not qualifying for housing recovery assistance under the government's Building Stamp Programme, which required legal land tenure status for eligibility.

Cuffe's survey, however, was conducted three months after the disaster (December 1988). At that time, only a small proportion of the building stamps were distributed and there was a strong reluctance among squatters to divulge their tenure status. Our survey may not have encountered this problem as extensively as the Cuffe survey did because it was conducted fifteen months after the disaster (December 1989), when about 90 percent of the building stamps had been issued. Thus we consider our data on housing distribution to be reasonably accurate.

4. The pattern of squatters suffering more damage than renters and owners is consistent with Cuffe's (1989) findings on damages by housing type.

TABLE 3.2. Housing Damage, St. James and St. Thomas

Damage	St. James Housing Type			St. Thomas Housing Type		
	Squatter	Renter	Owner	Squatter	Renter	Owner
No damage (%)	0.0	0.0	0.0	5.5	5.9	0.0
Light damage (%)	5.6	39.0	40.3	16.7	23.5	37.9
Heavy damage (%)	55.5	61.0	58.1	27.8	50.0	54.5
Destroyed (%)	38.9	0.0	1.6	50.0	20.6	7.6
N	18	41	62	18	34	66

Another explanation is that the informal sector accounts for 70 percent of all new construction on Jamaica (CRDC 1990). Homeowner builders and small-scale carpenters may pay less attention to the formal building code, which provides for disaster mitigation, than to prevailing building practices and the need to minimize construction costs. Moreover, the Jamaican building code covers only a limited area: incorporated municipalities and areas within a mile of the coastline. Furthermore, squatters tend to build on marginal land, which they can do since land use planning on Jamaica is rudimentary and largely ineffectual. The Town and Country Planning Act was enacted in 1957, but land use control and development guidance is weak, and the enforcement of existing provisions is limited. The primary authority for guiding land use is lodged in central government ministries, with parish authorities restricted to building and subdivision control, poor relief (welfare), cemeteries, sanitation, and street lighting.

Thus, land use authorities are not able to prevent the population's exposure to natural disasters, as illustrated by the situation in the Bambo River floodplain in St. Thomas. The Bambo River drainage basin is located in the Blue Mountains and has a steep gradient, which creates a narrow, high-velocity floodway. More than a hundred squatter residential structures in the Bambo River floodplain were destroyed by floodwaters associated with rainfall from Hurricane Gilbert. The parish building inspector readily admitted during an interview that St. Thomas Parish has little practical ability to prevent settlement and construction in this area and pointed out that a similar problem occurred along the Yallas River floodplain in St. Thomas. St. James Parish experienced comparable destruction by allowing housing for the poor to be built in steep hillside areas prone to landslides after heavy rains.

RECOVERY STRATEGIES

Recovery strategies on Jamaica included the government's Building Stamp Programme, relocation in temporary housing, and the acquisition of building materials.

The Building Stamp Programme

The primary formal housing aid program created after Hurricane Gilbert made landfall was the Building Stamp Programme. Under this government-backed initiative, with financial assistance from the World Bank, Canada, Germany, Japan, OPEC, and the United States, householders were issued building stamps based on extent of damages and financial need. Stamps could then be redeemed for their monetary value in lumber, nails, hurricane straps, zinc sheets, and other building materials. Stamps could be used only at building supply stores that were members of the Jamaican Hardware Merchants Association.

Stamps were restricted to householders who owned homes and had legal title to the land. Thus squatters and renters were not eligible to participate in the Programme (see figure 3.6). Since the Building Stamp Programme was the major source of aid for home repair or replacement, meeting the needs of the poorest in Jamaican society was a salient shortcoming during the aftermath of Hurricane Gilbert. Clearly, in this case international aid did not reach thousands of the most needy. Table 3.3 indicates the percentage of householders in the sample who received building stamps and the value of the stamps. A greater proportion of households in the St. Thomas sample received building stamps compared to households in St. James. Similarly, the value of stamps was higher in St. Thomas than in St. James.

A major reason St. Thomas respondents received proportionally more stamps and at a greater value was the great disparity in the length of time it took to initiate the Programme. In St. Thomas, assessment of damages and distribution of stamps were initiated in November 1988, two months after Gilbert. In St. James, residents did not begin to receive building stamps until April 1989, seven months after Gilbert, and then it was due to a change in the party in power (from the JLP to the PNP) precipitated by the national elections in February 1989. Recall that St. James is a PNP parish and thus in February became politically aligned with the newly elected national government. Indeed, this issue was quite salient among those interviewed in St. James. While no evidence was found on whether the delay in distribution of stamps to St. James

FIGURE 3.6. Squatter's house in village of Llandewy: family did not return due to their ineligibility for assistance under the Building Stamp Programme (photograph by Philip R. Berke).

was politically or administratively motivated, there was a widespread perception among those interviewed in St. James that the decision was political. One Montego Bay householder, commenting on the distribution of stamps, maintained that, "if it was up to them JLP boys we would never get nothing."[5]

Even for households that received stamps, there was concern that the value of the stamps was insufficient to undertake necessary repairs. We suspect that many households in St. James initiated repairs before the damage assessors of the Jamaica Defense Force (JDF) reached their homes. As a result, households either were ineligible for participation or they were eligible for considerably less aid because their homes were

5. A second, but less important, reason for the disparity between the two parishes was that St. Thomas householders whose homes were completely destroyed were issued a stamp for the maximum benefit (J$10,000) for buying either building materials or a complete housing kit known as the Hexcell House, but St. James householders were given only the option of the housing kit. This discrepancy, however, is not likely to induce major changes in findings presented in table 3.3, as only 1.6 percent of the houses of the eligible households in the St. James survey group were destroyed.

TABLE 3.3. Receipt and Value of Building Stamps, St. James and
        St. Thomas

	St. James	St. Thomas
Received building stamps[a]		
Yes (%)	30.8	57.1
No (%)	69.2	42.9
N	120	119
Value of building stamps[b]		
Less than J$1,500 (%)	37.8	39.7
J$1,500–J$3,999 (%)	56.8	29.6
J$4,000 or more (%)	5.4	39.7
N	37	68

[a] Chi-square 16.8, $df\,1$, p = <.001.
[b] Chi-square 19.6, $df\,2$, p = <.001.

partially repaired at the time of the damage assessments. Interviews in
both parishes with householders, building officials, and representatives
of community-based NGOs revealed that the shortfall was partially attributed to flaws in the JDF damage assessment methodology. Because
JDF soldiers conducted only a quick and crude assessment, with no follow-up, they often tended to underestimate the extent of damage. Comments like "They didn't look closely" and "They didn't look for cracks"
expressed the sentiments of many of those interviewed. Interviews also
revealed concerns about JDF "being unfamiliar with local geography,"
"missing entire neighborhoods," and "people not being at home when
JDF came." Evidently, an entire small residential district in St. Thomas
(Mt. Stewart, where two hundred people lived) was completely overlooked by the JDF damage assessment teams and thus did not receive
any building stamps. Apparently, the JDF, not knowing the local geography, did not expect people to be living in this particular area, the location of which was not obvious simply by looking on a map. A frequently cited problem with damage assessment was that, to get one's
name on the list to qualify for stamps, one had to be at home when the
JDF came through, which was problematic because people might be
working in the sugarcane fields or other places of employment, and if
their homes were destroyed or heavily damaged they were likely to be
living with family and friends.

Interviews also revealed a widespread perception that unscrupulous individuals presented themselves to JDF damage assessment teams as the owners of houses they did not own. The manager of a local bank in St. James Parish indicated that one family had received two $J10,000 ($US2,000) stamps for the same destroyed house. We also heard repeatedly from interviewees about two or three individuals receiving building stamps for the same damaged house.

Despite such concerns about the ineptness of the JDF, interviews revealed a consensus that damage assessments were not biased, politically or otherwise. As one homeowner indicated, "The army had no ax to grind." There was considerable suspicion, however, that political manipulation of the list of damaged homes occurred later, as certain names were added or taken off based on political affiliation. In the words of a local building supplier, "The whole system was rigged according to your politics, but the JDF was left out." Survey responses were consistent with interviews and gave high marks to the JDF: 94.3 percent of St. James respondents and 93 percent in St. Thomas rated the JDF as "highly effective" or "somewhat effective" during the disaster recovery period. The difference between parishes was not significant (chi-square = .6, df = 2, not significant).

During interviews we were told that damage assessments would have been more effectively conducted, and benefits more equitably distributed, if they had been undertaken by community-based NGOs like the Red Cross, the Association of Development Agencies (an organization representing some forty NGOs), and church groups. Many believed that local damage assessments would have been more complete and accurate, because local people have a much better understanding than the JDF of local circumstances; local assessment teams would have had a much better understanding of where people actually lived and would have been better able to assess claims of home ownership and to identify those in greatest need of housing assistance. In fact, many local NGOs, as well as specially formed parish disaster recovery organizations, compiled their own damage lists to use in distributing their own forms of assistance. There was, however, no effort by the central government to utilize these lists to verify the JDF lists.

Households receiving stamps were also asked how they used them. Table 3.4 indicates that, while a majority of respondents who received stamps complied with the formal guidelines by trading them to building suppliers for materials, there was a substantial difference in compliance rates between parishes: nearly all St. James respondents complied,

TABLE 3.4. Compliance with Building Stamp Programme, St. James
and St. Thomas

Compliance Decisions of Those Receiving Building Stamps	St. James	St. Thomas
Traded for cash (%)	0.0	5.9
Traded for goods other than building materials (%)	2.7	22.1
Traded for building supplies (%)	97.3	72.0
N	37	68

Note: Chi-square could not be calculated due to inadequate cell counts.

while about three-fourths from St. Thomas did. Additionally, our survey contained questions on the two primary ways people used stamps for informal or "unofficial" purposes. In St. Thomas, 22.1 percent of the respondents with stamps traded them for goods other than building supplies prescribed by the government, and 5.9 percent traded them for cash. In contrast, only 2.7 percent of St. James respondents with stamps traded for goods, and none traded for cash. Interviews, however, led us to suspect that the extent of unofficial uses were higher in both parishes than indicated by the survey results. It could be that unofficial uses of the stamps were underreported by survey respondents because of concern over revealing that they may have broken the law. Interviews further revealed that the occurrence of unofficial use was quite common.

A plausible explanation of the unofficial use of the stamps was that, according to householders in both parishes, the list of building materials that could be purchased with the stamps did not meet their rebuilding needs. There was widespread consensus among households interviewed that they wanted more flexibility in rebuilding their structures and could have utilized materials other than lumber, nails, and the few other materials permitted. Some people wanted paint, for instance. In partial recognition of this inadequacy, an exception was made in St. James Parish by the Ministry of Housing on Kingston to allow stamp holders to purchase two bags of cement. While the exception was helpful, hardware store owners noted that two bags of cement do not go very far.

One explanation for the differences between parishes in their compliance with the Stamp Programme is that St. Thomas is rural, while St. James is urban. Rural populations, particularly in developing countries, tend to be more isolated and self-reliant than urban populations (Bolin 1982). Thus, rural residents might be less dependent on aid and more likely to use it in ways not in compliance with formal government-backed initiatives, like the Building Stamp Programme. Another explanation is the failure of the Stamp Programme to provide for transportation to building supply stores in St. Thomas, where transport systems are less developed than in St. James. The provision of a cash allowance for transportation served to open the Stamp Programme to even greater abuses. The fact that stamp holders were going to get cash for transportation meant that it was probably easier for hardware store owners to provide even greater cash redemptions. Indeed, 91.2 percent of St. Thomas households receiving stamps indicated that they had difficulties with transporting materials due to high costs, while a lower but nevertheless substantial percentage (37.8 percent) in St. James indicated a difficulty with transportation. This difference is significant (chi-square = 39.0, $df = 1$, $p < .005$). One hardware store owner in St. Thomas estimated that van drivers were typically charging J$150 (US$30) or J$200 (US$40) to transport materials. He claimed that "people just don't have it." Some building supply stores made efforts to facilitate transportation, such as Baugh Hardware in St. James, which claimed to have made free deliveries to customers. Still others, like International Hardware of St. Thomas, arranged for transportation and then deducted the cost from the building stamp. But the mayor of St. Thomas observed that some hardware stores "were getting rich from the Building Stamp Programme." One building supply store owner observed that "80 percent of the supply stores are doing it." A local bank manager in St. Thomas maintained that "all the hardware stores were doing it."

Interviews with parish and other officials revealed numerous ways in which people unofficially redeemed stamps for cash or goods. In the case of cash redemption, a common scenario was for the building supply store owner to agree to change, for example, a J$10,000 (US$2,000) stamp for J$6,000 (US$1,200), retaining the remainder of the stamp as a profit for the cashing service. In the words of the head of the Building Stamp Programme in St. Thomas Parish, who acknowledged that such practices did occur, "Some people were desperate to get some money in their hands." It was apparently also common for stamp holders to redeem their stamps partially for building supplies and to receive back cash or goods that did not qualify under the guidelines. We were told of cases where individuals would redeem building materials and then sell them. Also, some store owners would provide cash for stamps but would calculate the profit they would have made and then deduct this from the amount of cash provided to the stamp holder. If one wanted to redeem a $5,000 stamp for cash, the shop owner might withhold $1,000 or more on the grounds that that much profit would have been made on the sale of $5,000 worth of building supplies.

There were also many reported cases of stamps being redeemed for goods and merchandise other than building materials. The Reverend Saunders of the Anglican Church in St. Thomas knew of a young boy who attempted to cash in a $10,000 building stamp for three bicycles (his mother worked in the department store where this was attempted). While this department store turned down the youth, Saunders later saw the boy riding a new bicycle and concluded that he had found a store willing to make such a trade. One bank official knew of an instance where stamps were used to purchase televisions and gas stoves. We were told of another case where stamps were used to buy rum and cigarettes. The attitude of some shop owners was, "If you want something we'll get it for you." We were told that some stores stockpiled such goods as mattresses and gas stoves to satisfy demand.

To many stamp recipients it was more important to have a little money in their pocket than to repair their homes to prestorm conditions. As long as they had made adequate repairs and the roof was not leaking too badly, priority was given to more immediate concerns. And, after all, many people were out of work following the storm and were undoubtedly in need of cash for normal living expenses. We heard stories of people who used building stamp supplies or cash to finance needed repairs to their businesses or farms. Indeed, some of the irregularity in the Stamp Programme was a result of individuals trying to obtain what most would agree are essential household items, such as mattresses and eating utensils. Several people observed that hardware stores were getting rich from the Building Stamp Programme. One bank official offered as evidence the dramatic change he saw in a hardware store in Port Morant, which had been a struggling and meager operation before the hurricane but which was now well stocked and had even bought a delivery truck. This observer believed the Building Stamp Program was responsible for the metamorphosis.

Not surprisingly, few building supply store owners would admit to irregularities, such as "changing" stamps for cash or for nonapproved goods. Most appeared to believe that these practices were widespread but were "not done here." The store owners who were interviewed understood that such practices were not allowed under the program. When pressed to identify which shops undertook such practices, there was great reluctance to point fingers. One store owner, a justice of the peace and a person repeatedly identified by individuals outside the building supply business as one of the more respectable among them, believed the majority of shop owners had engaged in these types of activities. The owner of a building supply store in village of Yallas in St. Thomas admitted that she allowed stamp holders to redeem the stamps for cash or for other goods such as televisions, believing that it was up to the people to decide what was most important to them. She indicated that this practice was permitted for about the first month following the issuance of stamps but that she stopped it after she received a warning from enforcement officials at the Ministry of Social Security. Another store owner, in Morant Bay, admitted that he allowed an individual to purchase a mattress with a building stamp.

The attitude on the part of many was that, while redeeming stamps for cash or other goods was not officially allowed, it was understandable and indeed O.K. A member of parliament representing the eastern constituency of St. Thomas Parish expressed these sentiments during an interview. While these transactions were unethical because "that's not what the donor agencies intended . . . who's to say they can't do it? . . . Its just between the shop owner and the homeowner, and nobody is going to prosecute them."

Rebuilding

The actual process of rebuilding presented numerous obstacles to households. Because of the extent and magnitude of the devastation, demand for wood, nails, and roofing quickly exhausted supplies. People were displaced from their homes for many months. The late arrival of building stamps and subsequent shipment of building materials further delayed recovery efforts, especially in St. James (see table 3.5). Table 3.6 provides additional information on the problems caused by the long delays in distributing of supplies in St. James. An open-ended follow-up question was posed to those respondents who indicated that they had relocated, asking them to specify the shelter strategy they had used. Moving in with friends was the most frequently cited strategy: 49.6 percent in St. James and 28.6 percent in St. Thomas. The remaining shelter strategies (10–20 percent) included moving in with relatives, going to an official shelter, or building a makeshift shelter. These interim living arrangements are obviously disruptive to the lives of the disaster stricken (Bolin and Bolton 1986). Thus, it appears that delays in distributing building stamps contributed to the suffering, particularly in St. James Parish.

Interviewees told of various formal and informal strategies they used to obtain building materials. Some salvaged materials from their damaged or destroyed homes, others relied on materials donated by family and friends, and still others took more extraordinary measures. In one case, several residents from a middle-class neighborhood in St. James flew to Miami to purchase plastic sheets for making temporary repairs to leaky roofs. But given the widespread devastation, seeking aid through such informal strategies only partially met the rebuilding needs of most households. Survey findings indicate that, of the five sources listed on table 3.7, the only formal source (purchased materials from a building supplier) was the most frequently used: more than three-fourths of the respondents bought materials from supply stores. Salvaging materials from the householders' previous home was the most common informal source. The three remaining informal sources (trades, material donated by family and friends, and material salvaged from the neighborhood) were used by 5.9 percent or less of the respondents. As discussed, in developing countries, self-help and informal aid from family, neighbors, and volunteers are typically more important to disaster-stricken households than formal aid from the government or the private sector (Bolin and Bolton 1983). However, because of widespread destruction across the entire country, rather than localized pockets typical of most disasters, makeshift forms of acquiring materials needed to be supplemented with large-scale assistance.

MITIGATION ACTIONS

Table 3.8 indicates that a majority of responding households from both parishes did not undertake mitigation actions during rebuilding. However, a greater proportion of St. James respondents undertook one or more mitigation actions than St. Thomas respondents, and this difference was significant. In addition, a follow-up, open-ended question was posed to those households that undertook mitigation to specify the type of measures used. The most frequently cited measures (25 percent or more from each parish) were hurricane straps and thicker gauge zinc roofing. A small percentage of households (10 percent or less form each parish) indicated that they installed anchoring systems, erected concrete roofs and walls, and relocated their homesites from high-risk to low-risk areas.

TABLE 3.5. Availability of Building Materials, St. James and
      St. Thomas

Number of Weeks for Materials to Become Available	St. James	St. Thomas
Less than 2 weeks (%)	32.1	61.2
2–6 weeks (%)	10.1	5.1
7–14 weeks (%)	10.1	5.1
15–24 weeks (%)	34.9	5.1
25 weeks or more (%)	12.8	23.5
N	109	98

Note: Chi-square 38.1, $df4$, p = <.001.

TABLE 3.6. Dislocation Time, St. James and St. Thomas

Number of Months until Moved Back into Own House	St. James	St. Thomas
Did not move or less than 1 month (%)	37.5	80.2
1–3 months (%)	16.7	10.5
4–6 months (%)	5.8	5.8
7–9 months (%)	37.5	2.3
10 months or more (%)	2.5	1.2
N	120	86

Note: Chi-square 45.5, $df4$, p = <.001.

TABLE 3.7. Acquisition of Building Materials, St. James and
      St. Thomas

Source of Building Material	St. James (%)	St. Thomas (%)	Chi-Square[a]
Purchased from building supplier	79.3	77.3	.1
Traded	0.8	2.5	1.1
Salvaged from previous house	26.5	18.5	2.2
Donated by family or friends	5.0	1.7	2.0
Salvaged from neighborhood	1.7	5.9	3.0

[a] Not significant.

TABLE 3.8. Recovery Decisions, St. James and St. Thomas

	St. James	*St. Thomas*
No mitigation measures taken (%)	58.7	71.4
One mitigation measure per household (%)	41.3	28.6
N	121	119

Note: Chi-square 4.3, *df* 1, *p* = <.05.

There are several plausible explanations for the limited mitigation activity in both parishes. Recall that most of the rebuilding effort occurred in the informal sector. Within this sector, new construction and reconstruction is largely undertaken by individual homeowners or carpenters who pay little attention to formal building codes and who do not obtain building permits even when they are supposed to obtain them. A second explanation was the difficulty in finding qualified carpenters. It is likely that, in response to the rise in demand for carpenters, many workers who were laid off from their jobs following the storm entered the carpentry market. Overnight, many people, often referred to as "hurricane tradesmen," with little formal training and knowledge of building codes, began to sell their "carpentry" services (CRDC 1990). A third explanation is that building codes still played a limited role in reconstruction. Recall that the Jamaican building code applied to only a incorporated municipalities and areas located within a mile of the coastline. Under code provisions, reconstruction did not require a building permit if the owner intended only to restore or replace the building to its previous condition. Further, code enforcement staff was inadequate: there were only one part-time inspector in St. Thomas and two full-time inspectors in St. James. And no provisions in the Building Stamp Programme tied the use of stamps to structural mitigation.

Because St. James respondents experienced longer delays in obtaining building stamps and supplies and in relocating to their original homesites, we expected they would be less likely than St. Thomas respondents to undertake substantial repairs. However, these expectations were not confirmed; a greater proportion of St. James respondents than St. Thomas respondents incorporated mitigation actions into rebuilding. In part, the difference may be due to a greater postdisaster educational effort in St. James. Between January 1989 and January 1990, some twenty postdisaster training workshops on rebuilding were conducted. Each

workshop consisted of a group of trainees (twenty or more) who actually constructed housing units under the supervision of trained carpenters. The trainees were taught about adequate anchoring, the use of
hurricane straps, and safe locations for structures. Short of a few posters
pinned to the office walls of the Ministry of Labour, Welfare, and Sport
in Morant Bay, there were no educational programs in St. Thomas to
encourage sound repair and reconstruction practices. Another possible
reason for the difference in mitigation practices between the parishes is
that, because of the rural character of St. Thomas, public policy issues
tend to be more parochial than in St. James. St. Thomas residents are
thus less likely to react positively to national concerns over reducing
risk from future hurricanes.

HOUSEHOLD EVALUATIONS OF GOVERNMENT

While identification of various actions taken by households to acquire
aid and to apply mitigation practices is pertinent, households' evaluation
of the adequacy of aid received is also important. That is, enumerations
of the sources and amounts of aid do not indicate a household's perceptions of the sufficiency of the aid. Key indicators of household perceptions are evaluations of government organizational recovery efforts.

Survey respondents were asked to rate how well eighteen different recovery issues (see table 3.9) were handled by the government. Two patterns of findings were derived from these ratings. First, both parish survey groups were somewhat more negative than positive in their
assessment of the overall government recovery effort. On the one hand,
six issues (demolishing damaged buildings, beautifying the community,
handling foreign aid, reconstructing medical facilities, reconstructing
schools, and providing permanent housing) were rated as poorly or very
poorly handled by a majority of both parish groups. On the other hand,
only three issues (restoring telephone service, clearing debris, and
restoring electricity) were considered very well handled or well handled by a majority of respondents from both parishes.

A comparison of our findings with findings from a survey of 749 randomly selected households one year after the 1985 Mexico City earthquake (Quarentelli, Dynes, and Wenger 1992) reinforces our interpretation. Households in Mexico City were asked to rate how well fifteen
recovery issues were handled by the Mexican government. These issues
are similar to the issues used in the Jamaican sample. Unlike the somewhat negative assessments of the Jamaican government, Mexico City

TABLE 3.9. Government Handling of Issues

Issue	Very Well 1	Well 2	Average 3	Poor 4	Very Poor 5	Chi-Square Significance
Assessing damage						30.5 (<.001)
St. James (N = 114)	14.0	15.8	29.8	28.1	12.3	
St. Thomas (N = 115)	1.7	10.4	20.0	28.7	39.1	
Restoring telephone service						6.6 (n.a.)
St. James (N = 109)	36.7	38.5	16.5	6.4	1.8	
St. Thomas (N = 113)	25.7	38.1	28.3	4.4	3.5	
Providing shelters						20.6 (<.001)
St. James (N = 114)	14.0	18.4	34.2	25.4	7.9	
St. Thomas (N = 116)	2.6	22.4	56.0	13.0	6.0	
Demolishing heavily damaged buildings						n.a.
St. James (N = 72)	8.3	6.9	29.2	31.9	23.6	
St. Thomas (N = 95)	1.1	5.3	28.4	22.1	43.2	
Clearing debris						25.8 (<.001)
St. James (N = 119)	57.1	23.5	8.4	6.7	4.2	
St. Thomas (N = 116)	34.5	49.1	13.8	2.6	.0	
Enforcing mitigation						44.5 (<.001)
St. James (N = 95)	11.6	23.2	26.3	23.2	15.8	
St. Thomas (N = 93)	2.2	2.2	20.4	19.4	55.9	
Beautifying community						6.8 (n.a.)
St. James (N = 102)	5.9	3.9	18.6	35.3	36.3	
St. Thomas (N = 108)	1.9	8.3	13.9	28.7	47.2	
Handling foreign aid honestly						21.5 (<.001)
St. James (N = 103)	8.7	9.7	13.6	31.1	36.8	
St. Thomas (N = 106)	.0	4.7	3.8	34.9	56.6	
Restoring streets						44.1
St. James (N = 114)	11.4	14.0	29.8	32.5	12.3	
St. Thomas (N = 115)	.9	8.7	20.9	19.1	50.4	
Providing housing assistance						30.0 (<.001)
St. James (N = 114)	12.3	16.7	27.2	30.7	13.2	
St. Thomas (N = 115)	.9	8.7	56.5	28.7	5.2	

(Continued)

Issue	Very Well 1	Well 2	Average 3	Poor 4	Very Poor 5	Chi-Square Significance
Reconstructing medical facilities						12.5 (<.05)
St. James (N = 118)	4.2	7.6	17.8	31.4	39.0	
St. Thomas (N = 116)	.0	6.0	8.6	29.3	56.0	
Informing public						13.6 (<.01)
St. James (N = 109)	11.9	17.4	30.3	24.8	15.6	
St. Thomas (N = 112)	17.9	33.0	25.0	18.8	5.4	
Restoring water						23.9 (<.001)
St. James (N = 120)	30.0	34.2	23.3	9.2	3.3	
St. Thomas (N = 112)	7.1	42.9	40.2	8.9	.9	
Reconstructing schools						8.5 (n.s)
St. James (N = 116)	3.5	13.8	30.2	32.8	19.8	
St. Thomas (N = 116)	4.3	12.9	22.4	24.1	36.2	
Restoring transportation						29.5 (<.001)
St. James (N = 114)	6.1	17.5	21.1	34.2	21.1	
St. Thomas (N = 111)	5.4	47.8	22.5	16.2	8.1	
Restoring electricity						n.a.
St. James (N = 120)	63.3	26.7	7.5	1.7	.8	
St. Thomas (N = 118)	63.6	29.7	5.9	.8	.0	
Making building materials available						25.6 (<.001)
St. James (N = 116)	24.1	31.9	24.1	14.7	5.1	
St. Thomas (N = 116)	8.6	25.0	19.8	23.3	23.3	
Providing permanent housing						10.6 (<.05)
St. James (N = 106)	4.7	12.3	22.6	31.1	29.3	
St. Thomas (N = 107)	1.9	3.7	15.9	45.8	32.7	

Source: List of issues adapted from Quarentelli, Dynes, and Wenger (1992).
Note: N.a. indicates that a chi-square could not be calculated due to inadequate cell counts; n.s. = not significant.

respondents consistently gave positive evaluations of their government. In fact, only one issue (handling foreign aid) was considered by a majority of households to be very poorly or poorly handled. The differences in findings between Jamaica and Mexico can be attributed in part to differing cultural values and beliefs. According to Quarentelli, Dynes, and Wenger (1992), the general absence of fault finding and blame of the government is consistent with Mexican cultural values. From the perspective of many Jamaicans, however, the Mexican reaction might seem passive and unchallenging of authority. Research indicates that Jamaican society is dominated by an aggressive value system with a violent undercurrent and that disaster-stricken people tend to be more active in their reactions to disaster-related problems and quick to blame organizations (Barker and Miller 1990).

The second pattern of findings derived from table 3.9 shows that St. James respondents generally gave the government higher ratings than did St. Thomas respondents in its handling of a range of recovery issues. Nine of the eighteen issues were rated significantly higher by St. James respondents, while only two issues were rated significantly higher by St. Thomas respondents. A partial interpretation of this finding might be that St. Thomas is rural while St. James is urban. Rural people in developing countries like Jamaica are more self-reliant than urban people (Bolin 1982) and are thus less dependent on—and more suspicious of—outside authorities' aid. Another interpretation might have to do with St. James being closely aligned with the PNP, which has been in power on Jamaica since the early stages (February 1989) of the Hurricane Gilbert recovery effort. St. Thomas, however, is largely supportive of the opposition party, the JLP. Given the widespread and deeply rooted system of political patronage in Jamaica (Stone 1989), it is likely that no matter what the actual aid allocations were, the party status of the parishes caused many residents to believe that politics were involved in all aid distribution decisions (Cuffe 1989). Thus, St. James residents might have believed that they benefited from government aid allocation decisions, and St. Thomas respondents might have believed that they suffered from these decisions. Recall that the government's Building Stamp Programme started five months sooner in St. Thomas than in St. James, yet St. James respondents rated the government's efforts at making building materials available significantly higher than did St. Thomas respondents. Specifically, 56 percent of St. James respondents rated this issue as very well handled or well handled, compared to 33.6 percent in St. Thomas.

Field interviews confirm the important role of politics in the aid distribution process. There was strong consensus among those interviewed in St. James that the parish benefited from government decisions, and all but one of the St. Thomas interviewees believed that they did not. Interviews also revealed a strong perception in both parishes that politics influenced not only the distribution of building stamps but also distribution decisions in other programs, such as water and health care and, especially, those under the control of central government ministries, like roads. The case of the government's zinc sheeting program depicts how this politicized decision-making process operates.

THE DISTRIBUTION OF ZINC SHEETING

Interviewees were unanimous in believing that the distribution of zinc sheeting for roof and wall repair was affected by politics. The program was set up in October 1989 (about one month after the storm). However, almost all of the sheeting was distributed after the February 1989 national elections. Households that were most in need, including those that did not qualify for building stamps, were eligible to acquire a few sheets of zinc to repair leaky roofs and damaged walls. The intention of the system worked out in parliament was to distribute the sheets in a politically balanced fashion to all parishes in the country. Sheets were allotted to each parish through its two members of parliament (MPs) and one "caretaker," representing the parish opposition party. The allotment was to be distributed through disaster recovery committees in different parts of each parish. Committees were to consist of local government officials, members of the Red Cross and youth clubs, and church leaders, among others, and the zinc was to be distributed according to the JDF's damage assessments.

According to the mayor of St. Thomas Parish (who was a member of the opposition JLP), most of the committees in the parish distributed the sheeting on the basis of need and to those who had not received aid from the Building Stamp Programme. The committees were described as being apolitical and close to the people. They were viewed as an effective organizational arrangement to ensure fair and equitable distribution. Distribution by St. Thomas caretakers, however, was described as much more political. We were repeatedly told during interviews that the zinc sheets had been passed along by caretakers to potential opposition candidates and distributed by these opposition party members as a way to "buy" votes for future elections. The mayor described a scenario in which a candidate distributed the sheets from a trailer to those who were willing to support him in the next election.

The parish's deputy mayor was even more adamant in his belief that the zinc distribution process had been heavily influenced by politics. Because St. Thomas is a JLP parish, he maintained, the government provided much greater amounts of zinc to members of the PNP. He was convinced that his PNP opponent had much more zinc to distribute than he did and that it was distributed for political purposes. He called the process "corrupt," claiming that "his people" had been unfairly overlooked. The deputy mayor further claimed that the "so-called caretaker," of the PNP, had received more zinc than the two parish MPs combined.

A major limitation of the zinc program in St. Thomas, regardless of the politics involved in distribution, was the length of time it took for distribution. When field interviews were conducted in June 1990, officials in the parish had received the zinc sheets only about three months earlier. The deputy mayor had received his zinc only two months prior to our interview and was that day in the process of distributing it. Thus some zinc was not distributed until nearly twenty months following Hurricane Gilbert. By this time, of course, many disaster-stricken people had already made repairs to their homes, some permanent and some temporary. Thus it was not surprising to hear widespread claims that zinc recipients commonly sold their zinc rather than use it for repairs. All householders interviewed considered this action a legitimate way to compensate themselves for the costs of the original repairs.

The distribution of zinc sheets received almost uniform criticism by those interviewed in St. James Parish. As in St. Thomas, much of the material was delivered long after Hurricane Gilbert struck, and the process for distributing the zinc was highly politicized. The parish council secretary indicated that attempts were made to create a sensible and apolitical mechanism for distribution: a special distribution committee, consisting of representatives of such NGOs as the Red Cross and Project Accord, was organized in each subregion in the parish. The committees, however, were never used for distributing the zinc. Rather, it was distributed directly by MPs, in the case of PNP allocation, and caretakers, in the case of JLP allocation. Under the original plan to use the special committees, the zinc was to have been distributed according to the JDF's damage assessment as updated by the parish's poor relief division, but the MPs generally relied on local government officials (in the PNP), and these local officials followed the pattern of the parish mayor. During an interview, the mayor described a process that relied heavily on a "network of local leaders," which did its own damage assessment and compiled its own list of needy households.

It was difficult to determine whether the sheeting was distributed on the basis of need, on the basis of political affiliation, or on some combination of the two. The St. James Parish mayor did not deny that politics played a role, but he did contend that those who received the sheeting were in need of it. Other observers agreed that the sheets were given to those who were in need but that, because need far outstripped supply, politicians favored those in their own party. The consensus among almost all people interviewed was that it was axiomatic that zinc would go to political supporters. In the words of one astute observer, "Where do you think the zinc's going to go? Its obvious! It would be difficult for an MP or any other elected official to pass over a constituent in his party for someone in the other party."

The actual distribution of zinc to St. James from Kingston suggests serious political manipulation. First, the distribution scheme specified that the two PNP MPs' share be much greater than that provided to the JLP caretaker: the MPs were to have sixty thousand sheets to distribute, while the caretaker was to have thirty thousand sheets. Second, and more serious, was that zinc supplies were delivered to the MPs but were never delivered to the caretaker. As of June 1990, the caretaker had not received a single sheet of zinc. The caretaker was told that he could pick up his allotment of zinc at a central government warehouse in Kingston. However, when he sent his staff to pick up the sheets, they were turned away. According to the caretaker, this happened three times. "Two years after the hurricane many of my people are still getting wet in their homes," he said. He maintained that some people who had not incurred damages got materials.

It was disturbing to see the distribution of postdisaster recovery assistance like zinc occurring some twenty months after the hurricane. In June 1990, we visited a train depot in Montego Bay that was being used as a zinc distribution center. Lines had formed and scores of people were waiting for the distribution center to open (see figure 3.7). Numerous people commented during interviews that such materials were being distributed too late to do any good. Many had already made necessary repairs, and some would now take the zinc and sell it. One individual, carrying zinc to his home, told us that if we were interested in buying any we need only go down to the depot, that there was plenty for sale there. Some people who did not have homes were also observed

FIGURE 3.7. People waiting for zinc sheeting (photograph by
Timothy Beatley).

taking zinc sheets. Interviews also revealed numerous instances of people who received zinc several times for the same damaged home.

In addition, there were complaints about the meager quantity of zinc being provided—each person was allocated five sheets, which was widely considered inadequate. There was also much concern about the disappearance of zinc; according to the parish council secretary, a good deal of zinc was stolen from warehouses, where it was in storage, and more had been lost in transit. This zinc was undoubtedly sold for a profit. However, several people waiting in line were clearly going to put the zinc sheets to good use; an employee of a local food market, for example, explained that, although she had made temporary repairs to her roof several months earlier, she planned to use the zinc for permanent repairs—and indicated that friends and acquaintances were taking similar steps.

SUMMARY OF MAJOR FINDINGS

What do the data from Jamaica indicate about the validity of the various claims for the process of disaster recovery and sustainable development put forth in chapter 2? The household recovery process on Jamaica was not linear, ordered, and predictable as depicted by some investigations (Haas, Kates, and Bowden 1977). Indeed, the process was altered for a variety of reasons. Interorganizational coordination efforts that encourage local participation (design principle 1) was posited to have a positive influence on household recovery efforts. The evidence supports and extends this principle. Given the magnitude of the devastation wrought by Hurricane Gilbert, the central government had to be involved in aid distribution throughout Jamaica. The experience further suggests, however, that great advantages can be achieved by central government reliance on decentralized institutions for aid distribution. Despite numerous imperfections, the Building Stamp Programme widely distributed building materials through local networks of the Jamaican Hardware Merchants Association. Survey findings indicate that a majority of households in St. Thomas and nearly one-third in St. James that sustained damages benefited significantly from the Stamp Programme, and building materials provided by the stamps made an important difference to most households affected by Hurricane Gilbert. Inaccurate and unfair aid distribution was far more problematic in the zinc program, in which aid was funneled solely through an interorganizational arrangement dominated by a centralized and bureaucratic national government.

While our data indicate that collaboration with local groups is critical, political neutrality should also be considered a critical attribute of successful interorganizational coordination. The distribution of zinc sheets was highly politicized, since the entire distribution system was controlled by central government MPs. The enduring division between political party factions suggests that almost any distribution system that relies solely on the central government will be influenced by politics. The evidence thus indicates a need to bypass political allegiances and to identify politically neutral, interorganizational arrangements for distributing aid. Indeed, the JDF was widely viewed as being fair and trustworthy in assessing damages, and the local hardware merchant networks were not susceptible to tampering by political party authorities. Interviews revealed that other politically neutral, local NGOs were also considered potentially effective in assessing damages and distributing aid. These grassroots organizations typically have an intimate understanding of local damage patterns, skills for rebuilding, and building material needs.

A low-cost system to monitor aid run by both aid recipients and field staffs (design principle 2) is crucial to ensure that aid is used for its intended purposes. The evidence provides considerable support for this design principle. The data suggest that local monitoring was not incorporated into the design of Jamaican aid programs. Unlike central government ministries, local people do not have to invest additional time and effort to monitor aid programs: monitoring is a natural by-product of local people's motivation to ensure that households receive their fare share of assistance. By not incorporating the knowledge of those with detailed knowledge of infractions in the distribution and use of aid, lack of transport in St. Thomas, delayed delivery of aid, and inadequate types and amounts of aid, many programmatic flaws were not corrected. As a result, the timing, type, and amount of aid poorly matched household needs and thus constrained recovery efforts. Many infractions occurred because households sought more logical ways to use aid to meet their most pressing recovery needs.

Enforcement and sanctioning (design principle 3) should lead to high levels of compliance. Although we do not have hard evidence of how many abusers could have been stopped if more stringent enforcement and sanctions had been employed, the evidence suggests that some aid recipients were confident they could get away with infractions since the use of sanctions was virtually nonexistent. It is possible that the absence of this design principle further perpetuated and encouraged abuse.

The rights of local people to undertake self-directed recovery initiatives (design principle 4) was posited to be a powerful indicator of a successful recovery. The evidence is that external authorities on Jamaica did not recognize the legitimacy of local knowledge and capabilities. Indeed, the stamp and zinc programs were designed from the top down and were inflexible, so they could not adapt to changing conditions. Local people had little or no influence in how these programs were designed and little opportunity to negotiate changes to ensure a better fit between program design and local needs.

The data provides some preliminary indication on the ways leaders influence the recovery process (design principle 5). The evidence is mixed. On the one hand, some leaders appear to have exerted a negative influence: the mayor of St. James Parish, for example, described how he used his "network of local leaders" to distribute zinc on what many considered to be a politically biased basis. On the other hand, interviews revealed that many local officials would have been in a stronger position to solve the problems at hand if well-established community-based organizations had been allowed to participate.

The linkage of the Building Stamp Programme and the zinc distribution program to long-term development (design principle 6) would have been a key factor in successful recovery. A weakness of the Jamaican experience is that the majority of households did not undertake mitigation practices during rebuilding. The Building Stamp Programme, in particular, should have tied mitigation requirements to stamp aquisition. The data do not indicate any attempts to link either program with ongoing development projects.

Fitting resources to the needs and capabilities of households (design principle 7) is crucial to a successful recovery. While building materials under the Building Stamp Programme reached a vast number of disaster-stricken households, there were significant mismatches between the timing, amount, and types of aid and household needs. The mismatches were even more problematic in the zinc program. Thus aid distribution was generally not supportive in building the capacity of local people to meet their own needs. Instead, aid was often used for unintended purposes, and households attempted to define their own needs and to meet them in their own way.

In conclusion, the effectiveness of Jamaica's disaster relief programs was mixed. The lessons learned from Jamaica's experience should be considered in the design of future international aid delivery programs and in the revision of existing programs. This information is used, in chapter 7, to develop specific recommendations.

4   MONTSERRAT

RECOVERY AFTER DEVASTATION

MONTSERRAT IS A SMALL, BRITISH COLONY OF ABOUT TWELVE THOUSAND people. It is located in the eastern Caribbean region and is part of the Leeward Islands. The economy of Montserrat is primarily dependent on tourism and, to a lesser extent, on agriculture. Over the past several decades the island has increasingly become a vacation and real estate investment locale, with many wealthy Europeans and North Americans building large second homes. Among the more relevant resources essential to the disaster recovery effort are a small seaport located on the east side of the island in the capital city of Plymouth and a small airport with a relatively short runway located on the west side.

The impact of Hurricane Hugo was devastating for Montserrat. In the early hours of September 17, 1989, the storm struck the thirty-nine-square-mile island leaving in its wake eleven persons dead and more than three thousand homeless. Physical damage to homes, businesses, and public buildings was extensive. Ninety-eight percent of all homes sustained damage. The island's tourist industry was also severely damaged, with the loss of more than 80 percent of its hotel rooms. All government buildings and schools were partially or totally destroyed. Damage estimates by the government exceeded EC$990 million (US$362.6 million), which is a catastrophic amount for this small island state.

THE PREDISASTER INSTITUTIONAL CONTEXT

At the time of the storm, Montserrat had a disaster plan. The document was completed in 1987 by the national disaster coordinator. According to the national disaster coordinator and officials from ministries involved with public works and housing, it was an updated, formalized statement of some previously understood disaster plans that existed within various ministries and agencies.

The National Disaster Plan is a sixty-nine-page document that primarily focused upon the emergency period. It delegated authority for disaster response to a six-member National Disaster Executive Committee composed of the permanent secretary, the disaster coordinator, the permanent secretaries of administration and of the Ministry of Communications and Works, the commissioner of police, and the commanding officer of the Montserrat Defence Force. In addition, there were six standing committees assigned to coordinate planning in the following specific areas: public utilities and works, telecommunications, information and education, food and supplies, health services and welfare, and shelters. Each standing committee had representatives from various government agencies and NGOs. Montserrat also employs a part-time national disaster coordinator within the Government Information Unit. This coordinator serves as a policy adviser and provides administrative assistance to the National Disaster Executive Committee. The coordinator also has the responsibility of promoting hazard awareness and planning in the country.

The National Disaster Plan divided the island into eleven districts, with each having a district disaster committee. The committees were to have responsibility for disaster response and recovery functions within their local areas. They were to develop their own plans. Furthermore, people assigned the role of district disaster chair were to play pivotal roles in the disaster response. Not only were they to oversee disaster operations within their locales, but they also were to serve as liaison personnel to the National Disaster Executive Committee. The plan was a somewhat standard, functionally based, document. In particular, it specified the planning responsibilities, and to a lesser extent the response activities, of various ministries and agencies within the government. However, the plan did not indicate the roles and responsibilities of government organizations for the disaster recovery period. Similarly, the responsibilities of various NGOs, such as the Red Cross, the Rotary Club, the Lions Club, and other service organizations, were specified for the emergency period but not for recovery.

In contrast to the National Disaster Plan, more elaborate planning measures were taken within various ministries and organizations at the subnational level. The quality of these planning efforts varied widely.

Some of the efforts were quite laudable and effective. For example, within the Ministry of Agriculture, Trade, Lands, and Housing (MATLH) a rather detailed and updated plan had been developed. The plan covered such tasks as monitoring weather reports and tracking storms, provided for protecting the ministry's vehicles and for battening buildings and equipment, and included detailed procedures for handling food distribution. It also delegated specific responsibilities for each officer within the unit. Perhaps most important, the plan had been updated as recently as two months before the Hurricane Hugo hit. Some limited planning had also taken place within the Ministry of Communications and Works. Basically, it involved some prior understandings regarding preimpact activities, such as measures to protect public property and buildings, the placement of heavy equipment at critical points on the island, and postimpact strategies for road clearance.

The capability for incorporating mitigation into development on Montserrat was low. The Caribbean Uniform Building Code was in place, but Montserrat's chief building inspector indicated during an interview that the natural hazards provisions in the code were almost nonexistent. He further maintained that even the limited provisions were rarely followed due to a shortage of trained building inspection staff. In fact, there was only one full-time and one part-time inspector on Montserrat at the time Hugo struck. He further indicated that code compliance was sporadic at best and, for the most part, was only done on a voluntary basis. In addition, land use controls that would direct development away from hazardous areas had not been adopted by the Montserrat government.

The uneven and generally inadequate disaster planning and mitigation activities on Montserrat can be partially explained by the country's limited experience with hurricanes. Although a series of hurricanes hit the island in the eighteenth and nineteenth centuries (major storms struck in 1737, 1740, 1744, 1766, 1772, 1866, 1867, and 1898), at the time of Hugo it had been more than sixty years since a hurricane had struck the island (see Markum and Fergus 1989). This lack of disaster hurricane experience was noted by a number of individuals, who felt that it had limited planning and mitigation activities for Hugo. One informant noted, "What Montserratians knew of a hurricane was from the older people, and they were very few in number. A lot of the older house roofs, one could see that they were built from experience. But there were no documents available to say, for example, that because of a storm in 1928 that our older houses have been built like this." Another respondent noted that "there was no sensitivity or realism of the nature of the problem before Hugo. Because of a lack of experience, we were not able to convince people of what they should do." In addition, while the island has a potentially active volcano and is located astride an active seismic fault, a disruptive event stemming from these hazards has not occurred for many generations.

Fortunately, however, one individual on the island (the Governor) had extensive experience with previous hurricanes because of his posting within the British Commonwealth. The governor personally had experienced five previous hurricanes, and his experience was to play an important role in the response of Montserrat to the wrath of Hugo. As will be discussed, his leadership and experience were most beneficial during the early stages of recovery, given the weaknesses of the predisaster planning effort.

In sum, prior to the arrival of Hurricane Hugo, the capacity for promoting hazard mitigation and the resources available for disaster recovery could be classified as meager. The island was not blessed with a plethora of resources that could be used for recovery. Its port and airport facilities were limited. While some disaster planning had taken place, it was focused on predisaster activities rather than on the postdisaster period. Furthermore, experience with disasters was virtually nonexistent, as it had been more than six decades since a disaster had struck the island. As the middle of September 1989 arrived, this small, vulnerable island stood directly in the path of one of the most ferocious hurricanes to ever strike the Caribbean region.

THE IMPACT OF HURRICANE HUGO

Throughout Saturday evening and Sunday morning, September 17 and 18, Hurricane Hugo smashed into Montserrat. The eye passed through Montserrat at about 7:30 A.M. on Sunday. Then the winds once again returned to strong hurricane force and pummeled the island until about noon. Thousands of trees were destroyed. Debris covered the roads and made them impassable. Utility poles were slammed to the ground throughout the island. Since all the meteorological instruments on the island were destroyed by the storm, no one knows the actual force of the wind. Estimates placed the sustained wind speed at 140 to 150 miles per hour. However, based upon an analysis of the damage that resulted, some investigators estimate that wind gusts of 240 miles per hour may have occurred (Gibbs and Brown 1989, 2.4).

At about 11 P.M. a sizable portion of the roof of Glendon Hospital was torn off. As the winds increased, the dock and port facilities were lost. While the runway at Blackburn Airport sustained only minor damage, the terminal was severely damaged, and all air traffic control facilities were destroyed (see figure 4.1). The radio transmission towers and microwave equipment on Chances Peak were turned into twisted rubble. The telecommunications mast on St. George's Hill was bent to the ground. All the major facilities for communicating both on and off the island were destroyed. Most shelters lost their roofs. All public buildings, with the exception of the police station at Salem, suffered damage (see figures 4.2 and 4.3). Government headquarters was severely damaged and lost major portions of its roof.

Private businesses and homes also received heavy blows. The tourist industry lost 80 percent of its hotel rooms. The storm wreaked havoc on the upscale Montserrat Springs and Vue Point hotels. Although damage to homes was particularly severe in Kinsale and St. Patrick's, no region was spared. Upper-class residential areas, such as Fox's Bay and Richmond Hill, and those housing the less affluent, such as Broderick

FIGURE 4.1. Roof of Blackburn Airport Terminal, with insufficient hardware holding the roof and too low a pitch to withstand high winds (Consulting Engineers Partnership 1989).

FIGURE 4.2. Traditional hipped roof on a public school; it was not destroyed by Hurricane Hugo (Consulting Engineers Partnership 1989).

FIGURE 4.3. Nontraditional low-pitched roof on a public school; it was completely destroyed by Hurricane Hugo (Consulting Engineers Partnership 1989).

FIGURE 4.4. Nontraditional low-pitched roof on low-income home; it did not survive Hurricane Hugo (Consulting Engineers Partnership 1989).

and Webbs, were all severely damaged (see figure 4.4). Some estimates of damage in the press stated that more than 90 percent of the housing stock had been destroyed. However, later reports produced more realistic estimates of 98 percent of homes affected, of which 50 percent suffered severe damage and 20 percent were totally destroyed (*Hugo News*, September 1989, 4). The island's utility infrastructure also received a severe pounding. There was no electrical power, as Montserrat Electricity Services (MONLEC) lost most of the power station roof and all of its transmission and distribution system. The phone system on the island was devastated, as Cable & Wireless lost its microwave equipment. The water system was severely destroyed, and the loss of electricity did not allow for pumping.

In addition to the painful loss of homes, property, and businesses was the toll in human life. Eleven people died during its impact. Most of the victims were elderly residents. Fortunately, there were very few injuries: most were minor, and only three persons required hospitalization. Compared to the catastrophic damage to property, the number of casualties was remarkably small. To some extent Montserratians were lucky in that Hugo did not produce a sizable storm surge nor a significant amount of rain; it was a vicious, but relatively dry, storm. Therefore, no bridges or culverts were lost, and low-lying areas were spared major flooding problems. Because of precautionary activities, there was not a significant loss of heavy equipment. Food warehouses and supermarkets lost little of their stock.

In summary, the sheer magnitude of the physical destruction brought major postdisaster problems for Montserrat. While there were considerable deficiencies in the recovery effort, it should be remembered that the tasks for rebuilding were daunting and required a tremendous effort.

THE STAGES OF THE RECOVERY PROCESS

There are four stages in the recovery process after a natural disaster: the emergency stage, the restoration stage, the replacement stage, and the development stage (see figure 4.5). The emergency stage in Montserrat came to an end about two weeks after Hugo made landfall. One of the first tasks was debris clearance, which was the responsibility of the Ministry of Communications and Works. There had been some prior, informal planning for road clearance. In addition, the director of Public Works had experienced previous hurricanes. Based upon this understanding, Public Works had undertaken a number of preimpact measures. It had extended its work shifts before the storm. It had also dispatched some equipment to Plymouth and to the eastern part of the island in case these areas became isolated. A major concern that had not been taken into account was establishing dump sites, and as a result, there had been considerable dumping of debris into gullies, or *guats*, before the storm. The capacity of these gullies to allow storm water runoff was thus significantly reduced.

Quick damage assessments were made to determine immediate emergency needs. Within one day after Hugo, it was known that the seaport had been destroyed; therefore, opening the road to the airport was particularly important because cargo and aid would have to come by air. By three days after the storm, it was determined that there was no culvert or bridge damage, which pleased officials at Public Works, one of whom noted, "It was great news, because then I knew it was mainly a cleanup job, which is much easier than a repair job." Some basic public facilities, particularly radio communication facilities, were also repaired to at least a minimal level of operation. Within a week the main

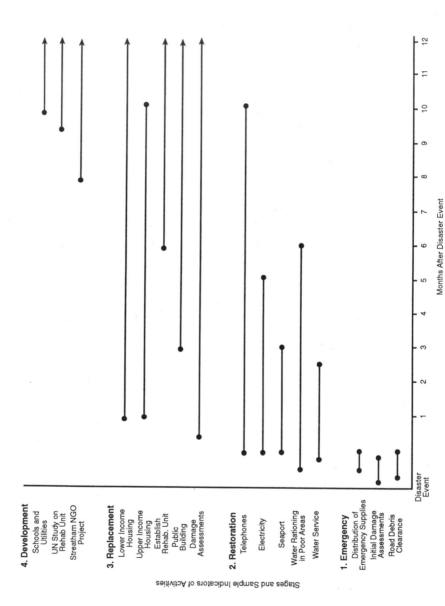

Stages and Sample Indicators of Activities

4. Development
Schools and Utilities
UN Study on Rehab Unit
Streatham NGO Project

3. Replacement
Lower Income Housing
Upper Income Housing
Establish Rehab. Unit
Public Building
Damage Assessments

2. Restoration
Telephones
Electricity
Seaport
Water Rationing in Poor Areas
Water Service

1. Emergency
Distribution of Emergency Supplies
Initial Damage Assessments
Road Debris Clearance

Disaster Event   1   2   3   4   5   6   7   8   9   10   11   12

Months After Disaster Event

Duration of Stages of Recovery Activity in Monterrat

roads were passable. Debris clearance continued during the emergency period. Later, Public Works became involved in providing emergency housing. It also assisted in the transportation of eighty thousand tons of material from the airport. Significant amounts of emergency food and medical supplies were acquired and distributed after the opening of the airport. The quick and effective clearance of the main roads and the rapid reopening of the airport testify to the benefits of disaster planning.

The restoration stage began during the emergency period, and its pace was not even. The restoration of water was accomplished first. A major problem with the water distribution system was the lack of generators to run the pumps for the island's deep wells. By the third week after the storm, two generators had been obtained, and one month after the storm water supplies were normal for 80 percent of the customers on the island. The system was back on-line when the pumping station in the St. George's Hill/Weekes area was restored in late in October. However, because of severe damage, leaks within the system had greatly reduced its efficiency, particularly for the older and poorer areas of Plymouth, where infrastructure had been decaying and in poor condition prior to the storm. In these areas water was rationed and was available for only two or three hours a day until six months after the storm, when the necessary repairs were made. The water shortages compounded the already difficult postdisaster recovery circumstances for the residents of these areas.

The restoration of the seaport, which was not fully functional until three months after Hugo, presented a major obstacle to recovery. No provisions had been made in the National Disaster Plan for the loss of the seaport. The solutions were thus ad hoc and poorly coordinated, and the structure of port management had to be improvised. The initial logistical problem involved finding a makeshift docking facility. After a delay of about twenty days, a flat-bottom barge with a crane was obtained from St. Lucia, in the eastern Caribbean. This makeshift port facility was in use for three months. Initially, the problem was not too severe, because building materials and other bulky items took some time to get to Montserrat. With their arrival, serious organizational problems surfaced. One NGO official noted that "there was confusion at the port. Generators were sent to us. They reached Montserrat, but they never reached us. It was difficult to keep track of things. Containers came to us, but there were no invoices, no idea at all of where it came from or who sent it. This confusion lasted about two weeks at the airport but continued on for months at the seaport." A long line of ships were waiting to unload.[1] Some had to leave and come back later. Some had perishable items, which rotted by the time of unloading.

The restoration of electrical power progressed slowly. Some areas did not have service until February 1990, five months after the disaster. Several essential buildings in the downtown Plymouth area were provided with electricity during the first two weeks. These included supermarkets, the port, and the hospital. However, progress on restoring the rest of the island was slow, due to the massive destruction of power poles. Some phones on the island were not affected because the wires were underground. However, Cable & Wireless lost all their microwave equipment on Chances Peak, and both internal and external communication was hampered for months. Although some priority buildings and areas, such as some ministry offices, had phone service within the first two weeks, phone service was not restored to the entire island until July 1990, nearly ten months after the disaster, which marked the end of the restoration period.

The replacement stage began early in the restoration period, starting with the initiation of a comprehensive, detailed, house-to-house damage assessment by MATLH three weeks after the storm struck. By about two months after Hugo, all major recovery aid donor organizations had established operations on Montserrat, and these made their separate damage assessments. Households were thus often surveyed several times, causing much frustration among residents and fueling unconfirmed rumors that much of the aid was siphoned away from those in need and sold on the black market by politically corrupt government officials.

A workable disaster plan could have provided better coordination among those government agencies and NGOs conducting the damage assessments and providing recovery aid. Further, MATLH had no pre-disaster plan for collecting and examining the damage data. As a result, there were unforeseen complications in making the assessments available to aid agencies: although the MATLH assessments were to be available within weeks, they were not available for about eleven months. Thus many households did not receive aid for months. Another cause

---

1. A key constraint on the recovery process was the design of the temporary port facility. One freighter with a large shipment of materials arrived at the port about six weeks after Hugo. However, because this ship was designed to unload from the stern and not from the bow, as is common, it could not be unloaded. The freighter was anchored in the harbor for two months before facilities were installed for unloading it.

for the long replacement stage was the sheer scale of destruction. Skilled labor and building materials were in short supply, and these were often siphoned off to rebuild the second homes of wealthy foreigners ("expatriates").

Two months after the storm, the government attempted to create a disaster coordinating committee involving disaster relief NGOs and government ministries. The resistance of the NGOs to participation on the committee and their unwillingness to work with government officials—and the resulting failure of this committee—contributed to the poor organization during the replacement period. Six months later, the government established the Rehabilitation Unit, with staff drawn from several government agencies, to coordinate and direct the overall housing recovery effort. Since its creation, the unit has widely been considered to be successful in monitoring and coordinating the recovery effort.

As of July 1990 (ten months after Hugo) the restoration and replacement stages were still ongoing, as many public facilities (e.g., schools and government headquarters) had not been repaired or rebuilt. Government officials in Public Works and MATLH estimated that, as of July 1990, upper-class residential areas, such as Fox's Bay and Richmond Hill, were nearly 90 percent rebuilt but that more than 40 percent of low-income households (about nine hundred households) had not received recovery assistance. Many of these poor households had used their own resources to rebuild.

The development stage began in the midst of the replacement stage. An apt indicator of the start of this final stage is the collaborative housing recovery program. Eight months after the hurricane struck, the Canadian University Students Organization (CUSO), the Caribbean Conference of Churches (CCC), and a local community action group began to link its recovery operations to long-term developmental activities in the poor rural village of Streatham. Initially, CUSO provided housing recovery assistance to the intermediary NGO (the CCC), which had been involved in development work in Streatham for several years before the Hugo disaster. The intermediary, in turn, worked with the community action group to initiate an assistance program. The program was successful not only in delivering housing aid during the replacement stage but also in strengthening the village's organizational capacity to undertake development work beyond recovery. Examples include the introduction of new agricultural cultivation and marketing practices and improvements in the public water supply and distribution system.

Another development event was the commissioning of a consultant report by the United Nations Commission for Human Settlements to assess the feasibility of permanently establishing the Rehabilitation Unit as the lead government organization for formulating and carrying out a long-range housing development program on Montserrat. Such a program obviously would not be solely directed toward disaster recovery. As of September 1990, a final decision by the United Nations and the Montserrat government had not been made regarding the status of the Rehabilitation Unit. Other long-term development activities included the use of recovery aid for a school building improvement program and the replacement of above-ground electric lines with storm-resistant, low-maintenance underground lines. These improvements were to be implemented over a twenty-four-month period after the disaster.

THE DIMENSIONS OF THE RECOVERY PROCESS

Seven important dimensions of the recovery process—organizational coordination, monitoring, compliance, recognition of local rights, leadership, staff and material resources, and the linkage of recovery assistance to development—were selected based upon their analytical importance to an understanding of the effectiveness and efficiency of recovery and development efforts.

Organizational Coordination

Several organizational coordination activities were particularly salient during the disaster recovery on Montserrat, including the National Disaster Plan, NGO collaboration, the damage assessment process, and the Rehabilitation Unit.

THE NATIONAL DISASTER PLAN

Evidence reveals that the effectiveness of the National Disaster Plan and the National Disaster Executive Committee in guiding long-term recovery and mitigation efforts was low. Informants gave several reasons for the failure of the plan, one being that the plan focused primarily on the predisaster period, not on recovery. In fact, only four pages of the sixty-nine-page plan addressed issues of disaster recovery and the mitigation of future disasters. Moreover, the plan gave only minimal attention to the posthurricane emergency response period. As one informant observed, "The plan focused on before the storm, and not after. The plan for activities before the hurricane worked pretty well; the problem is that there was no plan for after the storm. Everything that was done was an organizational nightmare."

The plans of individual ministries and agencies also tended to ignore the postdisaster recovery period. The MATLH plan, for example, did not give sufficient attention to the problems of disaster housing, a task that had been assigned to the ministry. As one informant noted, "The housing section of the ministry's plan was weaker than the section for food distribution. The housing capability within the ministry was very small. It's planning was 'in theory' but not 'in fact.' It was not our strong suit."

Exemplifying the lack of predisaster recovery planning were debris removal and damage assessment. While debris removal from main highways was rapid, long-term debris removal and disposal in damaged areas was slow. During the months after Hugo, it became increasingly difficult to remove debris from damaged areas due to a lack of suitable dump sites. Debris in residential areas in need of repair severely hampered reconstruction efforts for several weeks. In fact, the problem became so pressing that the government resorted to using open gullies as debris dumping sites in one large residential area on the west side of the capital city of Plymouth. And, as noted, damage assessment was undertaken by numerous government and nongovernment organizations with little coordination and a great deal of replication.

Another reason for the failure of the National Disaster Plan is that it makes limited reference to the responsibilities of the National Disaster Executive Committee in coordinating the numerous government and nongovernment organizations involved in disaster recovery. Although an organization like MATLH may have had a plan, the Disaster Executive Committee did little in acting as a focal point for coordinating the implementation of individual plans. Further, a high-level MATLH administrator told us that the emergency food plan was prepared "in-house" and that it had not been circulated to members of the Disaster Executive Committee before Hurricane Hugo.

Further, the national disaster coordinator was not given visibility as the leading advocate for disaster planning. The coordinator position did not have a separate organizational identity, as it is located within the Information Office of the Ministry of Communications and Works. The disaster coordinator, while very capable and possessing strong management skills, had never received training in disaster management. Nor was there adequate financial support to undertake proper disaster planning, as the annual budget for disaster planning prior to Hurricane Hugo amounted to only EC$5,000 (US$1,825). In addition, the position of disaster coordinator was part-time and tacked onto a position in information services.

The National Disaster Plan was not, as one government administrator noted, "a living document." When asked in 1991 if they were familiar with the plan, which was prepared in 1987, most public officials interviewed indicated that, while they were aware of its existence, they were not familiar with plan's contents nor the actions the plan specified for their organizations. One informant indicated that, except for a simulated volcanic disaster held in 1988, little attention had been given to disaster planning at the national level during the two years prior to Hugo and that there had been no executive committee meetings for reviewing and updating the plan. She repeatedly emphasized that "the plan was purely a paper document." Other factors were the low priority given to disasters by government organizations and an islandwide belief that a hurricane disaster would not occur because more than sixty years had elapsed since the last storm struck Montserrat.

Official hazard mitigation training or public education activity on the island prior to Hurricane Hugo was limited. While a few public address announcements regarding basic hurricane education and protective actions were aired and printed by the local media, a systematic program of public education did not exist. Furthermore, there was limited training for both government and NGO officials in how to plan for and recover from a disaster. This weakness is apparent in a number of areas but was particularly obvious in the lack of trained managers and district chairs. The plan placed significant responsibilities on the shoulders of the district chairs; however, it provided very little, if any, training. District chairs were not selected on the basis of their training or prior disaster experience; many were simply local business persons and community leaders.

There were, however, some planning efforts at the national level that did facilitate postdisaster emergency response efforts. Although no overall coordination came from the Disaster Executive Committee or any other government organization, representatives of MATLH indicated that the ministry had successfully implemented its disaster plan for food acquisition and distribution. In this instance, prior planning appears to have been beneficial. As one informant in the ministry noted, "Instructions were followed almost to the letter. For example, the ministry headquarters itself suffered roof damage, but files, typewriters, computers, etc. were safe because people took appropriate actions."

Similarly, Public Works spent the forty-eight hours prior to the storm boarding the windows of public buildings and making other preparations. An inventory of equipment and supplies was taken. Heavy equipment for debris removal was dispatched to Plymouth and to the eastern part of the island.

In sum, all informants noted that at both the national and individual organizational levels the plans paid too little attention to posthurricane recovery. Furthermore, the quality of plans varied significantly. As one informant noted, "The planning varied greatly in quality. The agriculture area was good, and the food planning within agriculture went well. The Public Works area was all right. But such areas as housing, building back stronger structures, and coordination between the aid donors, especially in the outlying districts, was very poor." Planning on Montserrat is indicative of the common view that planning is a product and not a process. Although a national plan was prepared and although one ministry undertook some positive predisaster actions, planning was not viewed as an ongoing process. The continuous updating of plans and the training and education of officials and the public were almost nonexistent.

Since Hugo, however, the government has given increased priority to disaster planning. The Disaster Executive Committee has held regular monthly meetings to review the disaster response and recovery strategies that did or did not work. Based on these assessments, the committee has been revising the National Disaster Plan and government organizations have been updating their individual plans. Further, the government has sponsored workshops on storm-resistant building design and on linking recovery to long-term redevelopment programs. Most officials interviewed indicated that, by the 1990 hurricane season, Montserrat was better prepared to respond and recover from a disaster than they were before Hugo.

NGO COLLABORATION

The following two cases of NGO collaboration had differing degrees of success. Each evolved on an ad hoc basis and had no relation to the predisaster planning activities on the island. Of most long-term significance was the collaboration between an international, development-oriented NGO from Canada (CUSO), an intermediary NGO from the eastern Caribbean (CCC) with long-standing external ties to foreign donor organizations, and a local community action group, which was an NGO as well. CUSO sought to provide housing recovery assistance

after Hugo by establishing a cooperative arrangement with the intermediary NGO, which was already involved in community development
work in Streatham.

Streatham, which is located in the hills above Plymouth and has a
population of about three hundred, is typical of many villages in developing countries in the Caribbean. Its economy is agrarian and poor. Before the storm, urban infrastructure was almost nonexistent, housing
consisted primarily of small, poorly constructed, wood-frame houses
with corrugated sheet metal roofing, electricity was available but only
a few households could afford to have it installed, and water service was
sporadic as there was just one public spigot, located on the northern
edge of the village. Almost all of the approximately hundred homes
were either severely damaged or destroyed by the storm.

The NGO collaboration was initiated about eight months after Hugo,
with CUSO providing the intermediary such reconstruction assistance
as financial sponsorship, building materials, and logistical support for
distributing the material. The CCC, in turn, worked with the community action group to initiate a new housing assistance program: it
trained local people and provided funds to temporarily employ a five-
member housing assistance team for a six-month period (April to October 1990). All team members were Streatham citizens and had been
volunteer members of the community action group, which had been
supported for several years by the CCC to undertake development activities. They included a foreman, two experienced carpenters, and an
apprentice carpenter (see figure 4.6). The fifth member, also a Streatham
citizen, was the volunteer project coordinator of the Streatham Community Action Group, who was employed as a part-time librarian in
Plymouth. Interviews with a local citizen and several public officials
whose government ministries had been active in Streatham revealed
that this individual was well respected for her local organizational
building and management capabilities.

The accomplishments of the new program were substantial. The
team conducted a series of local training workshops on rebuilding and
structural strengthening techniques, built twenty-two homes, and repaired the severely damaged community center. Of greatest significance, however, were the long-term developmental accomplishments.
During an interview, the local coordinator maintained that team members took great pride in their work and that the importance of the community action group was enhanced considerably as a result of its postdisaster reconstruction activities. The participation of local citizens in

FIGURE 4.6. Housing assistance team rebuilding in Streatham after Hurricane Hugo (*Links: Quarterly Newsletter of the Antigua Programme Center*, January–March 1990).

volunteer group activities was much higher than before the disaster. "We used to have just one or two people show up to help out. Sometimes nobody came. Now we often get ten coming, sometimes twenty who show up to pitch in." Such heightened interest and participation strengthened the community action group's capacity to undertake development projects not related to disaster recovery.

Before Hugo, the CCC and the community group had planned to undertake three local improvement projects: introducing new agricultural production practices, building a community center, and improving the distribution of potable water by installing two new public spigots. These projects were to be carried out on an incremental basis over a ten-year period. However, CUSO became convinced that additional external aid could be effectively used in Streatham. Indeed, the improvement projects were well under way two years after Hugo. Moreover, the community group appears to be self-sustaining in establishing and maintaining an economically viable local agricultural production and marketing cooperative.

CUSO sponsored a series of seminars in Canada on the accomplishments of the community action group by sending the local group coordinator to Canada for three weeks during the summer of 1990 to talk to the Canadian supporters of the project. These seminars provided a unique opportunity for a grass roots organizer to demonstrate how foreign aid was used—to give donors a first-hand account of the program, as opposed to the usual second-hand account given by the staff of the external NGO. The donors thus gained a better understanding of the issues and, in particular, of the fact that the success of a recovery project is measured not only in product (e.g., number of homes rebuilt) but also in organizational capacity building and long-term development.

The second case of NGO collaboration involved an agreement between the Montserrat government and the U.S. Peace Corps to undertake a housing recovery project. The project coordinator was an young, energetic, American architect with limited experience in project management. Under his supervision was a team of eight local full-time workers whom he had trained to construct prefabricated homes for those households that had participated in a pre-Hugo, low-income, public housing assistance program. His supervisor was a British engineer from the Montserrat Public Works Department. Interviews with public officials at the ministerial level revealed that the project was widely considered a success in terms of constructing many units. During the nine-month duration of the project (November 1989 to July 1990), 191 prefabricated homes were transported and erected. An additional accomplishment was that the workers gained basic carpentry skills and became more employable in the local economy.

This project, however, had a key disadvantage. According to three of the government agency staff interviewed, it did not exhibit a clear commitment to local Montserrat leadership and did not allow Montserrat authorities control of the program. Because the project director and his supervisor were not Montserrat citizens, "the project [took] on a life of its own," as one high-level government administrator indicated. She maintained that the project was not integrated with other housing recovery or development programs administered by the government and that, while the individuals in charge had good intentions, they were not familiar enough with the politics and culture of Montserrat to effectively link their projects with others.

Moreover, the Peace Corps units failed to meet local housing needs. The prefabricated construction techniques used for these homes bore little resemblance to the traditional style of construction of the eastern

Caribbean. While some structural strengthening techniques were incorporated into the new homes (e.g., hurricane straps), the two-sided, pitched design of the roof, for example, was poorly suited to withstand high winds from coastal storms. The traditional roof is four sided and pitched, which is more capable of surviving hurricane-force winds. Residents of the prefabricated houses also complained that the interior design violated the need for cross ventilation in the warm tropical climate of the Caribbean. Several residents attempted to approximate the traditional pattern by cutting holes in interior walls to attain better cross ventilation. Complaints were made to the Peace Corps representative and to Public Works, but no changes were made. The Peace Corps architect explained that it was impossible to make changes in the blueprints of the prefabricated houses due to cost and the need for additional training of the carpenters. This appears to be a case of an organization meeting its own needs rather than the needs of the people affected by the disaster.

THE DAMAGE ASSESSMENT PROCESS

As with many disaster recovery tasks, the assessment of damages on the island was prone to poor coordination, duplication of efforts, and lack of planning. As one government official noted, "We had no previous plan for damage assessment." Requests for and allocation of resources based on need and rebuilding priorities are dependent on understanding the magnitude, patterns, and location of destruction.

In the months following Hugo, separate damage assessments were undertaken by individual government agencies and NGOs. During the first few days after Hugo struck, the governor developed an ad hoc assessment group composed of architects, builders, and surveyors. The group traveled to the various districts, but as one informant noted, "Since there was no system in place, it took a while to get things organized." A questionnaire was developed to obtain data on homes and on schools and other public buildings. By about a week after Hugo a rough understanding of the extent of damage was available, and it was one of devastation. However, one official noted that "the estimate was low, because during the quick assessment they were not counting the housing that had disappeared." Another government official noted that "within the first few days, there was an overall image, a rough one, of the extent of damage. I knew after a couple of days that the police station was the only significantly undamaged building. It was readily apparent that there was almost 100 percent damage to government property. The sheer magnitude of the destruction made damage assessment easier, because everything was damaged."

Three weeks after storm landfall, MATLH conducted a comprehensive and detailed damage assessment on a house-by-house basis. Using eighteen enumerators, the assessment was completed in about one week. The assessment was to be used by the various government organizations (the Community Services Unit and the Public Works Department) with a role in housing recovery. Further, the Community Services Unit undertook a specialized damage assessment of only those low-income households that, before Hugo, had received assistance under a public housing program. Also during the weeks after Hugo several NGOs (e.g., the Red Cross, the CCC, the Salvation Army, and the Lions Club) conducted individual assessments. It was not surprising that interviewees consistently declared that they had been surveyed on more than one occasion. A local CCC staff member revealed that her home was assessed four times before her family finally received assistance. The recurring issue of multiple assessments caused much public anxiety and frustration, which was directed toward the government. It contributed to the widespread belief that many deserving households were denied assistance because it was distributed on the basis of politics rather than need.

An additional problem with the damage assessments was that they did not ask for data important to assessing the needs of the households that had sustained damage. According to the Community Services Unit staff, measures of socioeconomic status and housing demand were not collected. MATLH staff were also keenly aware of this problem, indicating that there was inadequate time in the days immediately following Hurricane Hugo to work with user organizations in designing a comprehensive survey questionnaire. MATLH's housing component was not as well developed as its agricultural component, and there was thus insufficient in-house expertise for questionnaire design. In fact, only one staff member of fifty-nine employed by the ministry operated its housing program.

Another difficulty was MATLH's long delay in making damage assessment data available. The delay was caused by difficulties in computerizing the data. The original intention for computerization was to enhance efficiency of data access and retrieval for user organizations. However, soon after the damage assessments were completed, MATLH staff discovered that there was insufficient expertise to use their software for data entry. (In July 1990—ten months after the storm—MATLH staff had acquired the expertise needed to use the software and were within weeks of completion of computerizing the data.) There were negative political consequences from the delay. The staffs of the Community Services Unit and the Public Works Department indicated that several weeks passed before a decision was made to not wait for the computerized data but to access the data manually. This delay ultimately "fueled many underlying turf battles," according to one agency staff member.[2]

THE REHABILITATION UNIT

Six months after Hurricane Hugo made landfall (March 1990), a housing recovery agency—the Rehabilitation Unit—was created by the Montserrat government. The unit's responsibility was to handle the many eligible households (twelve hundred) that had not received aid at the time the unit was established. While no accurate records were available, staff from Community Services and Public Works agreed that 70–80 percent of these households were poor. These officials were quick to point out that numerous households, particularly in rural areas, that had sustained damages had been overlooked because of foreign donor organizations' initial assumptions about local conditions.

The twelve-member Rehabilitation Unit staff (nine full-time and three part-time) is interdisciplinary and represents a range of government agency interests involved in housing recovery. The unit's director is a former high-level administrator with the Montserrat customs office with substantial management experience, particularly in dealing with international donor organizations. The remaining staff includes social workers, engineers, and an architect, who were drawn from Community Services, the Public Works Department, and MATLH. The Rehabilitation Unit's primary objectives are to assume direct administrative responsibility and coordinate all government housing recovery programs, to consolidate damage assessment data bases collected by MATLH and various NGOs, and to conduct an assessment of the twelve hundred remaining households to prioritize recovery needs based on level of dam-

2. Such battles centered on government agencies wanting to expand their roles in disaster recovery. For example, because the social workers in the Community Services Unit considered themselves the most informed about the housing needs of disaster victims, they also considered themselves the most qualified to take a leading role in the recovery effort. Public Works staff, however, felt that their agency was the most suited to manage the recovery effort because it had the most capability to store and distribute building materials.

ages and household resources.[3] As of July 1990, about eight hundred of the twelve hundred households had been assessed, with six hundred having received assistance in the form of building materials. In addition, many of those interviewed both inside and outside the unit agreed that the turf battles among government agencies had subsided due to the coordination efforts of the unit. Staff members from several NGOs (the Christian Children's Fund, the U.S. Peace Corps, and the Red Cross) also indicated that they have had better interorganizational relations with the government since establishment of the unit.

As a result of the unit's success, some discussion is under way within the Montserrat government on giving it permanent organizational status, with a full-time staff and budget. A study by a consultant was commissioned under the sponsorship of the United Nations Commission for Human Settlements to assess the feasibility of the unit as the lead government organization for formulating and carrying out a long-term housing development program in Montserrat (UNCHS 1990). The study, completed in July 1990, recommended that the unit be given permanent agency status. At the time of writing this report, it was too early to assess the impacts of the study recommendations on government policy regarding the Rehabilitation Unit's role in housing development.

Monitoring and Compliance

Activities involving the delivery of housing assistance, monitoring how the aid is used, and assurance that aid recipients comply with housing reconstruction guidelines varied among government and nongovernment organizations. The predominate government agencies responsible for housing for the first six months after the disaster were the Community Services Unit and the Public Works Department. The Community Services Unit was responsible for those households that, before the disaster, were receiving assistance under the unit's social welfare housing program. These households automatically qualified for either building materials for repairing their damaged homes or prefabricated homes if their homes were damaged beyond repair.[4] The Public Works Depart-

3. The first detailed damage assessment conducted by MATLH was determined by ministry staff to cover 73 percent of the forty-four hundred households in Montserrat. The remaining 27 percent (twelve hundred households) were to be assessed in a second survey conducted by the Rehabilitation Unit.

4. About a hundred households received assistance under the building material replacement program; an estimated two hundred households were eligible for the prefabricated home program.

ment administered a program for households that, before the disaster, were not participating in the Community Services program. Each household that incurred damage and requested assistance was given an equal amount of building materials. The Public Works Department was responsible for storing and distributing building materials for the Community Services Unit as well as for its own program.[5]

According to Community Services and Public Works staff, several factors disrupted their monitoring and compliance activities. One was MATLH's long delay in making damage assessment data available. Another was the ongoing problem of coordination and sharing information among government and nongovernment organizations. A third factor was the political bias in aid distribution. Thus, according to one Community Services social worker, "a culture of mistrust" deeply affected the organization. "It's been a big mountain to overcome when we try to get something done." Staff morale and commitment to support long-term recovery efforts was seriously eroded.

The use of building-strengthening techniques was effectively monitored under the prefabricated housing program, because the blueprint for these structures was prepared by a Peace Corps staff member and a team prefabricated the housing components at a Public Works warehouse. The problem in the prefabricated housing program was not with monitoring and compliance but, ultimately, with the houses themselves, which were considered far from satisfactory. Under other housing programs, houses were repaired on-site by either a carpenter or the aid recipients themselves, a procedure that obviously left decisions about construction to homeowners and local carpenters and thus did not ensure that structural strengthening occurred. Furthermore, although there was a national building code in place before the disaster, it lacked storm mitigation standards. During the months after Hugo, several housing reconstruction workshops were held to inform the public and the building professions about mitigation and repair techniques.[6] However, because of limited building inspection staffs in the Community Service Unit and the Public Works Department, there have been no field checks to assess the quality of reconstruction. In-

5. About twelve hundred households have received assistance under these programs. Once a household was considered eligible for assistance, it was issued a purchase order, which it turned in to Public Works to obtain building materials. The order specified the types and amount of materials to be distributed to the household.
6. These workshops were sponsored by the government, the United Nations, and an American university.

terviews with the staffs of these two organizations suggest that only a limited number of aid recipients made efforts to incorporate mitigation into their reconstructed homes and that the workshops had little impact.

The establishment of the Rehabilitation Unit should improve monitoring and compliance. The unit serves as a clearinghouse for records of households that have received aid and has conducted a detailed damage assessment of needy households. The assessment included information on housing needs and socioeconomic status, which was not included in the original MATLH assessment. This information helped the unit prioritize household assistance based on need. Also, the unit has sufficient staff (two engineers, one architect, and two social workers) to conduct field verifications on the use of the housing aid.

The effectiveness of NGOs in monitoring the use of aid and in ensuring that aid recipients complied with their organizations' objectives varied widely. Monitoring and the ensurance of compliance in the housing recovery program of the CCC and CUSO was very effective. This success was, according to a CCC organizer, due to a "well-staffed and trained, locally based, housing assistance team with a strong motivation to use community aid to the fullest extent." The organizer maintained that, because team members were local citizens, they could regularly observe how aid was used for reconstruction in their communities. The Red Cross was not, however, as effective in monitoring the use of its aid. Unlike the collaborative effort of the CCC and CUSO, the Red Cross effort did not have a well-staffed field organization to regularly conduct field inspections throughout the recovery period. Except for three volunteer local staff, almost all Red Cross personnel came from other nations in the Caribbean region to assist in assessing damages and distributing aid. Most of these individuals left Montserrat within two or three months after the hurricane's landfall.

The Recognition of Local Rights

Public officials consistently expressed concern about the difficulties the Montserrat government experienced during the recovery in working with foreign NGOs. These officials maintained that some foreign NGOs would not work with the government in distributing housing aid, using the word "resisted" to describe NGO responses. For example, eight weeks after Hugo the Montserrat government failed in its attempt to establish a coordinating committee consisting of representatives from ten government agencies and NGOs active in housing recovery. The objective of this committee was to coordinate the housing recovery programs of the member organizations. The key reason for the failure of the committee, according to those interviewed, was resistance on part of the NGOs to participate.

In particular, the staff of Community Services believed that NGOs did not recognize the organizational capacity of the government—and especially of the unit—in delivering housing assistance. The staff maintained that, as a social service agency, the unit had a better understanding of the housing recovery needs of Montserrat residents, particularly the poor, than the staff of foreign NGOs. They further believed that as Montserrat government personnel they had a legitimate right to be involved and familiar with foreign organizations' operations in their country. An interview with a foreign NGO program director in fact revealed that government offers to collaborate were passed over. Government staff did not have the experience in disaster response and recovery that the NGO official felt was needed. Because of the large number of people in need of aid, his NGO decided that it could not "risk" working with these inexperienced government agencies.

There were, however, exceptions among foreign NGOs. CUSO, for example, considered the disaster a special opportunity for setting into motion a process of collaboration and took a long-term developmental approach to disaster recovery.

Leadership

When asked if there were any organizations playing a leadership role in raising awareness and promoting the need for disaster planning before Hurricane Hugo, four of eight informants mentioned the Pan Caribbean Disaster Preparedness and Prevention Project. These individuals were well aware of the project's work over the previous four or five years. Key activities included conducting a tabletop simulation of volcanic eruptions, media awareness workshops, and disaster evacuation exercises.

While there was consensus among those interviewed that these activities had not translated into effective postdisaster recovery responses, they agreed that the Pan Caribbean Project was instrumental in raising awareness about hurricane disasters. One key ministry official suggested that this heightened concern and understanding was important to the disaster planning program currently under way on Montserrat: "The [Pan Caribbean Project] was involved in the planning. They organized meetings and they stressed the need to update plans.

They promoted planning and having people know what their roles would be. They provided expertise and literature, although not much finances." Another official maintained that "the impetus for the national plan came from [project]. Also significant was the perception of the importance of [the project's] activities by high-level people like the governor. . . . The [project] provided some training at the management level and generated an awareness of the principles involved in disaster management." A representative of a well-known NGO said that the project provided her with the technical assistance to conduct an audit of her organization's capability to respond to future disasters. The audit revealed several weaknesses, which the NGO is currently addressing.

One organization (the Development Unit of the Ministry of Finance) and one individual (the governor) were also mentioned frequently (by three of eight informants) as effective leaders during the postdisaster recovery period. The governor, it was clear, assumed executive management responsibility on the basis of his prominent position, his leadership style, and his disaster experience during his ten-year service as a public administrator in the South Pacific. He motivated the country through numerous media appearances. During the initial phases of the restoration stage of recovery he provided leadership in identifying and coordinating the roles of various government agencies. As chairman of the Disaster Executive Committee, he effectively revived the committee as a viable disaster planning organization. One government official summed up public sentiment: "The governor ran the country for a month after the storm. There are provisions in the Constitution that allowed him to assume control of the country under emergencies. But this was not spelled out in the National Disaster Plan. The government, including the permanent secretaries, felt that this was best. The governor did a terrific job." Unfortunately, the governor's term in office expired a few months after the disaster, and he was not an active participant during the recovery.

The Development Unit was appointed by the governor as the lead agency in coordinating the acquisition of international aid. Because of its predisaster responsibilities in acquiring outside aid for economic development, the organization had a well-established network of international donor groups. The network was useful in making requests for, and in acquiring, disaster recovery funds, materials, and personnel.

Interestingly, none of those interviewed indicated that the national disaster coordinator played a leadership role during the recovery process. Low visibility and insufficient staff allocated to disaster coordination were no doubt behind this perception. It also can be traced to the coordinator's lack of training in disaster management.

Resources

STAFF

The adequacy of staff varied by organization and type of recovery activity. The MATLH damage assessment staff consisted of eighteen agriculture extension agents, each with a college degree or a postsecondary school degree. Before Hugo, most agents worked on agricultural development projects, which gave them considerable familiarity with local geography and with political and social conditions. The agents also had some experience as enumerators for population and agriculture censuses conducted by MATLH. Given these skills, it is not surprising that the data they collected were widely considered accurate. As mentioned, however, there were several shortcomings in ministry staff expertise in assessing housing needs and in computerizing the damage data, which led to questions about the usefulness and availability of the data.

While the Peace Corps housing assistance team was sufficient in terms of absolute numbers—eight full-time carpenters plus an architect, who was in charge of the team—it unfortunately operated from a housing blueprint that poorly fit the needs of Montserrat's poor. Throughout its existence the team had virtually no contact with or feedback from the disaster-stricken people about their housing needs. The team also remained isolated from other organizations like the Community Services Unit and the CCC, which had considerable knowledge of local needs and capacities.

The government program for delivering aid to the general public, which was run by the Public Works Department, was not adequately staffed. Once a householder received assistance, there were no follow-up, on-site inspections to verify use of the aid. In fact, the department employed only one part-time building inspector, and he was assigned to other duties during the first nine months after the disaster.

By relying on well-established and highly trained field staffs, the CCC and CUSO project had considerable success in delivering aid and monitoring construction practices. Also, as in the case of Antigua, the Montserrat Red Cross drew on the network of Red Cross chapters in the Caribbean to conduct effective damage assessments. However, staff assigned to assessing damages were not available for working with local organizations in building their capacity to undertake long-term recovery activities, such as the distribution and monitoring of aid as well as long-term development.

BUILDING MATERIALS

Montserrat experienced a severe shortage in building materials for about seven months after the disaster.[7] The shortage was caused by two factors. One was inadequate seaport unloading facilities, which caused a three-month delay in distributing materials. The other was that upper-income households, or those with relatives or friends overseas who sent them money, bought all the available materials. Although there are no accurate data available, one social worker in Community Services maintained that more Montserrat citizens lived overseas than on Montserrat and thus the magnitude of expatriate aid was substantial.

These two factors, according to several informants, increased the prices for labor and building materials to three or four times predisaster levels. Interviewees often suggested that building suppliers, contractors, and carpenters were "price gouging" or "taking unfair advantage of the situation," or "thriving off the misery of others."

The Linkage of Recovery to Development

While no linkages of recovery programs to ongoing development projects were preplanned, several successful linkages were improvised after Hurricane Hugo. Of greatest significance was the linkage of housing recovery activities to long-term development initiatives in Streatham. Because the disaster recovery was viewed as a long-term development issue by international, regional, and local community development organizations operating in Streatham, the cooperative arrangements that evolved did not terminate at the end of the replacement stage of recovery. Instead, the disaster recovery period was used as an opportunity to strengthen ties among the three levels. Since the goal of the international NGO was to empower local people, and not to do the work itself, the local organization became accustomed to the new way of doing things during the recovery. Thus the shift of the collaborative partnership from recovery to development activities did not require a depar-

7. As of July 1990, Montserrat was $EC 500,000 short for buying building materials for two to three hundred of the twelve hundred remaining households still in need of assistance.

ture from ongoing activities. The infusion of resources resulting from the disaster reinforced the village's capacity to undertake a variety of development projects that were built on the momentum gained from recovery work.

Three other links between recovery and development were identified. Before Hurricane Hugo, the Ministry of Education had a long-term school improvement plan in place, which included the refurbishment or replacement of schools. Since Hugo destroyed or severely damaged most schools on the island, the ministry allocated international recovery aid funds on the basis of the plan. Another link was the replacement of damaged aboveground electric utility lines with lower-maintenance and more storm-resistant underground lines. This replacement was compatible with the long-term plan of the power company to replace existing lines with underground ones. A third link involved the establishment of a housing rehabilitation agency. The original purpose of this organization was to consolidate and coordinate government and non-government housing recovery assistance programs. However, because the agency has been effective, government officials are considering permanently establishing the agency to carry out long-term housing development programs.

A missed opportunity for integrating disaster recovery activities and long-term development was the Peace Corps housing reconstruction program for the low-income population. Many recipients of the prefabricated homes were dissatisfied with the way the program was organized and with the housing blueprint. Their requests to modify the housing design were ignored. A well-informed Community Services staff member, who knew many of the recipients, said that his organization had initially requested some type of loan program that would allow the disaster-stricken poor an opportunity to design and build their own homes. The intent was for individual loan recipients to pay back the loan in cash and for those involved in a cooperative housing reconstruction project to pay back through community service, like housing construction, within their respective villages. This view corroborates the findings of Harrell-Bond's (1986) study of self-help housing, which suggests that housing programs have a better chance of success when participants are loaned money outright and are free to use their own networks of contacts to buy locally available materials in a timely manner.

SUMMARY

The Positive Components

First, the Pan Caribbean Project played an effective leadership role during the predisaster period in raising awareness and knowledge about hurricanes and in giving technical assistance. Much of this work served as a precursor to postdisaster planning efforts. In addition, the governor provided much-needed leadership in identifying and coordinating the roles of various government agencies. His prominent position, leadership style, and prior disaster experience enabled him to take control. As evidenced by his designation of the Development Unit as the lead organization for coordinating and distributing aid, he decided soon after the storm made landfall what had to be done and who should participate in carrying out the recovery effort.

Second, the establishment of the Rehabilitation Unit was an important, although belated, step in coordinating the overall housing recovery effort. This organization was effective in serving as a central clearing house for damage data, in distributing housing recovery aid to those in need, and in monitoring the use of such aid. Given such success, the possibility was being considered of giving the unit permanent agency status with an independent budget. The unit's role would be to address housing improvement issues.

Third, some organizations recognized that the disaster provided a window of opportunity to pursue activities unrelated to the disaster. CUSO sought to advance its development work, and the government carried out public school and electric utility renovation plans at a more rapid pace than it might have if Hugo had not struck. In particular, the collaboration between CUSO, the CCC, and the local community group in Streatham village led to a strengthening of the capacity of the local organization to undertake sustainable development projects. CUSO's goal was to empower the local group to do the work and not to do the work itself. The local group was thus able to undertake a variety of developmental activities that were an extension of its disaster recovery work.

Fourth, CUSO's reliance on an intermediary NGO with a well-established and well-trained field staff that had been active for years in predisaster development activities in Streatham was an effective recovery strategy. Even though the intermediary NGO did not view itself as a disaster aid organization, its field staff had considerable knowledge of local needs and capacities, which enabled it to make accurate damage assessments, to know which households were in need and eligible for assistance, to closely monitor construction practices, and to understand how best to promote local involvement in self-directed recovery and development after the hurricane struck.

Fifth, CUSO sent a community action group leader from Streatham to Canada to give lectures to CUSO sponsors about its long-term developmental work. The local leader was able to give sponsors a first-hand, developing country, perspective and to explain that a successful recovery project involves local organizational capacity building as well as the more widely recognized "brick and mortar" issues.

Sixth, Hurricane Hugo was a "dry" storm," with limited rainfall. A "wet" hurricane could have caused much greater damage to an already devastated island, particularly in areas that had been built in floodplains. Montserrat was also fortunate that, compared to the catastrophic property losses, the number of casualties and injuries were remarkably low.

The Negative Components

THE PREDISASTER PERIOD

First, the National Disaster Plan was ineffective in guiding long-term recovery activities. While the plan emphasized preimpact provisions and, to a lesser extent, postimpact emergency responses, little attention was given to recovery. Thus the plan was widely considered a product and not part of a process. An indicator of this problem was the unfamiliarity of government and NGO officials with the plan's contents. Such lack of knowledge was attributed to the infrequency of meetings focused on reviewing and updating the plan.

Second, local development regulations, particularly building codes, did not have adequate provisions for incorporating mitigation measures. Even the minimal structural-strengthening standards incorporated in the codes were not implemented because inspection procedures were lax and not enforced during the years before Hugo struck. Thus the housing stock was not designed with storm-resistant construction techniques.

Third, national government staff and district chairs assigned to carry out disaster recovery programs were not trained before Hugo and were inadequate in terms of numbers. For example, MATLH's long delay in releasing damage assessments, causing major delays in the delivery of recovery aid, were caused by lack of staff expertise in computerizing damage data. Also, there was an inadequate number of building inspectors, with only one part-time inspector available for the entire rebuilding effort.

Fourth, the national disaster coordinator did not provide effective leadership. While she was capable and possessed strong management skills, she had never received training in disaster management. Other factors that hampered the coordinator were that the position was only part-time and that the administrative budget for the position was inadequate for carrying out even minimal disaster planning activities.

First, the absence of a predisaster recovery plan led to poor interorganizational coordination, low understanding of foreign NGO disaster recovery programs, and limited knowledge of what external resources were available. Interorganizational conflicts and duplicative actions used up staff time and resources that could have been used for other pressing needs. The case of households being surveyed by damage assessors from several organizations exemplifies this problem. Consequently, most postdisaster recovery activities were undertaken on an ad hoc basis. Since such improvisation dominated recovery response decisions, the pace of recovery was inevitably slowed and inefficient.

Second, significant opportunities to prevent or mitigate future disaster losses during reconstruction were lost. The narrow approach of "just put it back" dominated. In many instances, damaged structures could have been reconstructed to be safer from future storms or to enhance long-range development efforts. The most notable case was the decision by the Peace Corps to build a two-sided pitched roof, as opposed to a traditional four-sided pitched roof, on its prefabricated homes for low-income people.

Third, a heavy dependence on foreign assistance and a lack of interorganizational coordination led to a loss of control on the part of Montserrat authorities. Consequently, many of the decisions made by foreign NGOs were based on their own perceptions and values, which poorly reflected the needs and capacities of the disaster-stricken people. Only after the Rehabilitation Unit was created six months after Hugo did Montserrat begin to exert substantial control over its recovery and its future.

Fourth, much relief and recovery work on the part of the international NGOs was not held to development standards. Some NGOs (e.g., the Red Cross and the U.S. Peace Corps) used their field staff to conduct recovery activities but did not build on local organizational capacities.

For example, although the Peace Corps' prefabricated housing project was successful in delivering new homes, it had limited impact on local organizational capacity building. Further, NGOs' control of a significant amount of recovery resources and their resistance to the Montserrat government's attempts to collaborate, constrained domestic organizational influence in managing the recovery.

Fifth, the disaster was not viewed as an opportunity to reduce the future vulnerability of Montserrat to coastal storms. Building codes were not modified to incorporate structural strengthening measures during the recovery period. Moreover, even if mitigation measures were included, it was unlikely that codes could have been implemented given the lack of qualified building inspectors to monitor construction practices.

Long-Range Recovery

Several positive changes have occurred regarding disaster recovery planning since Hurricane Hugo made landfall. Many of these changes are in response to the problems encountered during the Hugo disaster recovery period. They can also be attributed in large part to the predisaster planning efforts by the Pan Caribbean Project.

Most notably, the national disaster coordinator has held a series of regularly scheduled, monthly, post-Hugo workshops to review and evaluate disaster recovery strategies. According to the coordinator, the workshops have been well attended by the Disaster Executive Committee. Members of the committee have also attended three workshops sponsored by the Caribbean Conference of Churches in Antigua. These workshops were regional in nature and focused on storm-resistant building design and construction practices and on linking recovery to long-term development. Based on the knowledge gained from these workshops, the Disaster Executive Committee has been revising the National Disaster Plan, and some government organizations like Public Works and MATLH have been updating their individual plans. In addition, NGO officials involved in the Streatham effort regularly attended the workshops, the first time their organizations had been involved in disaster planning on Montserrat.

There are, however, several limitations to this disaster planning. One is that the government has only made a marginal increase in the budget for disaster planning (EC$5,000 to EC$8,000). These funds are obviously not sufficient to undertake the tasks required for developing an effective disaster recovery planning program. A second limitation is that as of fall

1990 an updated National Disaster Plan had not been adopted by the government. The national disaster coordinator expressed concern that the government's interest in disaster planning was waning as the Hugo experience "fades into the distant past." Finally, the major portion of post-Hugo disaster planning reflects the predisaster trend of emphasizing emergency preparedness instead of disaster recovery.

5   ST. KITTS AND NEVIS

DIFFERENTIAL RECOVERY AND DEVELOPMENT CAPACITIES

THE FEDERATION OF ST. KITTS AND NEVIS IS IN THE EASTERN CARIBBEAN and is part of the Leeward Islands. Agriculture is the dominant sector of the economy, employing over one-third of the labor force. Over the past twenty years in St. Kitts, and more recently in Nevis, tourism has been encouraged in an effort to diversify the economy. The recent expansion of the Golden Rock Airport on St. Kitts, to accommodate large commercial jets, has had a considerable impact on the tourism sector. Both islands have small seaports, while Nevis also has a small, single-runway airport. St. Kitts is sixty-eight square miles and had a 1990 population of thirty-six thousand; and Nevis is thirty-six square miles and had a 1990 population of nine thousand.

The two islands comprise a loosely knit federation. Parliament is located in the capital city of Basseterre in St. Kitts, but Nevisians refer to Charlestown as the capital of Nevis. St. Kitts and Nevis operate with considerable independence, as each island has its own executive and administrative branches of government. St. Kitts has a prime minister and Nevis has a premier. Each head of state serves with a cabinet of ministers and associated ministries.

On Sunday, September 17, 1989, Hurricane Hugo struck St. Kitts and Nevis. Housing loss was substantial, with EC$126 million (US$46 million) in damages and thirteen hundred residents left homeless. The islands' agriculture sector sustained severe damage, particularly to sugar, the primary export earner. Forests suffered extensive damage mainly by defoliation, which induced severe soil erosion and threatened drinking water quality. Damage to public facilities and businesses, especially tourism, was also extensive. Electric, water, and telephone transmission systems were devastated, and most hotels experienced substantial damage.

THE PRESTORM INSTITUTIONAL CONTEXT

The St. Kitts and Nevis National Disaster Preparedness and Prevention Committee is the lead disaster planning organization in the Federation of St. Kitts and Nevis. The forty-member committee is composed of representatives from various government organizations (e.g., health, agriculture, and public works) and NGOs (e.g., the Chamber of Commerce, the Conference of Churches, and the Red Cross). The prime responsibilities of the National Disaster Committee are to carry out the St. Kitts and Nevis National Disaster Plan and to mobilize and coordinate domestic and international disaster response actions. The National Disaster Committee also consists of five subcommittees: public information and education, damage assessment, transport and road clearance, emergency shelter, and health services. St. Kitts employs a part-time national disaster coordinator. The coordinator also holds a high-level government position as the permanent secretary of the Office of the Prime Minister. In addition, an unfunded deputy disaster coordinator position was created to provide administrative assistance to the coordinator. The primary responsibility of both disaster coordinator positions is to serve as the country's chief advocate for hazard awareness and planning.

The National Disaster Committee, however, provides only limited coordination between St. Kitts and Nevis, as its membership overwhelmingly represents St. Kitts. The National Disaster Plan indicates that a "Nevis Island Administrator" (St. Kitts and Nevis . . . 1989a, 1) is the only representative from the Nevisian government on the committee. Two members—one from the St. Kitts and Nevis Port Authority and one from the Telephone and Telex Services—jointly represent the interests of both islands. The National Disaster Plan also indicates that "Nevis operates autonomously" (ibid.) in relation to St. Kitts disaster planning activities. Nevis has its own disaster plan and a separate organizational arrangement for carrying it out: a ten-member Coordinating Committee. It has ten subcommittees dealing with a variety of disaster-related issues similar to those of the Disaster Preparedness and Prevention Committee. The island has a part-time national disaster coordinator who also holds a high-level government position as permanent secretary of the Office of the Premier.

While the disaster plans for both islands were updated by a consultant five months before Hurricane Hugo, overall predisaster planning was more active on St. Kitts than on Nevis. The Emergency Operations Center on St. Kitts was well staffed and had adequate communications equipment, but the center on Nevis did not. During the year before Hugo struck, the St. Kitts Disaster Planning Committee also conducted a national disaster awareness campaign and disaster planning workshops for government officials and NGO representatives. These disaster planning activities, however, focused only on predisaster emergency planning and the immediate postdisaster response; they ignored long-term, postdisaster, recovery and development issues. Nevis, however, had no such predisaster planning efforts under way, and its recovery responses were thus ad hoc and poorly organized. Although most responses were ad hoc on St. Kitts, partly due to the absence of a workable disaster plan, they were better organized and more effective than on Nevis.

The ad hoc nature of planning on both islands can be partially explained by the federation's limited experience with hurricanes. While the islands have been struck by tropical storms about once every twenty years from the late eighteenth century to the present, they had not experienced a severely damaging hurricane in nearly seventy years (since 1928). Seismic and volcanic hazards also pose a threat. Mt. Misery of St. Kitts and Mt. Nevis of Nevis are both part of a chain of volcanic islands referred to as the Lesser Antilles. Both islands experience periodic seismic tremors, indicators that the volcanoes and the earthquake fault system are not dormant (St. Kitts and Nevis . . . 1989b). A disruptive event stemming from these hazards has not, however, occurred for many generations.

Similar to Montserrat, St. Kitts and Nevis has limited controls for guiding development. The Caribbean Uniform Building Code was in place before Hugo but has had little effect on construction practices. Moreover, when the code does apply—primarily for large structures requiring extensive investment—enforcement tends to be lax. There are no land use controls in place, such as zoning and subdivision regulations, that might restrict development from occurring in hazardous locations.

The disaster coordinators on both islands believed that the limited experience with natural disasters severely hampered planning and mitigation actions prior to Hurricane Hugo. The St. Kitts disaster coordinator, for instance, maintained that "people are just not interested in a disaster that might happen in the distant future. There is no sense of urgency about hurricanes, earthquakes, and the like. Its hard to get people motivated to do disaster planning when they are more worried about keeping their jobs and making ends meet."

In summary, prior to Hurricane Hugo, the capacity for undertaking disaster planning and mitigation was limited on St. Kitts and almost nonexistent on Nevis. Seaport and airport facilities for receiving recovery aid were adequate on St. Kitts but limited on Nevis. While some disaster planning had taken place on St. Kitts, it did not focus on disaster recovery. And no predisaster planning occurred on Nevis. Moreover, experience with natural disasters was virtually nonexistent, since, when Hugo struck, it had been sixty-one years since the previous major disaster struck the islands.

THE IMPACTS OF HURRICANE HUGO

Hurricane Hugo was the most powerful storm to strike the Federation of St. Kitts and Nevis in this century. Hugo struck the twin islands on September 17, with estimated sustained wind speed of more than 120 miles per hour. Rainfall was about ten inches. The eye of the storm passed forty-three miles south of the two islands. While Montserrat was the most severely damaged island in the Caribbean, Nevis and St. Kitts were second and third, respectively. Nevis suffered more damage than St. Kitts as it is further south (a channel of one to two miles in width separates the islands) and was closer to the eye of the hurricane.

Agricultural crops on both islands sustained major damage. Sugar, the main export earner in St. Kitts, was particularly affected, with destruction of nine thousand of the twelve thousand acres under cultivation. St. Kitts experienced a EC$28.8 million (US$10.5 million) crop loss, with Nevis losing EC$15.1 million (US$5.5 million). Total damage to the fisheries sector on both islands was more than EC$14.3 million (US$5.2 million). The forests in the upper reaches of the mountainous areas suffered extensive damage, mainly the uprooting and defoliation of trees. Such damage has induced extensive soil erosion in the upland, steeply sloped watersheds and has adversely affected the ground and surface water used for drinking.

Public facilities received a severe pounding. The main pier of the deepwater port in Basseterre was damaged. The only pier at the Nevis seaport sustained damage but remained in working condition. Severe beach erosion and damage to shoreline roadways was extensive on both islands. About 20 percent of all public buildings on the islands sustained structural damage; for example, 20 percent of all school buildings were destroyed and 60 percent were damaged. Roof failures and the subsequent destruction of the buildings' contents were the primary losses to schools and other public buildings on both islands (see figures 5.1–5.4).

Public utilities on St. Kitts and Nevis suffered extensive damage. While electricity-generating plants received only some roof damage, the electric transmission and distribution systems were devastated. The Skantel telephone system was devastated on both islands, as overhead lines, high-tension wires, and regional and international lines were disrupted. Finally, the water systems were severely damaged. Many intakes were silted up due to upland soil erosion, pipelines were broken by fallen trees, and the loss of electricity did not allow pumping.

Private businesses and homes also incurred heavy losses. Factories at the Ponds and Bird Rock Industrial Estates on St. Kitts experienced widespread damage and work stoppage. More than a hundred rooms at Jack Tar Village, the largest resort hotel on both islands, were damaged. Most hotels suffered substantial damage and were closed to guests between two weeks and five months. Others, like the Lemon Hotel on St. Kitts and the Zetlands on Nevis, temporarily went out of business. Damages were devastating to homes, and thirteen hundred residents in the federation were rendered homeless. An estimated 12 percent of all homes were

FIGURE 5.1. Church in Nevis: major roof loss resulted from nontraditional construction. Walls are intact because of traditional construction (photograph by Philip R. Berke).

destroyed, with an additional 25 percent sustaining severe damage. The value of damage to housing exceeded EC$126 million (US$46 million).

Although the destruction on St. Kitts and Nevis was not as catastrophic as on Montserrat, damages were nevertheless severe and widespread. The task of rebuilding was daunting and the impacts will be felt for years to come.

THE STAGES OF THE RECOVERY PROCESS

The emergency stage in St. Kitts ended about one week after Hurricane Hugo made landfall but took about an additional week in Nevis (see figure 5.5). Debris on major roadways was cleared, the homeless were provided with temporary shelter, and immediate food, medical, and potable water needs were met by the first week on St. Kitts and the second week on Nevis. Some basic public facilities, including the water distribution system, airports, and radio and television communication systems, were repaired to at least minimal operational levels during the emergency stage on both islands.

On St. Kitts, damage assessments were made from the air and from the ground within a day after Hugo to determine the need for external

FIGURE 5.2. House of substandard construction: part of roof remains intact but is completely dislodged from structure (photograph by Philip R. Berke).

FIGURE 5.3. Roof of upper-income home, which resisted Hurricane Hugo (photograph by Philip R. Berke).

FIGURE 5.4. Outside view of home shown in figure 5.3 (photograph by Philip R. Berke).

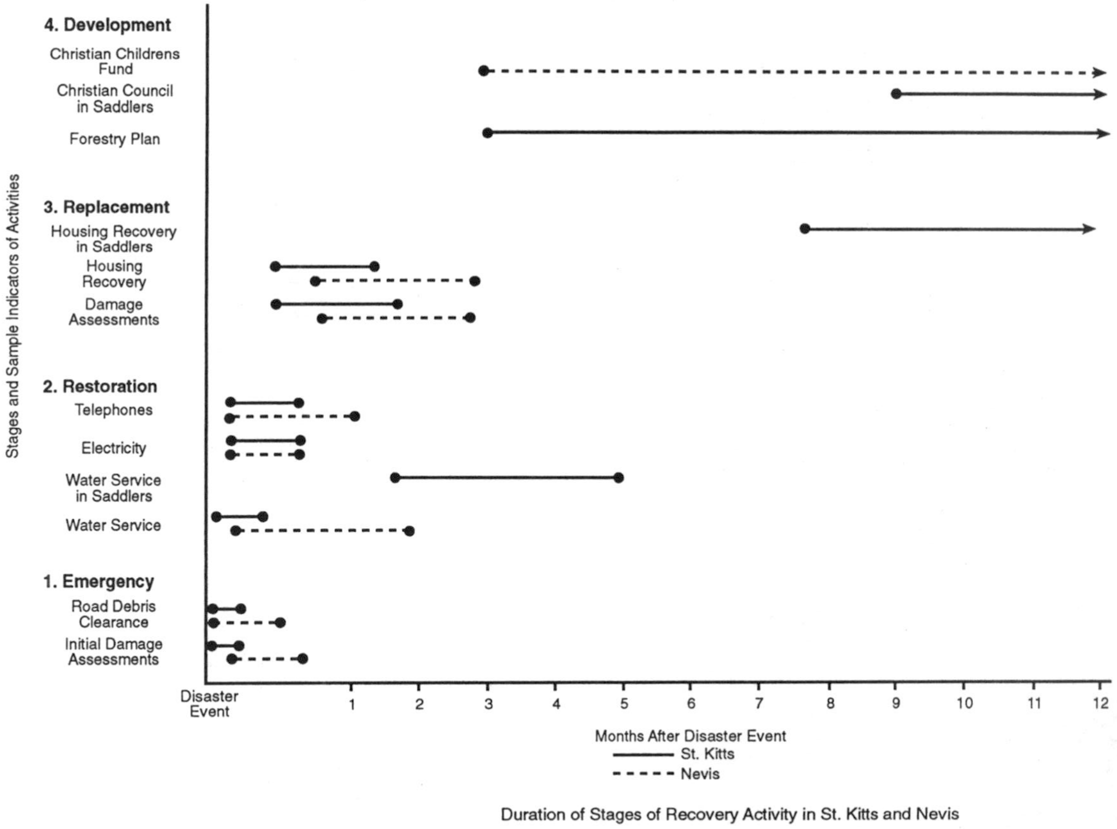

Duration of Stages of Recovery Activity in St. Kitts and Nevis

FIGURE 1.1. Duration of stages of recovery, St. Kitts and Nevis

assistance. These rapid and accurate damage assessments were credited to prior disaster planning and to an adequately staffed Emergency Operations Center. On Nevis, there was much confusion about whether a damage assessment should be conducted in the first place and, if it should be done, who should do it and what information should be collected. In fact, during the week following Hugo, the disaster coordinator encouraged all government staff to remain home. After several days passed without assistance, Nevisian government officials realized there was a need to assess damages to make realistic requests for outside aid.

The restoration stage, which began during the emergency stage, was uneven. Almost all water service on St. Kitts was restored within the first few days after Hugo, with one notable exception: water service restoration in the small, poor, coastal village of Saddlers took more than five months, during which water was available only from a stream running down a steep gully at the outskirts of the village. Such shortages posed obvious health problems and compounded the already difficult postdisaster recovery circumstances for the residents of Saddlers. The long delay was particularly disturbing as restoration consisted only of replacing one public water tap in the center of the village. With the exception of Saddlers, water restoration on Nevis was slower than on St. Kitts because of the more extensive damages to the water service distribution infrastructure in the Charlestown area. Restoration on Nevis required almost eight weeks in many areas.

Fortunately, the seaports and airports on both islands sustained only minor damages and were restored quickly: within a few days on St. Kitts and in one week for the airport and two weeks for the seaport on Nevis. The quick restoration of these facilities on St. Kitts was particularly important because of their capacity to receive large quantities of aid for both islands. The restoration of telephone service to most residents and businesses required about two weeks on St. Kitts but about four weeks on Nevis. Electricity was restored in the two primary cities (Basseterre and Charlestown) within two weeks. Other areas on both islands did not receive electrical service until three months after the storm, which marked the end of this stage.

The replacement stage began early in the restoration stage on each island. On St. Kitts, it started with the initiation of a comprehensive housing damage assessment two weeks after Hurricane Hugo struck. Damage assessments were independently initiated by various government agencies, with mixed success at coordination. On the one hand, the Housing Authority, Public Works, and the police department assembled damage assessment teams on their own and were unaware each other's activities. In many cases, multiple assessments were conducted for the same buildings, and the information that was collected was not standardized, making the data incomplete and difficult to compare. On the other hand, the Department of Agriculture and local agriculture development cooperatives used their long-standing ties among farmers and fishers to effectively assess their needs after the storm.

On Nevis, after a slow and indecisive start during the emergency stage, the damage assessment effort during the replacement stage experienced additional difficulties. Assessment teams were poorly staffed, and there was virtually no coordination among them. Consequently, after about two months of work, assessment data were considered highly inaccurate in estimating the housing needs and capacities of the disaster-stricken population. There was a widespread perception on Nevis that the inaccuracies could be traced to political manipulation to ensure that some households benefited more than others.

The duration of this stage was minimized on St. Kitts due to an effective Emergency Operations Center staff. Its well-organized efforts translated into positive working relationships with NGOs and government organizations in acquiring and distributing aid for rebuilding housing and public facilities during the first few weeks of reconstruction. The commitment and skill of the center's staff was especially crucial because St. Kitts did not have a workable reconstruction component in its National Disaster Plan. All public structures, such as the hospital and schools, were repaired or replaced by October 1990 (thirteen months after Hugo), and almost all households in need of housing assistance received aid within four to six weeks.

However, the much-publicized replacement effort on St. Kitts did not include the reconstruction of Saddlers, which did not receive housing aid until May 1990 (eight months after the disaster). Knowledgeable NGO officials maintained that Saddlers was ignored because its recovery was not in the interests of the government officials in power. The pace of replacement (with the exception of Saddlers) was generally slower on Nevis than on St. Kitts. Several public facilities, such as the school in Gingerland, still had not been completely repaired as of February 1991 (seventeen months after Hugo). Most households received assistance for reconstruction by December 1989 (three months after the disaster), but some were passed over due to what was generally considered inequitable and politically motivated resource allocation decisions by the government. Another factor making this stage more time consuming was that Nevis experienced more severe damage than St. Kitts and thus required more human and material resources. Other factors extending the duration of this stage were that Nevis did not have an operational Emergency Operations Center or a workable disaster plan, which led to confusion, delay, and poor coordination among NGOs and government organizations in acquiring and distributing the appropriate type and amount of aid.

The development stage began during the replacement stage on both islands. The Ministry of Agriculture in St. Kitts initiated the Tropical Forestry Action Plan during the fall of 1989 (about three months after Hugo) as part of the regional reforestation effort supported by the United Nations Environmental Programme. This plan was a response to the severe defoliation and subsequent soil erosion induced by Hurricane Hugo. Additionally, after Hugo struck, parliament increased the annual national disaster planning budget by tenfold in order to employ a full-time disaster coordinator and to provide more support for disaster planning. Also on St. Kitts, a collaborative housing recovery program involving the Caribbean Conference of Churches (CCC) and the St. Kitts Christian Council was initiated in June 1991 to link recovery operations to long-term development in Saddlers. On Nevis, about three months after Hugo struck, the Christian Children's Fund (CCF) initiated a similar effort, linking recovery activities to developmental efforts. Also, during spring 1990 several St. Kitts community service NGOs (e.g., the Rotary and Lions Clubs) began to take a more visible role in national emergency planning and response activities.

The tourist industry experienced substantial postdisaster capital improvement investments. Several hotel owners took the opportunity of expanding their properties while repairing the damage caused by Hugo: Jack Tar Village Resort added forty rooms and Timothy Beach Resorts added twenty-four (as of January 1990). Finally, the rebuilding of several major public structures, like schools and electric power plants, incorporated structural strengthening measures.

THE DIMENSIONS OF THE RECOVERY PROCESS

Organizational Coordination

Four organizational coordination efforts were of particular interest on St. Kitts and Nevis during the disaster recovery period: the national disaster planning program, damage assessments, NGO collaboration, and interisland coordination.

THE NATIONAL DISASTER PLANNING PROGRAM

Interorganizational coordination during the disaster recovery was generally considered successful on St. Kitts because of three members of the National Disaster Preparedness and Prevention Committee, whose combined skills gave the committee a high level of technical credibility and organizational management capacity in coordinating the recovery effort. Interorganizational coordination was also attributed to two events. The month before Hugo made landfall (August 1989) the National Disaster Committee committee sponsored a National Safety Month campaign intended to heighten awareness about disasters. Also, committee members attended a hurricane disaster planning workshop a few weeks before Hugo made landfall. These events, according to a high-level government official, "had the crucial effect of making ministerial and government decision makers, and St. Kittians in general, at least aware of the existence of an emergency structure and the existence of an EOC."

Interorganizational coordination efforts on Nevis, however, were not as successful, a key reason being that the lead disaster planning organization in Nevis (Nevis Emergency Organization) was totally inoperable during the immediate postdisaster emergency response and the disaster recovery periods. Unlike St. Kitts, Nevis had no viable disaster planning organization to serve as a focal point of disaster recovery activities. Nor did any individual play a crucial leadership and management role.

None of the informants interviewed on either island attributed the success of interorganizational coordination during the recovery effort to national disaster plans, which were generally viewed as "paper plans" and of little use during the recovery. The St. Kitts plan was prepared by a private consultant five months before Hugo struck, so there was minimal participation in plan preparation by individuals whose organizations would be involved in plan implementation. An official from Public Works, who was a member of the National Disaster Committee, commented that "on a couple of occasions I popped my head into the office where the consultant was writing the plan, but I was not asked to attend any meetings or give any feedback. Only after a few weeks had passed was I asked to give any comments. I was under the impression that the plan was only being prepared to satisfy some administrative rule or law, which requires that a plan be prepared. There was a plan all right, but one that could not be implemented."

Consequently, members of the National Disaster Committee were only vaguely familiar with the plan: of the six individuals interviewed on St. Kitts who were members of the committee, four indicated that they were not familiar with the responsibilities of their organizations as specified in the plan. These four members were aware of the existence of the plan but had not read it. One high-level administrator in the Ministry of Agriculture maintained that, although the consultant had provided much-needed expertise in preparing and writing the plan, some or most of the funds used for hiring the consultant should have been used to support in-house government efforts to develop the plan. The consultant, according this individual, should also have been used as an expert facilitator and coordinator of the plan formulation process. Even the two informants who had read the plan reported that it was somewhat confusing to understand. A content analysis of the plan document substantiated this claim. The title of the plan itself was inconsistent, changing from "National Disaster Plan" on the front cover, to "Federal Emergency Delivery and Services Plan" on the introductory page, to "Federal Disaster Plan" in chapter 3. Titles of the various disaster-related planning organizations and the tasks of these organizations also varied between chapters.

Furthermore, although the forty-three-page St. Kitts plan specified the emergency-related responsibilities and tasks (e.g., public information and education, damage assessment, transport and road clearance, emergency shelter, and health service delivery) to be carried out by various government and nongovernment organizations, it contained no discussion of long-term recovery responsibilities and attendant actions by relevant organizations. Also, the plan made little reference to the responsibilities of the National Disaster Committee in coordinating these activities. Although the Nevis plan was less confusing to read than the St. Kitts plan, other problems were prevalent. The Nevis plan was prepared by an outside consultant in 1985 with no involvement from Nevis officials. In fact, none of the four individuals interviewed on Nevis who were members of the Nevis Emergency Organization had participated in plan preparation, nor had they ever seen the plan. Also, there had been no plan updating activities. The Nevis plan focused almost entirely on the emergency preparedness and response phases of a disaster, with no emphasis on disaster recovery. With the exception of a half-page review of damage assessment procedures, there was no discussion of disaster recovery.

Since Hugo, the governments of St. Kitts and, to a lesser extent, of Nevis have given higher priority to disaster planning. Most notably, the

St. Kitts Parliament increased the national disaster planning budget ten-fold, from $EC5,000 ($US 1,825) before Hugo to $EC50,000 ($US18,250) after Hugo. This increased funding is to be used to employ a full-time national disaster coordinator and to provide additional support for dis-aster planning activities. Subcommittees of the lead disaster planning organization on each island have also been holding occasional meetings to review the successes and failures of Hurricane Hugo disaster re-sponse and recovery strategies. As of February 1991, however, no effort had been undertaken on either island to revise the disaster plans, nor had a full-time coordinator been hired on St. Kitts.

DAMAGE ASSESSMENT

Evidence on the effectiveness of interorganizational efforts to assess damages on St. Kitts was mixed. On the one hand, NGO and govern-ment collaborative arrangements were highly successful. On the other hand, collaborative activities among government agencies were gener-ally unsuccessful.

The evidence on government damage assessment revealed several in-stances of poor interorganizational coordination, in particular the du-plication in damage assessment by the St. Kitts police and the Housing Authority. About two weeks after Hugo struck, the police had assem-bled field teams to conduct damage assessments on a house-by-house basis. The assessment was originally intended to determine the amount of aid required by households. A high-level Housing Authority admin-istrator charged with directing the housing recovery effort on St. Kitts revealed that, during the first few days in the field, neither he nor his staff were aware of the ongoing police assessments. Collaboration in both data collection and field teams could have reduced the time re-quired to conduct the assessments "by several days at the least, or even a week or more." The police assessed only structural damage and did not assess needs based on family socioeconomic conditions. As a result, Housing Authority damage assessment teams had to return to hundreds of households that had been assessed by the police to collect informa-tion on need. Further, the Housing Authority damage assessment teams were understaffed, with only six part-time positions (or two full-time equivalent positions). The pooling of staff would obviously have facili-tated the assessment process. Another instance of poor interorganiza-tional coordination in assessing damages occurred between Public Works and the Housing Authority. During the first two weeks after Hugo, staff from both organizations conducted damage assessments on many of the same public buildings. A Public Works official maintained that "at times the problem became obvious . . . the damage assessment staff from both organizations were actually bumping into each other in the narrow hallways of some buildings."

On Nevis, there was indecision over whether the Nevis government should be involved in damage assessment in the first place and whether the first order of business for government officials was not to take care of their own households and to help their kin and neighbors. This response was, according to the disaster coordinator, consistent with the customary practice on Nevis of reliance on family, friends, and neighbors rather than on formal government and nongovernment organizations. Besides, most Nevisians felt that somehow aid would be coming from St. Kitts, since "they were not hit that bad and they had the big airport and seaport for receiving aid."

All five individuals interviewed who were knowledgeable about the Nevis damage assessment process maintained that it was further delayed by the absence of an effective disaster plan. An informed government staffer suggested that "damage assessments were organized on a totally ad hoc, seat-of-the-pants basis." One Red Cross staffer indicated that, as a consequence of poor planning, "the government rounded up whoever they could to get the damage numbers down on paper. It didn't matter whether these people were trained to do this type of thing. The bottom line was that they [the government] needed the numbers to get international assistance." Personnel used to assess damages included, for example, schoolteachers on vacation, government clerical staff, and manual laborers from the Department of Public Works, people with obviously limited or no expertise in building construction practices. As expected, after about four weeks of effort the assessment data were considered by all those interviewed on Nevis to be highly inaccurate.

NGO COLLABORATION

Three cases of NGO collaboration on St. Kitts were identified. Of most long-term significance was a collaborative arrangement between external, intermediary, and local NGOs. With support from a variety of NGOs in North America and Europe, the external NGO (the regional office of the Caribbean Conference of Churches) on Antigua worked with an intermediary NGO (the Christian Council of St. Kitts), providing funds to purchase housing materials and to partially support a full-time staff person. The intermediary NGO, in turn, worked with a community-based NGO (Saddlers Community Sports Club) to facilitate housing reconstruction and, most important, to promote long-term development in the community.

The circumstances in Saddlers was particularly disturbing and urgent. About nine months after Hugo struck (May 1990), housing repair in Saddlers, a rural village of about five hundred people on the north coast of St. Kitts, was neglected. It was a "disturbing fact," according to the CCC quarterly newsletter, "that the much publicized rapidity of the recovery of St. Kitts did not take into account the more than 60 percent of the houses in Saddlers that were severely damaged" (*Links*, April–June 1990, 14). An administrative staffer of the Christian Council of St. Kitts reasoned that Saddlers did not receive assistance because the village was poor and "in the backwaters of life in St. Kitts." A Saddlers community official further maintained that the provision of recovery aid to the village was "not in the political interest of those in power."

Unlike the circumstances in Streatham, on Montserrat there were no community-based development organizations in Saddlers before Hugo. In addition, NGO recovery work on Montserrat was initiated within several weeks after Hugo, but in Saddlers several months passed before action was taken. The challenge, according to *Links*, was "to refuse to accept the status quo, to refuse to accept that, because there were no formal groups in Saddlers, people could not be mobilized and motivated to come together and to assist each other" (ibid.). Moreover, the problem was not one of material or physical assistance, because in May 1990 the government did finally provide housing aid. The problem was that labor was scarce and expensive. A Christian Council staffer maintained that the Saddlers situation raised the need to focus staff "understanding of development beyond economic variables and to take a deep look at the [village] social/organizational processes, where people are not organized, motivated, and conscientized to enable the community to self-improve" (ibid., 5).

The Christian Council's strategy, with staffing support from the CCC, was to undertake a series of workshops in Saddlers, starting in June 1990, to enhance community leadership and organizational capabilities. A key local group involved in these workshops was the Saddlers Community Sports Club, which had been active in organizing village youth sporting events. Serious attention by Christian Council staff during the workshops was given to enhancing the organization of the Sports Club so it could undertake housing recovery and long-term developmental work. As of February 1991—eight months after the Christian Council initiated the workshops—the results of the collaborative NGO efforts were mixed. The physical and material outcome was somewhat disappointing—only three damaged homes were targeted for repair, and only one of these was to undergo rehabilitation, with the other two scheduled to be repaired during the spring and summer of 1991. The main obstacles to rebuilding were difficulties in obtaining government building permits and a lack of carpentry expertise in Saddlers. From an organization capacity-building perspective, however, the results appear to have had some potential benefits. The director of the Sports Club indicated that the workshops encouraged and taught members of the group and solidified the group as a unit. In fact, several club members are becoming competent carpenters and look forward to applying these skills to rebuilding many more homes in Saddlers.

A second case of NGO collaboration involved an arrangement between the National Disaster Committee staff at the Emergency Operations Center and local public service NGOs on St. Kitts—the Lions Club and the Rotary Club—in acquiring and distributing aid. The center relied on the Lions and the Rotarians to assess local needs for rebuilding materials, particularly roofing materials. Further, the organizational networks of these NGOs ensured that aid was distributed to those in need. This arrangement, according to a National Disaster Committee staffer and a Lions Club member, facilitated the timely delivery of appropriate housing aid during the three to four weeks after Hugo struck. Interviews consistently revealed that the arrangement also stimulated a positive political atmosphere and a sense of mutual trust between disaster-stricken people and the government. Interestingly, this successful interorganizational collaboration was due in part to the long-time membership of the deputy national disaster coordinator in the local Lions Club chapter.

A third case on St. Kitts involved collaboration between the Department of Agriculture and local rural development cooperatives. The department had been involved for several years before Hugo struck in initiating and promoting local agriculture development cooperatives. This locally based institution-building effort paid off in facilitating disaster recovery, according to both a high-level Department of Agriculture administrator and a local fishing cooperative representative. That is, during the first three to four weeks after Hugo struck, fishers and farmers reported their damages and their recovery needs to their local cooperative representatives, who reported this information to the national headquarters of the Department of Agriculture. According to the two officials interviewed, the entire distribution of fishery and farm recovery aid was timely, effective, and accurate. One of the officials maintained that the presence of the cooperatives was a key reason for not encountering delays in the delivery of aid, because they "helped us to quickly answer the question, Who needs what and how much?"

While several NGOs (e.g., the CCC, the CCF, and the Red Cross) were active in disaster recovery on Nevis, most of their activities were separate, independent efforts. Collaboration with the Nevis government was nonexistent. A collaboration of particular interest involved two nonprofit NGOs (the CCC and the Nevis Red Cross) and a local merchant. As in the cases of St. Kitts and Montserrat, CCC staff at the regional headquarters on Antigua wanted to support the Nevis rebuilding effort and found the Red Cross a deserving candidate for assistance. The staff thus committed funds on request from the Red Cross to purchase building materials for repairing low-income homes that had been severely damaged or destroyed. In addition to CCC funding, the Nevis Red Cross also received funds from expatriates in the United States for the purchase of materials (EC$50,000, or US$18,500) .

The Nevis Red Cross director was also successful in reaching an agreement to use a vacant grocery store building as a distribution center for housing materials. According to the store owner, the agreement was based on his long working relationship with the Red Cross and especially with its director. The two individuals had been involved in a variety of community service projects (e.g., improving local recreation facilities and conducting community first aid workshops) for several years before the disaster.

Overall, this collaborative effort was quite successful. As of July 1991, eight months after the housing program began, all but six of the twenty-seven households participating in the program had their homes repaired.

INTERISLAND COORDINATION

Interorganizational coordination between St. Kitts and Nevis was limited during disaster recovery. Recovery programs in housing, agriculture, and education, among others, generally operated independently on each island. Indicators of such limited coordination can be found in the *St. Kitts and Nevis National Disaster Plan* (St. Kitts and Nevis . . . 1989a). As mentioned, these include separate disaster plans and separate disaster planning committees for each island, with very limited discussion of how the plans and committees were to coordinate. Interviews also revealed that coordination between the islands was limited. Representatives of organizations (Agriculture, Housing, Public Works, and a variety of NGOs) active in the recovery effort were asked if stronger inter-island collaborative efforts would have improved their organizations' disaster recovery programs. All maintained that, with the exception of needing to improve the apportionment and distribution of aid between the islands, enhanced collaboration would have had a minimal impact on their organizations' recovery activities. The dominant reason given was that, historically, collaborative efforts have been limited and that, long before Hugo, there existed a sense of mistrust between the people of the two islands. Comments from people of both islands like "we're like two worlds apart," "they are a funny people," and "you can't trust them" exemplify the uneasy relationship between the two islands.

This uneasy relationship was reinforced by two incidents that oc-curred at the outset of the disaster response. One involved the percep-tion by Nevis officials that St. Kitts was keeping an unfair portion of the recovery aid. Because St. Kitts has a larger seaport and airport than Nevis, most recovery aid destined for Nevis had to be shipped through St. Kitts. One high-level government official from Nevis suggested that "those St. Kittians could get away with keeping that which was not theirs—it is obvious they took care of their own before they thought of us." Another commenting on the aid distribution said, "They speak so highly of an island federation, but only when it works to their advan-tage." In fact, this perception was likely to be accurate in some in-stances. Interviews with officials of international donor organizations, including UNDRO and the Red Cross, revealed that immediately after Hurricane Hugo struck St. Kitts government officials announced that St. Kitts intended to keep 80 percent of all recovery aid donated to the Federation of St. Kitts and Nevis, with the remaining 20 percent going to Nevis. The logic for this ratio, according to St. Kitts officials, was to reflect the proportional difference in population between the two is-lands. International officials expressed irritation with this apportion-ment rationale and demanded that aid be split fifty-fifty, since the Nevis population experienced more severe damage.

The second incident generated mistrust on the part of St. Kitts officials toward Nevis. Three St. Kitts government officials active at the Emer-gency Operations Center expressed concern that an individual suppos-edly representing the Federation of St. Kitts and Nevis on the CARICOM (Caribbean Community) Regional Disaster Unit (known as CRDU) had not been officially appointed by the St. Kitts and Nevis federal govern-ment. These officials maintained that he was appointed to the unit by influential Nevis interests, particularly large coconut plantation owners, in order to watch out for the interests of Nevis. More than a week passed after the unit was in operation before St. Kitts officials were able to have him removed from it. While no evidence was found to substantiate that Nevis officials were behind the appointment, the perception was that they had participated in behind-the-scenes maneuvering.

In sum, problems in apportioning and distributing aid between the two island states further constrained an already uneasy relationship. One informed observer of an international NGO maintained that tensions over aid allocation partly contributed to growing support in Nevis for secession. During the spring of 1991, Nevis elected officials were openly discussing—through newspapers and the radio—the possibility of secession from the federation.

Leadership

When interviewees were asked which organizations or individuals had played a leadership role in raising awareness and promoting disaster planning before Hurricane Hugo, six of eight interviewees on St. Kitts and five of eight on Nevis mentioned the Pan Caribbean Disaster Preparedness and Prevention Project. These individuals pointed to a range of project-backed activities during the four- or five-year period before Hurricane Hugo. Activities considered useful were the distribution of hurricane tracking charts and pamphlets on how to prepare households for disaster, technical assistance in disaster plan preparation, and hurricane disaster planning workshops. There was consensus that the project's activities raised awareness on the two islands but that this awareness had not triggered much predisaster planning activity, particularly on Nevis. Two informants on St. Kitts, however, suggested that the awareness and knowledge gained was making a difference since Hugo. One building permit administrator in the Housing Authority noted that he was currently following hurricane-resistant housing design guidelines in reviewing building plans. The guidelines appeared in a pamphlet distributed by the Pan Caribbean Project about a year before the storm. This individual admitted that he had ignored this information before Hugo struck but had "dug it out from under a pile" after Hugo.

Five St. Kitts informants said that the deputy disaster coordinator had also played a key role in raising awareness before Hugo, that he had been persistent and tireless in conducting disaster planning workshops and in promoting hurricane awareness through the media. Although he had multiple government positions (i.e., meteorologist, air traffic controller, and deputy disaster coordinator), these positions were mutually reinforcing. For example, his knowledge of meteorology helped him to assemble storm landfall prediction data and to explain the causes and the consequences of hurricanes, which helped him be more effective in the limited time he could devote to actual disaster planning activities.

St. Kitts informants also claimed that government organizations played a stronger leadership role than NGOs during the disaster recovery. The St. Kitts and Nevis National Disaster Preparedness and Prevention Committee was mentioned by seven of nine informants: the combined skills, commitment, and innovative decisions made by three members of the National Disaster Committee working at the Emergency Operations Center had, in their opinion, greatly facilitated the acquisition and distribution of recovery aid. One of these members was the deputy disaster coordinator, whose work during the first three or four weeks after the storm was crucial. Representatives of government and nongovernment organizations who had requested and received materials by coordinating with Emergency Operations Center staff consistently expressed a high opinion of his performance. "Worked tirelessly for hours on end in holding the ship together," "much competency and dedication," and "displayed exemplary management skills over the long haul." During the initial recovery period, the close ties this individual had with the Lions and Rotary Clubs before Hugo struck were indispensable to timely and accurate assessments of local needs and the distribution of aid.

The executive director of the St. Kitts Chamber of Commerce, who was also executive director of the National Disaster Committee at the time Hugo struck, also played a crucial role at the Emergency Operations Center. According to other members of the committee, the deputy disaster coordinator and the executive director had a close working relationship and a twenty-year friendship dating back to their high schools days. The executive director also used his knowledge of business sector operations—in particular, of domestic and international building supply companies—to acquire much needed recovery aid, especially building materials.

The third instrumental individual was the prime minister of St. Kitts, who chaired the daily meetings of the National Disaster Committee during the first weeks after Hugo struck. The deputy coordinator maintained that the prime minister provided strong personal leadership throughout the recovery period—identifying and coordinating the roles of government agencies and taking control of the recovery—and that his presence and involvement were crucial.

In contrast to the strong leadership role provided by the St. Kitts government, leadership provided by the Nevisian government was not effective. The limited leadership on Nevis was credited to NGOs. The most frequently cited organization (by four of eight informants) was the Nevis Red Cross. Although the Red Cross is normally active immediately following a disaster, these informants said that the performance of the Nevis Red Cross, especially its director, was exemplary. The Red Cross "set the standard for leadership" not so much for the number of homes receiving assistance from the organization (sixty) but for the "honesty and high standards by which it handled foreign aid."

Interestingly, none of those interviewed reported a government organization or official who played a leadership role during the disaster recovery. The omission of the national disaster coordinator was particularly noteworthy. One informant summed up the feelings of several of those interviewed by indicating that the coordinator was placed "in an impossible position," given his multiple responsibilities as the permanent secretary of the Office of the Premier.

LINKAGE

All instances of linkage between recovery and development encountered on St. Kitts and Nevis occurred on an ad hoc basis. There were no predisaster plans to identify ongoing programs that could be linked to the recovery effort. Nevertheless, several development programs were linked to and facilitated by the disaster, notably the recovery activities of the Lions and Rotary Clubs. Once these organizations completed their recovery activities (about three weeks after the disaster), they undertook follow-up work that took advantage of the positive image created by their earlier successes on St. Kitts. Now, these NGOs have a more active role in assisting the government in emergency planning and response than during the pre-Hugo period. For example, in April 1991 the government relied on volunteers of these organizations to organize a crew of more than 150 people to help clean up a tanker ship oil spill on St. Kitts beaches. According to the deputy disaster coordinator, such large-scale government collaboration with NGOs would have been "unimaginable" before Hugo.

Another notable case of linkage resulting from the disaster was the initiation of development work by the Christian Council in the village of Saddlers. The council had long wanted to be involved with the community but had no predisaster ties there. The minister of the Moravian

Church in Basseterre, who also served on the council, indicated that Hurricane Hugo provided the council an opportunity to initiate development activity in Saddlers. According to the executive secretary of the Christian Council, Hugo motivated its staff to get involved and provided the council with material and staff resources that would not have ordinarily been available. Further, the CCC staff at the regional office on Antigua provided support for the council, in order to improve the council's capacity to work with local people. The CCC staff was especially motivated, given its developmental successes in Montserrat. Although as of February 1991, housing rehabilitation in Saddlers was limited, those involved in the effort held out considerable hope for its future success. The CCC newsletter noted that "the hope is to do more than simply restore the community to a state of normalcy, but to enhance the community's local leadership and organizational capacity to undertake long-term development activities" (*Links*, April–June 1990, 14). "We hope it [the development activity in Saddlers] will be the beginning of a more long-term agreement with the community, one in which we will do more than simply restore the community to a state of normalcy—one in which we can work towards reducing vulnerabilities of the community, and enhancing its capacities" (5).

The local Sports Club was also active in development work in Saddlers. Its leader believed that the club "now commands more respect and authority in Saddlers. The club's self-motivation is much higher compared to what it was before the storm." The leader hoped that the club's improved self-confidence would translate into community housing, public infrastructure, and other development efforts. Sports Club members have enhanced their skills in carpentry and have also undertaken several activities that are not disaster related, including resurfacing a cricket field and cutting sugarcane, with the earnings going toward community improvement projects like renovation of the community center and installing better public water services.

Another case of linkage involved the CCF, which had been active in two self-help housing development projects on Nevis for two years before Hugo struck. Each project had a field coordinator and a community-based board of directors. As with the CCF's work on Antigua, the field coordinators were trained by CCF staff in basic carpentry and organization-building skills. CCF viewed Hugo as providing a window of opportunity for extending its development work into long-range disaster recovery. The strategy used by CCF was to involve its staff and its well-developed field network in disaster reconstruction. With funds from in-

FIGURE 5.6. New home built in Nevis with Red Cross Aid: it is constructed in the risky shape popular for houses built with international aid funds. Low-pitched, hipped roof with substantial overhang is more likely to lift from structure during storms (photograph by Philip R. Berke).

ternational CCF donors, the regional CCF office on Antigua supplied building materials to disaster-stricken, low-income households with children. As of July 1990 a total of seven new homes had been built or were under construction by the CCF-led community teams.

In a similar arrangement, the Nevis Red Cross acquired assistance from the CCC and expatriates to link its ongoing disaster response efforts to a long-range housing development project. The Red Cross used its pre-Hugo organization and field staff to assist low-income households in acquiring building materials and in rebuilding damaged homes. Unlike the CCF effort, however, the Red Cross staff was not involved in organizing self-help groups. Instead, it provided the funds and the materials and hired carpenters to do the rebuilding (see figure 5.6).

While most cases of linkage involved NGO coordination, one involved a government organization linking up with an external NGO to undertake environmental protection. According to the chief scientist at the Ministry of Agriculture, the quality of drinking water on St. Kitts declined markedly after Hurricane Hugo due to runoff—a consequence of the destruction of much of the vegetation on the island. Thus his ministry was embarking on a major reforestation program. Although ministry staff had been aware of the United Nations Environmental Programme for the reforestation of the Caribbean, there was minimal participation in the program by St. Kitts and Nevis. After Hugo, however, there was a renewed interest in reforestation, which led to a new department initiative to collaborate with the UN effort and prepare a "tropical forest action plan." Consequently, St. Kitts and Nevis can become eligible for technical assistance and financial support once the plan is approved by the UN.

Finally, the rebuilding of public and private structures often incorporated structural strengthening measures. Of greatest significance were the structural improvements made to the electric power plant located downstream of the St. Kitts airport. This plant, which is the island's sole source of electric power, is located in a floodplain and so experienced substantial flooding from hurricane rainfall. According to the public works director, much of the flooding was caused by the recent expansion of the airport terminal, which had increased the impermeable surface area in the drainage basin, increasing storm water runoff. The director maintained that the additional runoff and the resultant impacts on the power plant were not taken into consideration at the time of the expansion but that appropriate grading and landscaping have been undertaken since Hugo. Other mitigation measures incorporated into the rebuilding of public facilities include the structural strengthening of damaged roofs on schools, the installation of new utility poles, and the use of reinforced concrete to replace damaged concrete block seawalls and bulkheads.

The assistant planning officer for the Housing Authority indicated that the materials used for the reconstruction of the roofs of many of the damaged homes on St. Kitts addressed several local concerns and that, as a result, repaired homes were structurally stronger, more aesthetically pleasing, cooler, and generally more comfortable. These materials (asphalt shingles and plywood, rather than the light galvanized steel and plasterboard prevalent before Hugo) happened to be readily available from overseas suppliers at the time of Hugo, while, fortunately, galvanized steel and plasterboard roofing was not. This individual had no data on the number of households that made these structural improvements, but he was sure that mitigation was generally not of concern to carpenters during rebuilding.

Monitoring and Enforcement

The strategies used to monitor the distribution of aid and to ensure that aid recipients complied with reconstruction guidelines had varying degrees of success. The more successful monitoring and enforcement activities generally stemmed from NGO activities rather than government-initiated recovery work. Lions Club and Rotary Club recovery activities, for example, were widely considered successful in ensuring that much of the recovery aid was used appropriately. A Lions Club official explained that because the volunteer members of his organization had long been involved in service activities in their communities "they had a pretty good feel for the needs and the situations of the people affected by the disaster." Since the volunteers were local people, they could observe how aid was used for recovery in their neighborhoods. This close contact served as a deterrence to using aid for unintended purposes.

Another example of effective monitoring and compliance was the work of local agriculture and fishery development cooperatives, which provided a supportive role in ensuring that appropriate types and amounts of aid were distributed to farmers and fishers in need. A Department of Agriculture official indicated that a key reason for the successful monitoring of aid to local fishers was that they already had well-established arrangements for monitoring one another's catch limits (to ensure that the local fishery was not depleted). These institutionalized arrangements, according to the official, were effectively adapted to the distribution of aid.

Insurance companies also experienced considerable success in monitoring the distribution of aid to claimants. Interviews with two claims adjusters of the primary home insurer on St. Kitts and Nevis—the National Caribbean Insurance Company—revealed that about three hundred claims were filed with the company on St. Kitts and about sixty on Nevis. The staff of more than thirty people "scrutinized all claims with a fine-tooth comb" to ensure that claims payments matched insured damages. In addition, the company became more effective at monitoring household insurance needs: because home values are continually changing, there is a need for people to regularly update their insurance. On St. Kitts and Nevis home values had been increasing during the pre-Hugo period. Thus when the storm hit many people were underinsured and unable to claim all damages incurred. Since Hugo, the company has instituted policies to inspect all the buildings it insures and to include a notice on customer billing forms to remind people of the need to regularly update their insurance.

Although the monitoring of claims and insurance needs has been effective, compliance with the legitimate use of claims payments has been somewhat suspect. Claims agents maintained that the company relied on Housing Authority inspection staff to ensure that rebuilding complied with the national building code, but as discussed previously, the Housing Authority's inspection staff was inadequate for monitoring all the structures undergoing repair, which included not only those being repaired with insurance payments but also six hundred structures that housed low-income, uninsured occupants.

Inadequate mitigation requirements in the national building code and shoddy workmanship by unqualified people further constrained effective monitoring and enforcement. A Housing Authority planning officer summed up the situation: "Many people suddenly became overnight carpenters and building contractors, and there was a lot of sloppy work as a result. We just did not have the building inspection people to go out and keep track of all of these characters. Besides, even if we could track them, the rules of the game, the codes, just weren't adequate to require any really effective mitigation."

Another concern with government monitoring and compliance involved politically motivated aid distribution, as opposed to distribution based on need. Interviews revealed that there was great concern regarding the situation in Saddlers among NGO officials involved in long-range development. Because Saddlers was overlooked for so long in the recovery effort (aid was distributed eight months after Hugo), many began to question why such a desperate situation was allowed to develop in the first place. An atmosphere of mistrust and ill will developed between the residents and the government. An NGO representative involved in development work on St. Kitts suggested that—whether it was oversight, bad politics, or both—the adverse political atmosphere created by the Saddlers incident seriously eroded any NGO initiatives, at least for the near future, that might require collaborative work with the government. "If there were any hint that we were involved in any way with the government, the Saddlers people would not have anything to do with us." One indication of his NGO's effort to distance itself from the government were the blue T-shirts that all of his organization's field staff were required to wear when working in the village. The T-shirts were emblazoned with the slogan, "Work Together for the Better," symbolizing staffers and residents working together to build for the future. The NGO representative indicated that the T-shirts have helped residents distinguish the staff from government officials.

The situation on Nevis regarding monitoring and enforcement was similar to that on St. Kitts. That is, NGOs generally were more effective at monitoring the distribution of aid and in ensuring that aid recipients comply with guidelines specifying how the aid should be used. The CCF and the Nevis Red Cross effectively used their well-established field networks to ensure that aid was distributed based on need and that it was used for its intended purposes. In contrast, the Nevisian government was widely accused of distributing building materials based on political favoritism. In fact, a Public Works employee maintained during an interview that he personally witnessed galvanized sheets for roofing being given to people in such inordinate amounts that their homes could have been "reroofed twenty times over." Compounding the problem was an inadequate building inspection staff (there was only one building inspector on the island). Also, as in the case of other island states in the eastern Caribbean, there was widespread dissatisfaction with the Nevis building code, as it did not stipulate building strengthening standards to guide reconstruction.

The Recognition of Rights

The right of domestic NGOs and governments to formulate recovery strategies and to adapt them to the changing needs and demands of disaster-impacted populations is crucial. If external donor organizations impose inflexible and stringent conditions on how aid is to be used by domestic organizations, the pace of recovery will be constrained due to aid that does not fit the needs of disaster-stricken people. Moreover, the commitment and capacity of domestic organizations to carry out recovery programs can dramatically decline (Anderson and Woodrow 1989; Harrell-Bond 1986).

Fortunately, external organizations generally recognized the legitimacy of St. Kitts and Nevis authorities to manage the recovery process. On St. Kitts the National Disaster Committee exerted substantial control in coordinating the distribution of externally donated aid. CCC regional headquarters on Antigua had an effective relationship with the St. Kitts Christian Council, which had the capacity to undertake development work during the disaster recovery period. The council, in turn, depended on the Saddlers Sports Club's capacity to do development work. On Nevis, the Red Cross benefited from CCC's recognition of its capacity to undertake housing recovery activities. However, foreign recognition of domestic rights and capabilities was not as important in explaining successful recovery on St. Kitts and Nevis as it was on Montserrat, since these islands (especially St. Kitts) did not experience the level of devastation that occurred on Montserrat. Thus, although the demands on domestic organizations were extensive and in many instances exceeded their capabilities, St. Kitts and Nevis organizations were not nearly as overwhelmed in dealing with foreign disaster relief organizations as those on Montserrat.

Resources

STAFF

The adequacy of staff varied by organization and type of recovery activity. In general, the governments on both islands had insufficient staffing in terms of number of positions and expertise. The St. Kitts Housing Authority had only two full-time positions for damage assessment. While the authority did receive some assistance in damage assessment from the police department, coordination in using staff from both organizations was lacking, resulting in duplication of effort. The Housing Authority also lacked inspection staff to ensure that appropriate building practices were used during reconstruction. Similarly, Nevis had inadequate staffing to carry out damage assessments and to inspect structures undergoing repair. For example, the Nevisian government employed only one building inspector.

On the positive side, however, the St. Kitts Emergency Operations Center was adequately staffed. As mentioned, the combined skills of the staff members led to a high level of technical credibility and organizational management capacity. Moreover, since Hugo the St. Kitts government has appropriated funds to make the part-time national disaster coordinator position full-time. This positive step will obviously provide additional support for future disaster planning activities.

In contrast to the government, the staffing situation of NGOs was better. The numerous volunteer members of the community service organizations were used effectively during the disaster recovery by the St. Kitts Emergency Operations Center. Additionally, plans have been implemented to further integrate these NGOs into ongoing emergency preparedness and response activities, as evidenced by the oil spill incident. Also, NGOs involved in long-range development (the Christian Council on St. Kitts, the CCF on Nevis) and in emergency response (the Nevis Red Cross) relied on their field staffs for undertaking disaster recovery activities. Finally, private insurance companies had well-established and trained staffs to conduct damage assessments and to monitor the distribution of claims payments. A shortcoming of the insurance industry efforts, however, was their reliance on the government to monitor the construction practices of claimants. This was particularly unfortunate because they were adequately staffed to handle building inspections, while the government had inadequate staffing to carry out this task.

BUILDING MATERIALS

In general, building supplies on St. Kitts and Nevis met most of the needs for reconstruction. Several factors accounted for this. First, there was a substantial prestorm stock of building materials available for reconstruction on both islands. Interviews with building supply store owners revealed that their businesses were well stocked because prior to Hugo they had been supplying large resort-based construction projects with building materials. Second, building suppliers on Nevis gave a 10 percent discount for building materials, which alleviated the potential of selling materials at inflated costs. Third, compared to Montserrat, St. Kitts and Nevis had smaller portions of their housing stock damaged, which minimized heavy reliance on foreign sources of aid. Thus unlike Montserrat's high level of dependency on foreign aid, recovery on St. Kitts and Nevis was not substantially constrained by time and effort spent seeking such aid. Fourth, the CRDU helped the two islands acquire external aid on a timely basis. Aside from initial problems of appointing an official representative, this organization was recognized as playing an effective regional role in securing assistance.

Of concern, however, was the extraordinary eight-month delay in providing housing recovery aid to Saddlers. There was a consensus among officials interviewed on St. Kitts that the delay did not stem from resource shortages but was politically motivated. Comments like "it was an unsettling fact that Saddlers was ignored" and "once the government got involved, then anyone can assume that some people will automatically get more than they deserve and others, like those in Saddlers, get less" reflect an awareness and concern over the Saddlers situation.

SUMMARY

Positive Components

First, the St. Kitts Disaster Committee, particularly the three members who participated on the Emergency Operations Center staff, provided much needed leadership. During the predisaster period the committee conducted a variety of activities that raised awareness and knowledge about hurricanes. The deputy disaster coordinator was especially effective, conducting workshops and promoting hurricane awareness through the media. During the recovery the center's staff provided leadership in identifying and coordinating the roles of various government and nongovernment organizations. For example, the close ties the staff maintained with public service NGOs (the Lions Club and the Rotary Club) before Hugo struck were indispensable during the recovery period in assessing local needs and distributing aid. The limited leadership present on Nevis, however, came from NGOs, and not the government. In particular, the Nevis Red Cross was given high marks for acquiring and distributing foreign aid.

Second, the Pan Caribbean Project provided a strong leadership role during the predisaster period on St. Kitts and Nevis in raising awareness and knowledge about hazards. This organization undertook numerous useful activities, such as distributing hurricane tracking charts and pamphlets on how to prepare households for disaster, providing technical assistance in disaster plan preparation, and conducting a variety of disaster planning workshops. Much of this work also provided the ground work for undertaking postdisaster planning actions, especially on St. Kitts.

Third, interorganizational coordination was generally considered successful on St. Kitts. A key reason for such success was the presence of three dedicated staff at the emergency operations center. The combined skills of these people gave the center a high level of technical credibility and organizational management capacity in coordinating the recovery effort. Other reasons explaining the success were the undertaking of a National Safety Month campaign by the National Disaster Committee, and the active participation by committee members in a disaster planning workshop the month before Hugo.

Fourth, effective collaboration occurred between domestic public service NGOs (e.g., Lions Club and Rotary Club) and the St. Kitts Emergency Operations Center. This arrangement led to a strengthening of interorganizational capacity to assess needs and distribute appropriate types and amounts of recovery aid on a timely basis. It also led to an improved capacity among the public service organizations and the government to undertake collaborative emergency response activities, as demonstrated by the post-Hugo oil spill incident.

Fifth, on St. Kitts the Emergency Operations Center staff were aware of the availability of external resources and understood how to gain access to foreign government and NGO programs that administered use of these resources. The pace and efficiency of recovery was thus improved by such awareness and knowledge.

Sixth, some organizations recognized Hurricane Hugo as providing a window of opportunity to initiate activities unrelated to the disaster. The St. Kitts Ministry of Agriculture sought to become involved in reforestation planning and management. The St. Kitts Christian Council extended its developmental activities to impoverished conditions in Saddlers. The Christian Children's Fund on Nevis also made advances in its developmental work. Public service organizations on St. Kitts viewed the disaster as providing an opportunity to become involved in disaster planning and response activities. Still other organizations sought to use the disaster to extend their traditional activities to long-range recovery. The Nevis Red Cross shifted from its traditional role in emergency response to housing recovery, and the local fishery and agriculture co-ops of both islands became involved in recovery operations.

Seventh, collaboration between a national level and a local NGO strengthened the local NGO's capacity to undertake long-range development activities. The goal of the national NGO (St. Kitts Council of Churches) was to empower the Sports Club in the village of Saddlers—and not to do the work itself. The Sports Club was thus able to initiate several developmental activities that built on its disaster recovery work.

Eighth, private insurance companies were able to provide accurate, rapid damage assessments and deliver housing recovery aid to claimants on a timely basis. The companies were staffed with experienced adjusters and claims agents to ensure that accurate damage assessments were conducted quickly. They also closely monitored all claims payments to ensure that claimants received payments that reflected actual damages.

Ninth, Hugo generally caused moderate damage on both islands, but on Nevis some areas suffer severe losses. Thus the islands were not heavily dependent on foreign assistance, as was Montserrat. As a result, compared to the Montserrat situation, domestic authorities were more likely to have control of the recovery process and were better able to devise programs and strategies that accounted for local needs.

Negative Components

THE PREDISASTER PERIOD

First, the national disaster plans for both islands were ineffective in guiding long-term recovery. The plans emphasized emergency response, and little attention was given to recovery. Thus the plans were generally considered to be "paper plans." Government and NGO officials were not familiar with the contents of the plans, which was attributed to infrequent meetings focused on the plan and a lack of participation in reviewing and updating the plans. As a result, recovery responses on both islands, especially Nevis, were ad hoc and not a product of prior recovery planning.

Second, government staff assigned to carry out disaster recovery programs were not trained before Hugo and were inadequate in terms of numbers. For example, the St. Kitts Housing Authority had only two full-time-equivalent building inspector positions to assess damages, monitor aid distribution, and ensure structural strengthening during rebuilding. Also, the Emergency Operations Center on Nevis was not adequately staffed with people who had the expertise, time, and energy to undertake the crucial predisaster task of identifying and coordinating the roles of organizations involved in disaster response and recovery.

Third, the national disaster coordinator on Nevis did not provide effective leadership in prestorm disaster planning. This individual had many other critical roles to fulfill, particularly as the permanent secretary, which precluded his ability to effectively carry out the coordinator role.

Fourth, development management and land use planning programs, particularly building code regulations, and inspection and enforcement procedures were not effectively carried out on St. Kitts and Nevis during the years before Hugo. Thus the housing stock and many public structures, such as schools and electric power plants, were not designed with storm-resistant construction techniques.

THE POSTDISASTER PERIOD

First, residents in need of assistance on St. Kitts did not have equal access to housing aid, as there was substantial disparity in allocation of such aid. That is, residents of the poor, working-class village of Saddlers did not receive assistance until eight months after the storm struck, while residents on the rest of the island received assistance within one or two weeks. Whether this incident resulted from a conscious politically motivated decision or from simple neglect, the outcome resulted in much suffering, which clearly could have been avoided if greater priority was given to aid distribution policies that accounted for equity.

Second, although interorganizational coordination was effective on St. Kitts, it clearly was ineffective on Nevis. The Nevis Emergency Operations Center was not operational, and the island's Disaster Committee was not a functioning entity. Decisions were thus made on an ad hoc basis, and there was little effort to coordinate ongoing recovery efforts.

Third, post-Hugo leadership on Nevis was weak. The limited leadership that was present primarily stemmed from NGOs, the Nevis Red Cross director being particularly successful. Government, however, provided little if any leadership in guiding the recovery effort.

Fourth, while some NGO human and material resources were successfully used during the initial weeks of the recovery in St. Kitts, development-based NGOs were not initially used on either island. On Nevis it took more than two months after Hugo before the CCF got involved, and on St. Kitts the Christian Council did not become active until almost ten months had passed.

Fifth, many opportunities to mitigate the hazards of storms and to make rebuilt housing structures less vulnerable to future storms were lost on St. Kitts and Nevis, primarily due to the lack of adequate building codes and government inspection staff. Further, although insurance companies were successful in delivering and monitoring the distribution of aid, they did not seek involvement in monitoring reconstruction practices. This inaction represents a missed opportunity to ensuring that rebuilt structures are less vulnerable to storms.

Post-Hugo Changes Regarding Long-Term Recovery

Since Hugo, St. Kitts and Nevis have taken several positive steps to improve their disaster recovery planning capabilities. These changes are in response to the problems encountered during the Hugo recovery effort and to the predisaster efforts of the Pan Caribbean Disaster Preparedness and Prevention Project and St. Kitts National Disaster Committee.

Most notably, St. Kitts parliament has increased funding for national disaster planning by a factor of ten, relative to predisaster levels. The additional funds will be used to create a full-time national disaster coordinator position and to support more disaster planning activities. Several post-Hugo workshops have been sponsored by the National Disaster Committee and the Christian Council. They have focused on sharing personnel and organizational disaster response and recovery experiences. Other activities on St. Kitts include increased participation by community service NGOs in emergency planning and response, initiation of a tropical forestry management planning program by the Ministry of Agriculture, and more active monitoring by insurance companies to ensure that customers have adequate insurance.

On Nevis, post-Hugo activity has been less ambitious. The only significant activity was several workshops sponsored by the government in cooperation with the Pan Caribbean Disaster Preparedness and Prevention Project. The workshops were on storm-resistant building design and on linking recovery to long-term development issues.

Disaster planning, however, has some shortcomings. One is that as of March 1991 the St. Kitts government still had not hired a full-time disaster coordinator. A second shortcoming is that neither island had revised their disaster plans to take advantage of the lessons learned from the Hugo experience. Another is that most of the post-Hugo disaster planning activity appears to reflect the pre-Hugo trend of placing great emphasis on emergency preparedness and a lesser emphasis on mitigation and recovery planning.

6 ANTIGUA

RECOVERY WITHOUT DEVELOPMENT

ANTIGUA IS LOCATED IN THE EASTERN CARIBBEAN AND IS PART OF THE chain of Leeward Islands. In 1990, this 108–square-mile island had a population of 78,500. Tourism is the main industry on Antigua and employs a majority of the labor force. The expansion of this economic sector fueled an economic boom throughout the 1980s. Light manufacturing industries, such as jam and jelly preserving, liquor and wine making, and assembly of electronic components, are of importance. Agriculture, particularly the sugar industry, was once the dominant sector of the economy but has declined considerably since the 1950s. The island also has a regional airport, which accommodates large passenger jets of international carriers, and a deepwater seaport for large cruise ships. Both the airport and the seaport are located in the capital city of St. Johns.

On September 17, 1989, Hurricane Hugo struck Antigua with devastating impact. After Hugo made landfall, fifteen hundred people were rendered homeless; 10 percent of the island's housing stock, or about 500 homes, sustained severe damage, of which 120 mainly low-income units were completely destroyed. Losses in housing were an estimated EC$219 million (US$80 million). Antigua's infrastructure and public facilities received blows. Electric power was lost, the water distribution system was severely impaired, and the roof was blown off the island's only hospital. The island's tourist industry was also severely damaged, with five major hotels sustaining considerable damage.

THE PRESTORM INSTITUTIONAL CONTEXT

At the time of Hurricane Hugo, Antigua had a National Disaster Plan, prepared in 1985 with assistance from the Pan Caribbean Disaster Prevention and Preparedness Project. The National Disaster Committee was the lead disaster planning organization and was responsible for formulating, revising, and carrying out the plan. The twenty-six member committee was composed of representatives from various government organizations (e.g., health, police, public utilities, and community development) and NGOs (e.g., the Red Cross, the Chamber of Commerce, and church groups). The Disaster Plan identified eleven functions of the National Disaster Committee, such as regularly reviewing and updating the plan, advising on legislation to mitigate the effects of disasters, and coordinating the activities of NGOs with government organizations during a disaster.

Antigua also employed a full-time national disaster coordinator within the Ministry of Home Affairs. The coordinator served as a policy adviser and provided administrative assistance to the National Disaster Committee. The coordinator also had the responsibility of promoting hazard awareness and planning in the country.

The plan was prepared based on a standard, function-based format. Emphasis was placed on identifying the roles and responsibilities of government agencies for predisaster planning and immediate postdisaster response, but virtually no discussion focused on the disaster recovery period. Moreover, the roles and responsibilities of NGOs in disasters were briefly discussed for the emergency response period, but there was no discussion of how they would be involved during the long-term disaster recovery period. Predisaster planning activities like reviewing damage assessment procedures, updating the plan, sponsoring workshops, conducting simulation exercises, and improving awareness of hurricane-resistant building practices were almost nonexistent, resulting in a predominance of ad hoc decisionmaking in responding to post-Hugo recovery demands. This mode of decisionmaking slowed the pace of recovery and resulted in lost opportunities for reducing local vulnerabilities to future disasters.

The capabilities for incorporating mitigation into development practices on Antigua were minimal. The Caribbean Uniform Building Code was in place before Hugo struck but, as on Montserrat and St. Kitts and Nevis, the code was not enforced. An engineering damage assessment study by Gibbs (1989) provided concrete evidence of what most building industry officials knew long before the storm: that most buildings did not incorporate even the modest hurricane-resistant construction practices required by the code. Further, Antigua had not adopted development controls, such as zoning and subdivision regulations, that might have incorporated mitigation standards for guiding land use patterns in hazardous areas. Thus with virtually no government control over land use practices, intensive development occurred in many low-lying, flood-prone, shoreline and inland areas.

The low level of disaster planning and mitigation activities in Antigua cannot be explained by a lack of disaster experience. Unlike Montserrat and St. Kitts and Nevis, Antigua had had recent disasters: moderate intensity earthquakes in 1974 and 1988 and periodic inland flooding every four to five years after heavy showers. Before Hugo, however, the island had had no recent experience with hurricanes. Although Antigua had on average been hit by a damaging storm about once every twenty years over the past two centuries, it had not been struck in almost forty years, with the most recent damaging hurricanes striking in 1928 and 1950.

This lack of planning was noted by several individuals, who believed that Antiguans were preoccupied with other concerns. Almost all people interviewed noted that the economic boom of the 1980s had led to big changes on Antigua and that most people were more worried about the country's inability to keep up with such growth than with preparing for hurricanes. Electric service prior to Hurricane Hugo was unreliable, with all parts of the island experiencing daily blackouts or brownouts for four to five hours at a time. There were also concerns with increasing crime, traffic congestion, schools inadequate to accommodate growth in student numbers, and other problems associated with a rapidly expanding economy.

In summary, prior to Hurricane Hugo, the capability for undertaking disaster planning and mitigation was somewhat low on Antigua. The island had some resources that could be used for recovery—its seaport and airport facilities had ample capacity for receiving recovery assistance. However, little predisaster planning had taken place, and there was only a minimal capability for organizing a recovery effort.

THE IMPACT OF HURRICANE HUGO

On Saturday, September 16, 1989, Hurricane Hugo struck Antigua. The eye of Hugo passed thirty miles to the southwest, but the island still took the brunt of one of the strongest storms to enter the Caribbean in the twentieth century. Peak gusting winds were estimated at nearly a hundred miles per hour (UNDRO 1989b), and rainfall caused significant flooding in many low-lying areas throughout the island.

While Antigua was less affected than the neighboring islands of Montserrat and Nevis, it still experienced substantial damages (Chin and Suite 1989; UNDRO 1989a, 1989b). A sizable portion of the roof on Holberton Hospital, the only hospital on the island, was torn off. The V. C. Bird International Airport terminal experienced moderate damage, and the air traffic control facilities were knocked out of commission. All major telecommunication facilities were damaged and rendered inoperable. The roof of the regional headquarters of the Pan Caribbean Disaster Preparedness and Prevention Project was blown off. Two schools and several government administrative buildings also sustained severe damage.

Private businesses and homes were also battered. The tourist industry experienced a heavy blow, as the storm wreaked havoc on the Antigua Hotel Training Centre and five major hotels, among them the upscale Jolly Beach Hotel. Damage to homes was primarily concentrated in the southern and southeastern portion of the island. About fifteen hundred people were rendered homeless. Old Road Village was the hardest hit community, particularly the houses of the less affluent, typically mounted precariously on concrete blocks (see figure 6.1). About 10 percent of Antigua's housing stock, or about 500 homes, sustained damage, and an estimated 120 of these were low-income units that were destroyed (see figure 6.2). The total value of damage in Antigua was estimated at EC$219 million (US$80 million).

The island's infrastructure received heavy blows. Electric power was knocked out when the Antigua Public Utilities Authority lost most of its transmission and distribution system. Utility poles carrying electric and telephone transmission lines were slammed to the ground throughout the island partly due to improper installation and poor maintenance. The water distribution system was severely impaired, as the loss of electricity did not allow for pumping. Dams and water storage and distribution facilities incurred considerable damage. Drinking water quality also deteriorated markedly due to soil erosion into the main surface water reservoirs. Antigua is particularly susceptible to erosion because only 8 percent of its original forest has not been cleared.

Although the damages suffered by Antigua were severe, they could have been much worse. Antiguans were fortunate that Hugo did not produce a sizable storm surge and a significant amount of rainfall; it was

FIGURE 6.1. Low-income home in Old Road Village: it remained intact because of traditional hipped roof and other construction details (photograph by Philip R. Berke).

FIGURE 6.2. Low-income home, nontraditional construction: concrete block foundations are not securely anchored (*Links: Quarterly Newsletter of the Antigua Programme Centre*, January–March 1990).

considered a "dry" storm. Unlike the mountainous terrain of Montserrat and St. Kitts and Nevis, much of Antigua is flat and low lying. Widespread inland flooding would have been devastating. While floodwaters undermined several roadways and bridges and caused damage to a few homes, much of the island was spared. The toll on human life was remarkably low. A resident of Urlings Village was the only fatality, and there were few injuries. Compared to the magnitude of the damage, the number of casualties was low.

In summary, the task of rebuilding was considerable for many Antiguans but was not as severe and geographically extensive as for residents of other island states in the eastern Caribbean. Most of the recovery effort, especially housing reconstruction, was restricted to a relatively small portion of the island.

THE STAGES OF THE RECOVERY PROCESS

The emergency stage on Antigua ended about one week after Hugo made landfall (see figure 6.3). Debris clearance was a major concern but was completed within the first few days after the storm. Because the director of Public Works had had experience with recent earthquake and flood disasters on Antigua, some preimpact measures were taken. Work shifts were extended prior to the storm, and debris removal equipment was made ready during the twenty-four hours before landfall. Short-term sheltering for the homeless, food supplies, and medical aid needs were met within the first week. There was a strong sense of relief that, although damages to public facilities were severe in some parts of the island, the emergency period was dominated more by cleanup operations than by repair.

A particularly troublesome task during the emergency period was damage assessment. Quick-response, visual damage surveys were undertaken by the Ministry of Agriculture, with assistance from the police and the National Defence Force, to determine the level of need for international assistance. However, government assessments grossly overestimated damages. Damage estimates by several NGOs (e.g., the Red Cross and the United Nations) failed to corroborate those of the Antigua government. Consequently, the government lost credibility during subsequent stages of the recovery. Two reasons were given for the divergence of government estimates from other estimates: one was that it was an innocent mistake made by government assessors who had no prior training in damage assessment; the other implied that the overes-

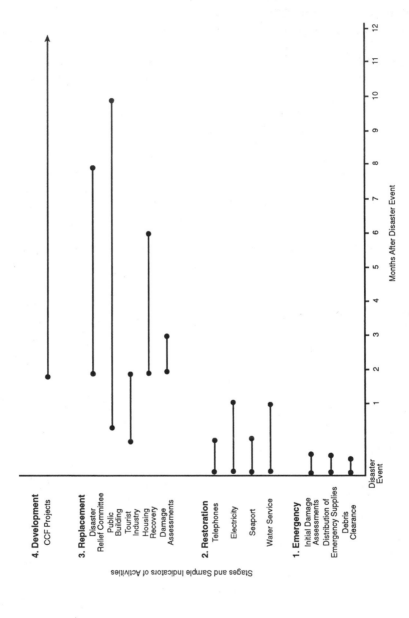

FIGURE 6.3. Duration of stages of recovery, Antigua.

timating was intentional, in order to ensure that a large amount of outside aid would be sent to Antigua. Both of these explanations fostered
considerable reluctance among international donor organizations to provide aid through government organizations.

The restoration stage was initiated during the emergency stage. Because damages were concentrated in the southern and southeastern
portions of the country, there were no significant variations in the pace
of public utility restoration among localities. Critical public facilities,
including airport, seaport, and radio and television communication systems, were restored to perform at minimal operational levels. Fortunately, because these facilities sustained only limited damages, basic
repairs were made in two weeks. The restoration of water and electrical
services for 80 percent of all residences was also completed in two
weeks, with the remaining 20 percent being restored within four weeks.
All telephone service was restored within two to four weeks.

The main electric power generation station in St. Johns was back on-
line within three to four weeks. As noted, Antigua had experienced
daily power outage prior to Hurricane Hugo, since the station had inadequate capacity to meet the demands of the rapidly growing economy.
Consequently, many Antiguans had adopted various coping strategies
to deal with the shortfalls, such as altering daily patterns of energy use,
acquiring backup power sources, and storing water. Thus for most Antiguans affected by the storm, the postimpact power loss was not as severe as it might have been.

The replacement stage on Antigua began during the restoration stage.
A key activity was the initiation of a comprehensive and detailed housing damage survey about eight weeks after the storm. Because of suspicion among international donors over alleged overestimates of damage
by the government, Red Cross damage estimates were used to determine the extent of housing assistance required by individual households. Various development NGOs, like the Christian Children's Fund
(CCF), also were active during this stage of recovery, relying on their
well-established field staffs for damage assessment, building material
acquisition and distribution, and construction practices monitoring.

The reconstruction of the tourist industry was initiated about two
weeks after Hugo (see figure 6.4). About two months after the storm
struck, all major hotel facilities had been completely repaired and had
either reopened or were ready to be reopened for the upcoming tourist
season. All public buildings and schools were repaired or replaced
within ten months. The initial part of this stage was, however, longer

FIGURE 6.4. Shoreline, Old Road Village, which suffered the greatest damage from Hurricane Hugo in Antigua: high-income resort condominiums were repaired but remain at the water's edge (photograph by Philip R. Berke).

for residents in need of housing assistance, since Antigua's Disaster Plan was not functional. A workable plan could have enhanced the government's ability to conduct accurate damage assessments and to seek and distribute housing aid. To improve domestic capacity to manage the housing replacement process, the government created the Disaster Relief Committee two months after Hugo struck. This organization, with a membership drawn from government agencies and NGOs, was created to monitor the use of international housing assistance donations, to acquire and distribute housing materials, and to minimize duplication of effort among the member organizations. By March 1990 (six months after Hugo), almost all households in need of assistance had their homes either replaced or repaired, marking the end of the replacement and reconstruction stage and the discontinuance of the Disaster Relief Committee shortly thereafter.

The development stage was initiated during the early part of the replacement stage, about two months after Hugo, when the CCF began to link disaster recovery to ten ongoing development projects in the disaster-stricken area. The staff of the CCF viewed the disaster as an opportunity to extend their developmental work, but with this exception, this stage could be characterized as one of missed opportunities: the country did not ensure that structural strengthening occurred during rebuilding, that watershed management practices improved, or that the lessons learned from Hugo were incorporated into recovery planning for future disasters. CCF officials maintained that the CCF could have enhanced its capacity to do development work if it had not been ignored by the government when it tried to undertake collaborative development and predisaster planning.

THE DIMENSIONS OF THE RECOVERY PROCESS

Organizational Coordination

Three organizational coordination efforts were salient during the disaster recovery on Antigua: the National Disaster Plan and the National Disaster Committee, damage assessments, and the Disaster Relief Committee.

THE NATIONAL DISASTER PLAN AND THE NATIONAL DISASTER COMMITTEE

Interviews with members of the National Disaster Committee revealed that the committee and the National Disaster Plan were failures and were totally inoperable during the postdisaster recovery period. Comments such as "the committee just collapsed . . . it was a complete failure," "nobody paid attention to the plan," and "the plan was worthless . . . it might have been a sound document, but it was just totally unworkable for our organization" expressed the common view of the plan.

Several reasons explain the ineffectiveness of the committee and the plan. First, the plan was never formally adopted by the Antigua cabinet as a stated national policy on disaster management. Because of this lack of legislative support, a lead disaster management organization, budget, and staff was not in existence at the time Hugo made landfall. Further, the national disaster coordinator position was not given separate organizational identity and visibility. There was no clear job description regarding the role, functions, and responsibilities of the coordinator. Nor was it clear to whom the coordinator should report. A United Nations–supported study of Antigua disaster planning claims that "there is tremendous lack of credibility in the co-ordinator with respect to developing a disaster management organization, program, and response systems" (Rodriguez 1990a, 6).

Second, the plan emphasized emergency preparedness and response and did not give guidance to organizations involved in long-term recovery and mitigation. In fact, the plan document did not have a chapter or even a subsection devoted to recovery and reconstruction. Third, although the plan specified the responsibilities of various organizations and the tasks to be carried out by such organizations, it made little reference to the responsibilities of the National Disaster Committee in coordinating these activities.

Fourth, the plan existed only on paper. That is, there had been no meetings to review and update agency responsibilities for three years before Hugo struck. Nor had the plan been tested regularly by drills, simulations, or even desktop exercises. All four of the committee members interviewed indicated that they had some familiarity with the domain of responsibility of their organizations as specified in the plan but lacked a working knowledge regarding plan implementation. When asked if the plan was used for resource acquisition and distribution or to facilitate interorganizational communication and coordination during the recovery period, members replied that they had not been familiar enough with the plan to use it as a working document.

Since Hugo, the Antigua government has given minimal attention to disaster planning. The National Disaster Committee has not met to review the success or failure of organizations involved in disaster response or recovery. Nor have any workshops or training sessions been held that have been attended by committee members. On the positive side, a UN–sponsored consultant has rewritten the National Disaster Plan (Rodriquez 1990b). This revision was completed in July 1990, but as of February 1991 it had not been adopted formally by the cabinet.

DAMAGE ASSESSMENTS

A glaring example of the ineffectiveness of Antigua's National Disaster Plan occurred a few days after Hugo, when extension specialists from the Ministry of Agriculture, with the assistance of the police and the National Defence Force, conducted a rapid visual survey of damages to determine the magnitude of housing needs. These damage survey results were to be used for requesting foreign aid. The resulting estimates, however, were widely considered to be extraordinarily high, with damages to housing exceeding EC$548 million (US$200 million). Other post-impact assessments conducted independently by the Red Cross (Antigua Red Cross 1989) and the United Nations (UNDRO 1989a), among others, estimated housing damages to be less than half the government estimates. The UN damage estimates were, for example, EC$210 million (US$80 million).

Evidence from interviews with government and NGO staff revealed that personnel assigned to do the assessments had never attended disaster planning workshops and had no prior training or disaster experience. But possibly the overestimation was intentional and politically motivated. Officials from the Caribbean Conference of Churches (CCC) and the CCF and midlevel management personnel from the Ministries of Agriculture, Public Works, and Home Affairs consistently maintained that top government officials deliberately inflated the damage figures to ensure that the country would qualify for additional outside aid. A comment by one CCC staffer was indicative of the sentiments of those interviewed: officials wanted "to get away with some loot . . . they wanted to skim cash off the top to line their own pockets." Both explanations fueled speculation among international donor organizations that the government was not capable of managing long-term recovery for the country. Such speculation led to considerable reluctance on the part of these donors to deal with the government and caused delays in the provision of aid.

THE DISASTER RELIEF COMMITTEE

In response to the speculation among international donor organizations about its handling of foreign aid, the Antigua government created the ad hoc Disaster Relief Committee to manage long-term recovery. The committee was established in November 1989 and consisted of representatives from two government organizations (the Ministries of Home Affairs and Public Works) and three NGOs (the CCF, the Red Cross, and the Salvation Army). The primary objective of the committee was threefold: (1) to acquire and keep track of twenty-one accounts created from international housing assistance donations, (2) to acquire building materials with these funds and to monitor their distribution, and (3)—and most important—to ensure that the housing assistance programs of the various organizations represented on the committee were complementary and minimized duplication and inefficient use of recovery resources.

The committee is widely considered to have been successful in achieving these objectives. The committee was established outside existing government organizations and was given a separate identity and authority to acquire and distribute housing aid. It was, therefore, not perceived as politically motivated, which is often the case with government-administered programs. Further, an Antigua public official chaired the committee, and thus member organizations of the committee were committed to Antigua leadership, as opposed to foreign NGO leadership. This action also suggested that Antigua authorities were in charge of the recovery effort in the country. The committee's participants had considerable expertise in housing. The Red Cross representative, for example, had been involved in disaster recovery throughout the Caribbean region for more than fifteen years. The Ministry of Home Affairs representative had more than twenty years of domestic and international experience as a social worker and had been involved in recovery work in two previous flood disasters in Antigua. The CCF representative had been active in housing assistance for the poor in Antigua for more than five years prior to Hugo.

Four member organizations delivered assistance to the 500 damaged or destroyed housing units: the Red Cross assisted 220 households, the CCF aided 20 households, and the Ministry of Home Affairs helped 200 households. The insurance industry, which had a representative on the committee, provided assistance to the remaining 60 households.

Interestingly, the Housing Department of the Ministry of Agriculture was not a member organization of the Disaster Relief Committee and did not play a significant role in housing recovery. Its absence resulted from the desire of member organizations to assume the major responsibility in managing the recovery effort and from their concern that the Housing Department, and the Ministry of Agriculture in general, had lost credibility from the highly politicized damage assessment. The membership wanted to assure the public and international donor organizations that the committee was capable of effectively distributing aid and of managing the overall long-range housing recovery effort.

Monitoring and Compliance

The strategies used to deliver housing recovery aid, to monitor how such aid was used, and to ensure that aid recipients complied with reconstruction guidelines had varying degrees of success among the CCF, the Red Cross, the Ministry of Home Affairs, and the insurance companies, which were the primary organizations involved in delivering housing recovery assistance.

Red Cross damage assessment teams prepared a list of the types of building materials needed to repair or replace each housing unit, based on the damages sustained. The Ministry of Home Affairs relied on these damage assessments to determine the extent of housing assistance required by individual households. Households that suffered damage would then apply for housing recovery aid: all low-income households that had been receiving government housing subsidies before the disaster were automatically eligible for recovery assistance from the Ministry of Home Affairs, and all other disaster-stricken households were considered eligible for housing aid unless they had disaster insurance for their homes.

Once a household was determined to be eligible for assistance, the homeowner was issued a purchase order specifying the building materials needed. The purchase order was to be turned in to a local building supply store. A copy of the purchase order was placed in the centralized files of the Disaster Relief Committee. Both member and nonmember organizations had access to these files, to ensure that householders did not apply for housing assistance more than once. Interviews with officials from the primary organizations involved in delivering aid revealed that the centralized files were used extensively for checking which householders received aid and who was in need. Sharing and contributing to a common information base, they claimed, greatly improved interorganizational coordination throughout the recovery period.

All aid recipients were required to use structural strengthening techniques when repairing damaged houses. While the national building code, which is based on the Caribbean Uniform Building Code, lacked hazard mitigation requirements, aid recipients were required to adhere to other code design requirements for plumbing, electrical wiring, and so on. During the first few months after Hugo, the Red Cross conducted a series of housing reconstruction workshops throughout the country to educate homeowners and carpenters on appropriate structural strengthening techniques and national building code standards. In addition, the Red Cross required its aid recipients to purchase disaster insurance. An additional intent of the workshops was to enhance prospects for compliance with these requirements. However, because of the limited field staffs of the Ministry of Home Affairs and the Red Cross, it was not possible to conduct on-site verification of household compliance. (Details about the adequacy of field staffs are discussed below.) While no exact figures were available, both ministry and Red Cross staff expressed concern during interviews that only a minority of aid recipients complied.

As mentioned, CCF's housing recovery strategy stemmed from ongoing housing development projects for the poor that were in place before the disaster. The CCF had ten ongoing projects on Antigua, each with a field coordinator and a community-based board of directors. Field coordinators were trained in basic building construction techniques and had substantial community organization-building skills. The strategy used by this NGO involved the supply of building materials to low-income, disaster-stricken households with children. Building materials were provided to individual households based on damages estimated by CCF field coordinators. In contrast to the Ministry of Home Affairs and the Red Cross, the CCF could rely on its well-developed field network to ensure that reconstructed homes complied with CCF housing design and construction standards.

Interviews revealed that participating households and CCF field staff were strongly motivated to monitor how aid was used. CCF staffers indicated that any cheating or attempts to take more than a fair share of aid was construed to be detrimental to the other participating low-income householders. It was understood that CCF aid was finite and that if any participant received more than what he or she needed, then other participants would suffer. Participants believed that the program would benefit them if there was widespread compliance. One participant said that she knew of another participant who was "double-dipping" into program funds by selling donated roofing material on the black market and then claiming it was stolen. She saw this participant make the transaction and then asked two corroborating witnesses to testify before CCF staffers about the incident. It was important to "blow the whistle" on such people, she claimed.

Insurance companies were also involved in housing recovery. One housing insurance company, for example, required owners of insured damaged homes to incorporate structural strengthening measures (e.g., to tie walls to concrete slab foundations) during reconstruction. One insurance claims adjuster in Old Road Village indicated that agents like himself would regularly inspect homes undergoing reconstruction to ensure that construction practices were in compliance with company mitigation policy. If the practices were not in compliance, insurance claims payments to owners were withheld. Of the twenty-two homes in his jurisdiction receiving insurance payments, three did not receive payments due to noncompliance (these homeowners have since undertaken appropriate construction measures).

The Recognition of Rights

The right of recipient countries to devise their own recovery strategies, without imposition of inflexible and stringent conditions on the use of external aid, is crucial for achieving successful recovery. External organizations generally were supportive of Antigua's responses to the disaster and recognized the legitimacy of Antigua authorities to manage recovery efforts. Such recognition was evidenced by the formation of the ad hoc Disaster Relief Committee, composed of an external NGO official, a representative of an Antigua NGO, and government officials. Further, the chair of the committee was Antiguan. Representation on the committee thus exhibited a clear commitment to Antigua leadership and suggested that Antigua authorities had control of the overall recovery effort.

Interviews revealed that committee members were aware of the loss of internal control of the recovery process to external NGOs on other devastated islands in the eastern Caribbean. They believed, however, that the organizational structure of the Disaster Relief Committee fostered internal control. The recurrent theme on Montserrat, for example, was that localized knowledge about these issues often escaped the notice of outside experts.

In some instances, however, we found external organizations' recognition of the legitimacy of Antigua authorities to be lacking. Commenting on the way some international donors demanded the use of recovery funds be tracked, a Ministry of Home Affairs staff member indicated that there was "too much red tape and too little flexibility." Another staffer, commenting on housing recovery aid provided by the British Development Division, said that "they don't let us work out our own way of doing things. . . . We're meeting their demands, but not ours." Another individual maintained that, although donor organizations' concern for the handling of their funds is understandable, they may not consider the enormous demands placed on recipient agency staff. This person indicated that the many late nights she spent writing proposals and filling out forms diverted her time and attention from other more pressing recovery activities.

Leadership

When asked if there were any organizations or individuals that provided a strong leadership role in facilitating hazard awareness and reduction before Hugo struck, six of nine informants mentioned the Pan Caribbean Disaster Prevention and Preparedness Project, especially its media awareness campaign prior to Hugo. The project was, in fact, the only leader mentioned. These informants also maintained, however, that the project had little impact on predisaster government action—and that in fact government officials had been and remained apathetic and had not given adequate attention or resources to disaster planning.

When informants were asked about leaders during disaster recovery, several organizations were identified. Again, the most frequently mentioned (six of nine informants) organization was the Pan Caribbean Project. While the project did not become directly involved in long-term recovery operations on Antigua, informants told us that it assisted their organizations by providing timely technical assistance. For example, during its workshops on housing rebuilding throughout the disaster-stricken area of Antigua, the project distributed illustrated manuals on how to reconstruct hurricane-resistant buildings. Project staff also appeared on television and radio talk shows to discuss recovery issues and the revision of the National Disaster Plan. Several respondents also mentioned that the project helped organize the international emergency relief effort at the airport immediately following the disaster. This effort required the collaboration of two other regional organizations (the Organization of Eastern Caribbean States and CARICOM) in the acquisition and distribution of emergency aid to the disaster-stricken nations in the region. This collaborative effort was known as the CARICOM Disaster Relief Unit (CDRU).

The next most frequently mentioned organization (by four of nine informants) was the Antigua Red Cross. Informants credited this Red Cross chapter with undertaking accurate damage assessments and conducting well-attended workshops on housing reconstruction techniques as well as delivering housing aid to those most in need. None of the respondents mentioned a government organization, giving as their principle reason an ineffective disaster coordinator and National Disaster Committee. (In October 1990 a new coordinator was hired.) Another reason was the exaggerated damage estimates used by the government as the basis for requesting foreign aid. By using such estimates, the government, and particularly the National Disaster Committee, lost credibility in dealing with external organizations.

An additional obstacle to leadership was Antigua's highly interpersonal political patronage system, which controls public resources acquisition and distribution decisions. A local Red Cross volunteer from Old Road Village, for instance, maintained that, although the intentions of individuals taking leadership roles to promote new initiatives like disaster preparedness and mitigation may be altruistic, most people in his community would perceive such intentions as politically motivated. As a result, individuals who might otherwise push for new initiatives tend to assume passive roles to avoid being ostracized by their neighbors.

Resources

STAFF

The government generally did not have adequate staff to take on the responsibility of building inspection. Even if the Housing Department of the Ministry of Agriculture, which was responsible for inspecting disaster rebuilding, had been active in the recovery effort, it did not have adequate staff to monitor rebuilding. The Ministry of Home Affairs did not have sufficient field staff to monitor rebuilding—and in fact had only one staff member prior to Hugo. The Ministry of Agriculture used the police and the National Defense Force to conduct the initial damage assessment (within days after Hugo). Due to a lack of adequate assessment skills, however, the initial damage estimates were not accurate and provided an inadequate basis for requesting foreign aid and for determining specific housing needs.

By relying on well-established and trained field staffs, NGOs were more successful than the government in undertaking disaster recovery tasks. The Antigua and Barbuda Red Cross chapter drew on the region-wide network of Red Cross chapters throughout the Caribbean, and these trained personnel conducted damage assessments on a house-by-house basis. These individuals, however, were not available for monitoring the use of the aid during rebuilding. The CCF relied on its well-established field staff for damage assessment, building material acquisition and distribution, and construction practice monitoring.

BUILDING MATERIALS

Aside from several unconfirmed reports related to politically motivated building material allocation decisions, building supplies on the island were generally sufficient for reconstruction. While there were some inevitable delays, no serious shortages were reported.

Unlike the near total devastation on Montserrat, only a small proportion of the Antigua housing stock was damaged, minimizing the need for outside assistance. Interviews with building supply store owners revealed that most of the materials were already in stock when Hurricane Hugo struck Antigua. According to one store owner, because the island had been experiencing steady economic growth prior to the disaster, building supply stores had enough building supplies in stock to meet the demand. Furthermore, building suppliers often gave a 10 percent price discount for building materials, which prevented the sale of materials at inflated prices, as often happens in areas struggling to recover from a disaster. An additional factor contributing to effective material acquisition and distribution was the Disaster Relief Committee, which was given high marks by two government officials and one NGO official in acquiring the appropriate type and amount of material on a timely basis.

Linkage

Several instances of linkage of recovery activities to ongoing development programs were cited. One was the use of NGO field teams that had been active before Hugo in development projects (construction of houses, schools, and public recreational facilities) to deliver aid and to organize recovery efforts. The Baptist Mission, the CCF, and the Lions Club, among others, were consistently cited as involved in recovery. Another linkage was the self-help, or do-it-yourself, housing reconstruction workshops conducted throughout the disaster-stricken region by the Red Cross.

However, all cases of linkage encountered in this study occurred on an ad hoc basis. That is, there was no predisaster planning effort to identify current and ongoing programs that could be applied to disaster recovery. Several staff members of government organizations and NGOs expressed concern during interviews that responses to the recovery could have been more effective if there was a careful consideration of the potential linkages between their organization and recovery demands. A high-level CCF administrative staffer, however, expressed concern that, since CCF did not normally function in a disaster housing reconstruction mode, there was a lack of expertise among field staff in disaster-related matters, particularly in building strengthening techniques. This individual maintained, however, that the CCF could have enhanced its capacity to deal with disasters if "we had not been ignored by the government in predisaster planning activities." Another CCF staffer had similar concerns, commenting that "governments don't own disasters, and they don't own the problems either. . . . Why are NGOs always used as a last resort when governments can't find anywhere else to go."

Another NGO staffer, for instance, felt that her organization could have been more effective in incorporating structural strengthening measures in rebuilding schools if NGO field teams had better knowledge of such measures. An official from the Ministry of Home Affairs reiterated this concern over mitigation, maintaining that there was "little foresight and know-how" in her organization regarding structural strengthening.

Finally, an opportunity was lost for linking the disaster recovery effort to an ongoing, UN-supported, reforestation and watershed management program. A UN case report on the recovery effort of agriculture production (UNDRO 1989b) indicates that drinking water quality on the island has declined markedly since Hugo and recommends that Antigua participate in a UN regional planning effort in watershed management. If Antigua prepared a draft plan, it would be eligible for funds and technical assistance in developing a comprehensive watershed management and reforestation plan. However, as of July 1991 (twenty-two months after Hurricane Hugo) the government had taken no formal action to participate in the program.

SUMMARY

Positive Components

The Disaster Relief Committee was widely viewed as successful in serving as a central clearing house for damage data, in acquiring and distributing housing aid, and in monitoring the use of such aid. The committee was established outside the existing governmental organizational framework. It had a separate identity and authority and was not perceived to be politically motivated in aid acquisition and distribution. Further, foreign donor organizations were supportive of this Antigua-based organization and recognized its legitimacy in handling aid. A public official chaired the Disaster Relief Committee, as opposed to leadership by a foreign NGO official. Member NGOs and government organizations were committed to domestic leadership in managing recovery operations. There was a widely held view that the recovery process was controlled by Antiguans for Antiguans.

By relying on well-established and trained field staffs, NGOs undertook a variety of recovery activities. The Red Cross drew on its region-wide network to conduct damage assessments, and the CCF relied on its field staff for damage assessment, building materials acquisition and distribution, and construction monitoring. The CCF sought to advance its ongoing development programs by becoming involved in disaster recovery activities and viewed Hugo as providing an opportunity to expand its overall development operations on the island and to empower local groups. The Red Cross extended its traditional work in emergency preparedness and response activities into housing recovery activities.

The Pan Caribbean Disaster Prevention and Preparedness Project played an effective leadership role in the predisaster period by raising awareness about hurricanes and about the need to plan for disasters. Although some weaknesses in prior planning were present, they would likely have been more severe without the Pan Caribbean Project. This organization also provided important technical assistance, made frequent appearances on local media, and helped to revise the National Disaster Plan during the postdisaster period. Private insurance companies played a key role in ensuring that claimants incorporated structural strengthening measures during rebuilding. The companies tended to be well staffed with experienced claims adjusters, who regularly inspected homes undergoing reconstruction to ensure that storm-resistant construction was incorporated.

Fortunately, damages from Hugo were not severe and were localized. Consequently, Antigua was not as dependent on outside aid as Montserrat and St. Kitts and Nevis. Domestic organizations were thus able to exert considerable influence over the recovery effort. Further, Hugo was considered a dry storm, and rainfall was moderate on Antigua. A wet hurricane could have wreaked tremendous damage, particularly to development located in low-lying floodplains.

Negative Components
THE PREDISASTER PERIOD

First, although the National Disaster Plan was considered well developed, it was never formally adopted as a stated national policy on disaster management. Because of the absence of legislative support, a formal disaster management organization, budget, and staff were not in existence at the time Hugo struck. The plan was widely viewed as a "product," and not part of an overall planning process. There were no meetings during the three years prior to Hugo, to review and update the plan regarding agency roles and responsibilities. Nor was the plan tested by drills, simulations, or tabletop exercises. Thus, there was a low level of working knowledge regarding plan implementation.

Second, the national disaster coordinator position was not given a separate organizational identity and visibility as the lead disaster planning advocate in Antigua, nor was there a clear job description of the coordinator's functions and responsibilities. These shortcomings were compounded by the inadequate experience and management skills of the coordinator. These problems led to a lack of credibility on the part of the coordinator, which severely constrained her ability to develop an effective disaster management organization and planning program.

Third, development management and land use planning programs, particularly building code regulations and inspection and enforcement procedures, were not effectively carried out during the years before Hugo. Thus the housing stock and many public structures were not built with storm-resistant construction techniques. Moreover, many of these structures were located in low-lying, flood-prone areas.

THE POSTDISASTER PERIOD

First, the lack of planning for disaster recovery resulted in (1) weak leadership by the national disaster coordinator, (2) a lack of organizational arrangements or coordination, (3) a poor understanding of the role of NGOs in recovery, and (4) little knowledge of what external resources were available. Thus, most postdisaster recovery activities were undertaken on an ad hoc basis. Because improvisation dominated decisionmaking, the pace of recovery was inevitable slowed and made less efficient.

Second, the Ministry of Agriculture's rapid damage assessment estimates were tremendously exaggerated. Such inaccuracy caused much foreign and domestic uncertainty over the ability of the government to effectively handle foreign aid. Because of this concern, international donor organizations became reluctant to provide aid immediately and thus delayed sending aid until the Disaster Relief Committee was established, two months after Hugo struck.

Third, Antigua did not take advantage of many opportunities provided by Hugo to undertake betterment and development work. Structural strengthening measures were not required in the rebuilding of public and private structures due to the absence of mitigation provisions in the national building code, improvements in watershed management practices were not undertaken, and lessons learned from Hugo were not incorporated into the recovery planning for future disasters.

Fourth, NGOs with substantial human resources and that had been involved in long-range development for many years prior to Hugo were not, at least initially, acknowledged or effectively involved in the recovery process. For instance, it took two months after the storm struck before the CCF became involved in the recovery—by participating on the Disaster Relief Committee.

Fifth, the housing recovery work of the Red Cross was not developmental in nature. While this NGO used its regionwide network of field staffs to conduct housing recovery activities, it did not build on local organizational capacities. And although its housing recovery work was successful in providing aid, it had limited impact on improving local organizational capacity to undertake long-range development.

Sixth, the government did not have adequate staff to undertake disaster recovery. For example, at the Ministry of Home Affairs only one staffer was charged with the responsibility of building inspection. Further, the police and the National Defense Force personnel who conducted damage assessments were inadequately trained.

Seventh, in some instances, recognition of the legitimacy of Antigua authorities by foreign donor organization was lacking. Public officials maintained that these organizations were often inflexible and required excessive accounting to ensure that the aid was used for its intended purposes. While this lack of recognition of local capability to manage aid may have had some legitimacy, given the incidents surrounding the inflated aid requests premised on exaggerated damage estimates, it nevertheless impeded the ability of domestic organizations to meet local needs and thus slowed the pace of recovery.

Post-Hugo Changes Regarding Long-Term Recovery

Since Hugo, Antigua has taken some limited positive steps to improve its disaster recovery planning capabilities. These changes can be attributed to the problems encountered during the Hugo recovery effort and to the postdisaster technical assistance activities of the Pan Caribbean Project.

Early in 1990 the Antigua government requested that the project assist it in reviewing and updating the 1985 National Disaster Plan. In May 1990, a revised plan was completed, in cooperation with staff of the Ministry of Home Affairs. In addition, a new, full-time, national disaster coordinator was hired. A series of post-Hugo workshops have also been conducted by the Red Cross to educate homeowners and carpenters on storm-resistant construction practices.

The increased emphasis on disaster planning, however, is limited. As of February 1991, the government had not adopted the plan as a national policy on disaster management. Nor had the government given the national disaster coordinator a separate organizational identity and visibility as the lead disaster planner on Antigua. Finally, there had been no regular meetings by the National Disaster Committee to review and evaluate lessons learned from the Hurricane Hugo experience.

7 LINKING DISASTER RECOVERY AND SUSTAINABLE DEVELOPMENT

CONCLUSIONS AND FUTURE DIRECTIONS

MANY BROAD LESSONS CAN BE EXTRACTED FROM THE HURRICANE recovery experiences of the four Caribbean nations discussed in previous chapters. In this final chapter we do several things. The first section summarizes the key findings of the study, generalizing across the several case studies. The second section of the chapter discusses the implications of these findings for future disaster and hazards policy in the region and puts forth a set of recommendations for future action (including needed future research). In the final section of this chapter we begin to identify the elements of a future vision of a sustainable Caribbean region, in which the exposure of people and property to natural disasters is minimized and in which the quality of the natural environment, as well as the built environment, is enhanced.

KEY FINDINGS OF THE STUDY
The Caribbean Basin at Risk

A number of key findings can be stated from our study. Perhaps the most obvious is the seriousness and severity of the natural hazards problem. These case studies of the response and recovery of four Caribbean nations to two major hurricanes illustrate the nature of natural disaster risks in the Caribbean basin. What is clear is that, increasingly, people and property are at risk and that the existing government and private framework for protecting people and property in advance and in the wake of hurricanes and other events is rudimentary at best—and severely flawed at worse.

While the loss of life in both storms was relatively small, future hurricanes and tropical storms may not be so kind. Particularly troubling is the vulnerability of the housing stock and the conditions of poverty that much of the basin's population lives in. And despite the existence of official building and construction standards, much of the actual construction in the Caribbean occurs in the informal housing sector, in which the standards are not enforced.

Recent demographic and development trends suggest that more people and more property will be at risk in future storms. Urban areas, in particular, will experience increasing population pressure. By the year 2000, more than 64 percent of the population in the Caribbean basin is expected to be living in urban areas, compared with 38 percent in 1960, a trend that can be observed in Jamaica and the Leeward Island countries included in this study (Potter 1989). Population expansion in greater Kingston, for example, has grown by 200 percent (from three hundred thousand to six hundred thousand people) between 1960 and 1985. This increase reflects high fertility rates, greater restrictions on overseas migration (especially to Canada, the United Kingdom, and the United States), and the continuing internal migration of the rural poor.

These statistics raise the question of where this additional population will be living, in what types of structures, and in what locations? Will this population be at more or less at risk from hurricanes and other natural disasters than the present population? Will they be living outside of high-hazard flood areas and in structures that will withstand winds and the other forces of nature? And will there be in place a set of mechanisms for effective recovery and reconstruction? Our study of the recovery experiences in these four Caribbean nations suggests reasons to be skeptical about positive answers to these questions.

Caribbean nations are subject to a variety of serious natural disasters. Hurricanes and coastal storms are common. Moreover, the these events may be much more disastrous as predictions of global warming materialize—namely, we may begin to see larger and more powerful events (see, e.g., Houghton, Jenkins, and Ephram 1990; U.S. Office of Technology Assessment 1993). Global climate changes also hold the possibility of a significant rise in sea level, and although many Caribbean islands will be unaffected because of high terrain, there have been few attempts to understand how such changes will affect the vulnerability of people and property. The basin is also threatened by earthquakes, with the Caribbean faults running in close proximity to population centers. Other natural hazards the area is subject to include landslides and mass movements, riverine and stream flooding, and shoreline erosion and long-term sea level rise.

In short, the region is prone to serious and repetitive natural disasters, and the trends suggest that vulnerability of people and property will grow ever greater. The hurricane events described and documented in this study indicate the extent of this vulnerability and the need for major, and more effective, programs for planning and management. Our case studies of the recovery efforts in Caribbean nations show a number of serious problems in the current disaster planning and recovery framework, in the role that external aid and development agencies play, and in the capability of bringing about long-term mitigation and sustainable development.

The Stages of Recovery: Differential and Dynamic

Our study suggests the need to substantially rethink the ways we conceptualize the recovery process and the ways we view the stages and sequence of recovery and reconstruction. Findings from Hurricanes Hugo and Gilbert suggest that traditional thinking about this may lead to inappropriate public policy responses. Specifically, much credence has traditionally been placed on the four-stage model of recovery developed by Haas, Kates, and Bowden (1977; the four stages are emergency, restoration, replacement, and development). These stages were described by Haas and his colleagues as "ordered, knowable and predictable" (xxvi). However, similar to a limited but growing number of investigations on disaster recovery (Harrell-Bond 1986; Oliver-Smith and Goldman 1988; Oliver-Smith 1990) in developing countries, our data do not entirely support the Haas, Kates, and Bowden model. While the four stages are useful in understanding the dynamics of recovery and development, we found that they are not uniformly sequential and orderly for an entire impact area.

Our findings, then, suggest that it may not make sense to discuss recovery in terms of a single stage. Rather, the stage of recovery will depend on which political, economic, or other group one is a member of and the geographical location or local community in which one lives. The role of political affiliation was seen most dramatically in Jamaica, in which the allocation of recovery resources, such as roofing material, depended on whether the individual (or the community) belonged to the "right" party—that is, the party in power at the national level. We heard numerous credible stories of disaster recovery materials being distributed as a form of political patronage. While Jamaica's Building Stamp Programme was more immune from politics than most, even it suffered from the problem. In our comparison of recovery in two Jamaican parishes—one a PNP stronghold (St. James), the other a JLP stronghold (St. Thomas)—the availability of building stamps was much delayed in the PNP parish, a delay widely attributed to political party affiliation, as the central government administration was under JLP leadership. The allocation of central government resources to rebuild such government facilities as hospitals, schools, and roads was also heavily influenced by the political affiliation of the parish or community. Politics and political factors do significantly influence recovery, and the pace of recovery will vary significantly from community to community, depending on these political factors.

These findings reinforce concerns about the differential effects of disasters. It is clear that some groups, particularly the poor and poorer communities, are slower to recover from a major disaster than other groups, particularly the wealthy. This raises significant questions about equity and fairness. For many already living on the edge, a hurricane will likely deepen conditions of poverty and further exacerbate social and economic inequities. Certain poor communities clearly recovered more slowly. Impoverished Saddlers Village, on St. Kitts, is one of the most dramatic examples of the much slower recovery of a poor community. Here, restoration of basic services and the provision of disaster aid were dramatically slower than on the island as a whole. While water service for most parts of the island was restored within five days, it took some five months in Saddlers Village. Housing aid was not provided until some eight months after the disaster. Many local people interviewed strongly maintained that political reasons explained this slower allocation of aid and services. Some disaster assistance programs explicitly excluded the poorest citizens. To qualify as a recipient under Jamaica's Building Stamp Programme, one had to prove homeownership; those renting property or without clear title were generally excluded.

An Ineffectual Disaster Recovery System: The Pitfalls of Top-Down Approaches

The case studies examined here illustrate that the existing disaster recovery system is largely ineffective and faulty. In particular, our evidence suggests that top-down aid delivery programs, managed by central government and international NGOs (e.g., the Peace Corps housing rebuilding project on Montserrat, the zinc roofing program and the Building Stamp Programme on Jamaica) did not work well and were almost always unable to deliver aid that matched local needs and that built on local capacity to undertake self-directed recovery initiatives. As such, they could not address long-term development needs, which involved a complex relationship between people and their social, physical, and economic environment. Because they ignored the enormous range and variety of local needs and priorities, even well-intended programs were often counterproductive, especially for the poor. Despite the increasing number of investigations of people's social and economic conditions and behavioral responses to disasters, top-down recovery programs failed to take into account the range of factors that went into people's decisionmaking. While a program might build homes for disaster-stricken people, it might at the same time ignore or even undermine the local institutional capacity for recovery and long-term development.

Because of their vast resources, their politicized values (in the case of central governments), and their reliance on specialized skills, top-down aid delivery programs tend to be carried out without local involvement in planning and decisionmaking. People's participation is reduced to providing minimal labor in externally organized rebuilding schemes. Programs are inherently uneconomical, because they exclude the principal resources available for undertaking recovery and sustainable development actions: the people themselves, their local knowledge, and their leadership skills. Because they are unable to make use of these resources, top-down recovery programs rarely achieve their goals and often waste scarce external resources.

Potentially, the most serious criticism of top-down aid delivery programs is that, because of their concentration of power and knowledge, they are particularly vulnerable to political manipulation by powerful groups, especially in the case of central government programs. Recovery aid becomes an instrument for maintaining the status quo or for actually making the poor more vulnerable. Disaster recovery and delivery systems are thus motivated more by political and economic self-interest than by humanitarian motives. Central government programs, and sometimes external NGO programs, tend to disregard information about the needs and capacities of local people, especially the poor and their organizations, either through outright repression or through simple neglect. The role of autonomous local organizations in recovery and, by implication, in sustainable development initiatives is inhibited or even undermined, which serves to repress political consciousness and challenges to the existing power structure.

While most top-down government disaster aid programs are essentially authoritarian (like Jamaica's Building Stamp Programme and zinc distribution program), top-down NGO programs tend to be paternalistic, but they can be equally damaging to autonomous community organizations, as in the case of Montserrat. Top-down management has a strong orientation toward ideological control. Disaster has come to be synonymous with emergency relief, and relief with large international agencies. Emergency relief organizations consider each disaster an isolated event that requires a unique set of crisis-oriented societal responses. Disaster-stricken people are viewed as helpless victims in need of charity. The underlying problems associated with poverty, underdevelopment, and vulnerability to future disasters are thus not addressed. There is no real devolution of power and resources to local people and their organizations. Development organizations, which do not account for hazards in their project investment decisions, are often not included in disaster recovery operations, even though they may have well-established, community-based field networks that could be used for aid distribution and reconstruction.

Our findings support the accuracy of the interorganizational design principles identified in chapter 2. Recovery programs that promote bottom-up approaches and mechanisms do appear, for instance, to more effectively satisfy the principles of monitoring and enforcement, recognition of rights, intergovernmental coordination and communication, local control through local leadership, and resources that fit local needs and capacities.

Missed Opportunities during Recovery and Reconstruction

Understandably, following Hurricanes Gilbert and Hugo, there was a desire to return impacted people and communities to predisaster normalcy. This is a typical reaction following disasters in both developed and developing nations (Anderson and Woodrow 1989; Godschalk, Brower, and Beatley 1989). Moreover, the recovery and aid distribution programs studied here did not place a high priority on, or incorporate adequate procedures for, monitoring mitigation measures. Much of the housing reconstruction occurred with little adherence to official building codes. Rebuilding on Jamaica, for instance, usually happened in the informal housing section, especially in rural areas and well outside of the existing building permitting and regulatory system. Opportunities to relocate people and structures out of floodplain and high-risk locations were generally not taken.

One important measure of the success of recovery and administration is whether people and property are safer than they were before the event. Each disaster offers opportunities to rebuild and reconstruct with more attention to safety (as well as other objectives). In many of the places examined in this study, recovery and reconstruction failed by this measure, suggesting the need to give greater attention to mitigation in the Caribbean, both before and following disaster events. A range of mitigation measures must be incorporated, including building codes and construction standards, more effective land use and community planning, and environmental management measures that reduce vulnerability.

Building and Development Control

The hurricane damage examined in this study illustrates that Caribbean island nations currently have a limited capability to influence the quality and location of development and growth. Many structures and entire communities are located in high-risk locations, and few opportunities to relocate or prevent rebuilding in these risky areas were taken advantage of in the aftermath of the hurricanes of the late 1980s.

These disasters illustrate, as well, that much of the construction and reconstruction occurring in the Caribbean does not adhere to basic building codes and construction standards. Typical of the situation in many developing nations, there is a stark contrast between the requirements or standards on the books and what is actually enforced. All of the case study nations had officially adapted the Caribbean Uniform Building Code before the hurricanes, but it appears to have been only occasionally enforced. The mere adoption of codes and regulation, without a system or framework for enforcement and implementation, will ultimately be ineffective.

Linkage

We found in the case studies examined here a number of opportunities to link disaster recovery and reconstruction, and also predisaster mitigation, with long-term, sustainable development—or with other important issues of perhaps greater political saliency. Long-term, sustainable development would include reduced environmental degradation (e.g., deforestation, soil erosion, habitat degradation) and improved housing, living conditions, and community services.

Such linkages would have enhanced the political importance and feasibility of disaster reduction programs but generally did not occur in the cases we examined. One positive example was on Montserrat. Here, efforts were made to link funding for housing recovery to other long-term development initiatives in the community of Streatham. Because of the greater community capacity that developed following the storm (in constructing and repairing houses), the community embarked upon three additional long-term development projects—introducing new agricultural production practices, building a new community center, and improving the community's water distribution system. Postdisaster recovery funding and activities were explicitly linked, then, to these long-term development projects. Other examples from Montserrat include implementing portions of the long-term school improvement plan, replacing above-ground utility lines with more storm-resistant underground lines, and establishing a housing rehabilitation agency.

Recall from chapter 2 that linkage of external disaster recovery aid to well-established local development activities is an important design principle. Unfortunately, we found relatively few examples of this and many missed opportunities.

Disaster Planning

All of the Caribbean countries investigated in the study had engaged in some disaster planning, and all had prepared some form of a national disaster plan. Generally, these plans and the framework in place to implement them, however, were largely ineffective. Among other things, such plans can be useful in identifying in advance the recovery and reconstruction needs following a disaster, in coordinating the various agencies and organizations involved in recovery and reconstruction, and in establishing response and recovery priorities and procedures in advance of an event.

We found, though, that the plans in place prior to the hurricane suffered from several basic flaws. First, most disaster plans focused heavily on emergency response and preparedness issues and did not give adequate attention (if any) to recovery and reconstruction. It is evident, as well, that these plans were frequently "paper plans"—that is, they existed on paper but were not generally referred to or acknowledged in disaster management decisionmaking. Our case studies indicate that many public officials and decisionmakers were not aware of the content of the plans and were certainly not taking actions or making decisions based on them.

Another problem is that the plans tended to be viewed as end products rather than as dynamic instruments and the bases for ongoing dialogue and processes. The problems that arise during recovery and reconstruction are, as we have seen, tremendous, and the need for a coordinating structure are great. We did not find an adequate or successful disaster plan in any of the cases investigated, however, nor were there other mechanisms or institutions that could have provided needed coordination and guidance in the aftermath of a major disaster event.

FUTURE DIRECTIONS IN CARIBBEAN DISASTER PLANNING

Our case study analyses of recovery and reconstruction suggest a number of problems and limitations in the current system, but we believe that certain role changes and future initiatives can address many of these problems. Of key importance is the building of an effective disaster planning and recovery framework. While what follows is by no means a comprehensive list or discussion of this framework, we do identify the major implications of our research.

Sustainable Development: A New Vision

We have made the argument throughout this book that sustainable development is the overarching framework in which to consider disaster recovery and natural hazards management. While the precise definition of sustainable development is debatable, the concept presents an extremely useful framework in which to evaluate the efforts of Caribbean nations, external donor organizations, and others to promote long-term recovery from natural disasters. While disagreement exists about what sustainable development includes or how it might be defined, achieving a pattern of human settlement that generally keeps people and property out of harm's way is increasingly viewed as an essential element. Land use patterns that fail to acknowledge the location of high-risk areas (e.g., floodplains, steep sloping terrain, and shoreline erosion zones) are not sustainable. And housing construction not built to withstand predictable physical forces (e.g., likely hurricane winds) is also not sustainable.

The concept of sustainability and sustainable development also offers a useful framework for integrating hazard reduction with other social and environmental goals. A new development project or public investment should be evaluated simultaneously by a number of sustainability criteria. Does the project provide for a sustainable use of, and relationship to, the environment and natural resources (e.g., does it minimize energy consumption, does it protect renewable resources, does it preserve biodiversity)? Does it address social needs and provide for a high quality of life? Does it provide for the needs of all social, ethnic, and income groups and for a just and equitable distribution of social resources?

Sustainability and sustainable development, moreover, explicitly calls for the adoption of a much longer decisionmaking time frame. Especially in developing countries (though certainly also in the developed world), short-term needs and considerations are frequently given priority. Actions that satisfy a short-term goal or need—such as allowing deforestation and environmental degradation to permit the expansion of agriculture—may make little sense when long-term goals and needs are considered (e.g., when the costs of soil erosion, loss of fresh drinking water, and increased flooding are considered). Sustainable development, as the now famous Bruntdland report definition suggests, is development that meets the needs of the present without compromising the ability of future generations to meet their needs (WCED 1987).

Particularly foolhardy are short-term actions that destroy or undermine natural ecosystems and that encourage or facilitate long-term growth and development patterns that put people and property in harm's way. An initial and primary point, then, is that sustainable development requires substantial attention to natural hazards both before and after disaster events.

A New Role for External Donor Organizations

A sustainable development focus for disaster recovery and mitigation implies commitment to a broad developmental process, which necessitates a different role for outside donor organizations than they currently play. While aid provided in the aftermath of a devastating natural disaster can be helpful, often its focus is on providing a short-term fix and dealing with immediate needs. While addressing short-term postdisaster needs (like shelter and water) is important, such aid could be, at the same time, contributing to broader, sustainable development goals and to reducing long-term exposure to natural hazards.

The evidence suggests that external donor organizations must expand their focus in several fundamental ways. External development agencies, such as the United States Agency for International Development and the World Bank, must increasingly incorporate natural disasters and natural hazards into the projects and programs they fund. Some of their projects not only are silent on the issues of disaster vulnerability but may actually serve to increase exposure and vulnerability. International disaster assistance organizations, like the International Red Cross and the Red Crescent, must take a more proactive view of disasters—promoting projects, programs, and aid distribution that do not simply treat the symptoms (i.e., immediate response and recovery needs) but address the underlying causes of disasters. Both types of organizations need to redirect their emphases toward nurturing and expanding long-term community development and in helping communities build the institutions and capabilities to reduce vulnerability and to deal, themselves, with recovery from future disasters.

Promoting Bottom-Up Recovery

A primary conclusion of our study is that a bottom-up, community-based approach to recovery will frequently be more effective and equitable than the traditional top-down approach. The definitive characteristic of the bottom-up approach documented in our case studies (Streatham Village, for example) is that the principal responsibility and authority for carrying out the program rested with a community-based organization. Because community-based NGOs are deeply rooted in the society and culture of a locality, they enable people to express their real needs and priorities, allowing problems to be correctly defined and responsive aid and development programs to be designed.

The presence of community-based NGOs also allowed people to respond to disaster situations in a timely and effective manner. In various instances (like Streatham Village on Montserrat and Christian Children's Fund projects on Antigua), the distribution of assistance by community-based NGOs was just and efficient, eliminating bureaucratic delays and politically driven corruption. An interesting comparison with the typical top-down approach is that, in one program (Streatham Village), a community-based participant was sent to explain to donors in Canada how long-term disaster recovery is a bottom-up, organization-building, and empowerment process and not solely donations of materials and food to helpless victims.

The cases show that the principal resource available for recovery linked to long-term development is the people, themselves, and their local knowledge and expertise. Through mobilizing this resource, positive results could be achieved through modest aid inputs. Under the control of community-based NGOs, resources were used efficiently and effectively. Community-based NGOs were typically multisectoral, combining disaster reconstruction with other development activities like housing, agriculture, and environmental protection.

The support activities of external NGOs and central governments were far more effective in community-based programs than in top-down programs. For example, the Streatham Village and CCF projects show how technical assistance and training served to reinforce and strengthen local organizational capacity, which in turn permitted the implementation of recovery, reconstruction, mitigation, and various developmental measures.

Some programs (Saddlers Village, the Lions and Rotary Clubs on St. Kitts, CCF on Antigua and Nevis, Streatham Village on Montserrat) show how disaster was viewed as a unique opportunity for change and brought into focus problems that normally are obscure and low in salience. The postdisaster recovery period offers a time to stimulate not only local organization capacity-building efforts for immediate concerns related to recovery but long-term development as well. These bottom-up approaches not only led to reconstructing damaged housing and public facilities but also induced change in the social, economic, and political relations that underlie sustainable development. They reinforced organizations, built up cooperative networks, and encouraged awareness. In this way, they increased people's potential for reducing their vulnerability to future disasters and to conditions of impoverishment.

The most interesting bottom-up approaches were those in which external organizational efforts supported and complemented community-based NGO activities through devolution of power and resources to the local level. Antigua's Disaster Relief Committee was widely viewed as successful in involving a cross-section of outside and local organizational participants. The committee was established outside of the central government. It had a separate identity and authority and was not perceived to be politically motivated in aid acquisition and distribution. Foreign donor organizations were thus supportive of this organization and recognized its legitimacy in handling aid. Local NGO organizations were represented as well, which allowed for expression of local needs and capacities. In another case, recovery was accelerated, especially for the poor, once the Rehabilitation Unit was established on Montserrat. The unit allowed for Montserrat local organizations to take control of the recovery effort, which had been dominated by external donor organizations.

Overcoming Politics

Politics is not necessarily a bad thing, but in the Caribbean countries we examined the allocation of scarce postdisaster resources presented certain problems. It led to differential distribution of aid, differential local recovery, and significant questions about equity and fairness. The significance of politics was perhaps most dramatically seen on Jamaica, where the division between the JLP and the PNP is sharp and contentious. The allocation of virtually everything, including disaster aid, is subject to these political divisions, and a sensitivity to political divisions is essential in designing mechanisms for distributing aid.

Despite its problems, the Jamaican Building Stamp Programme did manage to achieve a high degree of political neutrality. The program's aid allocation system was based on fairly clear and objective standards, its damage assessment was done (and perceived to be done) in a fairly neutral fashion (although there were certainly problems with it), and the allocation of aid was through the local private sector (i.e., local building supply stores).

Many of the other recommendations of our study would also enhance the goal of political neutrality. A detailed, usable, disaster plan, that lays out in advance coordinating responsibilities, required actions, and recovery and reconstruction criteria might minimize (though certainly would not eliminate) the role of politics.

Making Disaster Plans Relevant

The experiences documented here suggest that major reforms are needed in national disaster plans. These plans can provide an important coordinating framework following a natural disaster. More attention should be paid to making public officials, public and private sector organizations, and the general citizenry aware of the existence of these plans and how they can be useful during response and recovery. The plans, as we have seen, tend to focus primarily on preparedness and emergency response plans; they should be enhanced to explicitly address recovery and reconstruction.

We believe there will be many postdisaster opportunities for rebuilding in safer ways and in safer locations, and disaster plans could start to identify such opportunities in advance. A disaster plan should also be seen as a long-term process of dealing with natural disasters and not as a static end product. Plans should be widely disseminated and frequently updated. In this way, plans will stay current and relevant and are more likely to be implemented following a disaster.

Achieving Fair and Equitable Recovery

A considerable question has been raised by the case studies about the fairness of recovery and reconstruction. Poorer people and communities, for instance, are less likely to receive their fair share of disaster assistance or to receive it in a timely fashion.

Any program for disaster recovery, we believe, must incorporate the goal of social equity. Criteria and procedures for damage assessment and allocation of short-term and long-term disaster assistance should treat in an equal fashion all regions, communities, and socioeconomic groups, unless there are clear and compelling reasons to do otherwise. Indeed, resource needs may be greatest in poorer communities, in which the ability of residents to recover on their own may be much lower. Any disaster plan or recovery framework must explicitly address the issue of equity and strive to bring it about.

A number of specific actions might enhance equity in recovery. One is giving greater responsibility to locally based, nongovernmental organizations, which are likely to be more insulated from political pressure than government organizations and to have a better understanding of the needs of individuals and groups than an external organization.

In many Caribbean countries, the issue of land tenure needs to be addressed. Our cases illustrate that people without secure land tenure— those living in squatter communities—frequently did not receive the same level of disaster assistance as others. The Building Stamp Programme on Jamaica, for example, was restricted to those who could show property ownership. Those living illegally in squatter settlements were also less likely to seek out disaster assistance. Moreover, these tended to be the poorest of residents, in the poorest of communities, and frequently at the greatest risk in the wake of natural disasters. Achieving equity in disaster planning will require some strategy for dealing with the land tenure issue. Among the possibilities are (1) designing aid programs that are not contingent on showing land or property ownership, (2) land tenure reform to redistribute land or property ownership, and (3) special outreach programs designed to reach squatter communities.

TOWARD SUSTAINABLE DEVELOPMENT: STRATEGIES FOR LONG-TERM MITIGATION

Reducing the long-term exposure of people and property to natural disasters in the Caribbean will require a number of specific mitigation actions. These are actions that, for effective implementation, will require the concerted efforts and support of a number of actors, public and private. We discuss several of the more important of these below.

Strengthening the Housing Stock

Obviously, the low quality of the housing in much of the Caribbean region, and its vulnerability to wind and other forces of nature, is a major cause of damage and loss of life. In countries such as Jamaica, general conditions of poverty translate into large numbers of people living in housing that do not fare well in a hurricane or other natural disaster.

Substantial attention, then, will need to be given to strategies for strengthening the housing stock, both new construction and the retrofitting of existing units. There are many obstacles to these strategies in developing countries. The existence of an official building code is not an issue. The Caribbean Uniform Building Code has been widely adopted, and if it were implemented and enforced, it would go far in strengthening the building stock in the region. The problem in most cases is one of enforcement, and much greater attention needs to be directed here. There is an especially strong need for trained personnel and for an administrative structure for enforcing the code. In many urban areas in the Caribbean there already typically exists some form of construction permitting and inspection process.

But improvement in code implementation and enforcement is not an appropriate strategy in many parts of the Caribbean, since much of the construction (and reconstruction) occurs in the informal housing sector and does not go through a code review and inspection process. This is especially true in rural areas, which are often outside the jurisdiction and purview of permit review. Some of this housing is illegally built. The informal housing sector can be approached through programs to train carpenters and craftsmen and building trade workers in building strengthening techniques and designs and through the education of the general public about appropriate building techniques.

The informal housing sector in the Caribbean is even larger following a disaster. We found substantial anecdotal evidence that, on Jamaica following Gilbert, a large proportion of the recovery and rebuilding took place without any government review or approval. Indeed, in many cases the housing occupants, themselves, scavenged building materials and made the repairs. We also noted that, because of the large amount of repair and reconstruction work available and the higher demand for building tradesmen, many inexperienced and unskilled individuals were employed in rebuilding. There is a special need to find effective ways to promote mitigation and building strengthening during this informal rebuilding process. Local-based education and training programs are, again, one potentially effective approach. The efforts on Montserrat following Hugo, described in chapter 4, are an example of this approach, albeit on a small scale. A similar training program was instituted on Jamaica, through the Hexcell House program, but the program was short-lived and also relatively small.

Strengthening the Caribbean housing stock will require strategies for both the formal and informal housing sectors. External aid organizations should consider the long-term investments in disaster reduction yielded by developing programs that lead to safer building practices. It is important to remember as well that poverty has much to do with vulnerability to natural disasters. Much of the population of the Caribbean basin lives in the most rudimentary of housing—frequently, single-room wooden structures with tin roofs. Poverty prevents them from living in stronger, more substantial structures resistant to the forces of wind and water. Housing recovery programs, like Jamaica's Building Stamp Programme and the Hexcell House program, can go only so far in improving the postdisaster housing stock, given residents' low incomes and resources. Similarly, programs to educate people about appropriate building practices can go only so far, in light of these conditions. This further reinforces the importance of overall economic development programs and efforts to alleviate the basic underlying problem of poverty.

Sustainable Land Use Patterns

Generally, a natural hazard does not exist until people and property are placed in harm's way. At this point, a natural process or function becomes a hazard and, most likely, eventually a disaster. Our study finds that much of the past and recent development in these Caribbean nations has occurred in the most dangerous locations, for instance in low-lying shoreline and inland flood-prone areas.

Given the context of developing countries, promoting sustainable land use may require a number of different efforts. Greater attention at the national level should be given to land use planning. Countries such as Jamaica do have a rudimentary land use planning framework, modeled after the British town planning system. Although such systems, where they do exist, are quite limited in scope and effectiveness, they are useful regulatory and management frameworks on which to build. One problem has been a limited understanding of the spatial extent of the natural hazards present. Among the specific areas that should receive attention are the preparation of systematic and accurate maps of hazards zones (see below), indicating the type, magnitude, and spatial extent of hazards; expanded funding for planning and for the training of planners; and the strengthening of land use and town planning laws and of the processes through which building and development proposals are evaluated.

As with building codes, however, land use planning will have difficulty influencing the informal housing sector. It is not uncommon for squatter communities to evolve on public lands, often in the most dangerous locations—along floodplains, for example, or in areas vulnerable to mud slides and other hazards. This again suggests the need to supplement the formal procedures and processes of land use planning and control with informal mechanisms. Community-based NGOs (churches, civic groups, neighborhood organizations) have great potential in many Caribbean nations to help educate and advise about appropriate land use.

Environmental Protection and Natural Mitigation

Disaster planning can and should be integrated with environmental management and protection. The relationship between these two areas is clear, and assuming the overall goal of sustainable development, it is logical to view these goals together. First, evidence suggests that the exposure of people and property to natural disaster is greater as a result of environmental destruction. Second, many features of the natural environment serve important mitigation functions, so preserving these features is an effective disaster reduction strategy. Wetlands absorb floodwaters, for instance, while beach and dune systems serve as natural seawalls and absorb the force of surge and waves. Any long-term strategy for reducing exposure of people and property to disasters must work to preserve and protect these natural mitigative features.

Third, there are many opportunities to accomplish both environmental conservation and disaster reduction and recovery goals. Many nations in the Caribbean are beginning to take action to protect their environments and to realize that maintaining their natural heritage is important to achieving long-term economic development goals. Jamaica, for example, has established the Blue Mountain John Crow National Park, which has the potential to preserve significant parts of the island's natural heritage, to reduce and control loss of forests and vegetation, and thus to minimize erosion and flooding. A number of Caribbean countries have established parks and protected areas, which have the potential to help reduce natural disasters, and many more such areas will likely be designated or established in the future, as efforts at increasing tourism increase. However, many of these protected areas are as yet "paper" parks—established on paper with little or no management capability or personnel (e.g., see Salm and Clark 1984). Natural hazards must be taken into account in designing these parks and park systems, and sufficient resources and personnel must be allocated to ensure proper control and management.

Part of the answer here lies in expanding public awareness of, and concern about, the environment. Local and community-based environmentalism is beginning to emerge in many parts of the Caribbean. On Jamaica, for instance, a group called PEPA (Portland Environmental Protection Association) has been instrumental in expanding environmental awareness and in mobilizing local resources to oppose certain environmentally destructive practices (see Berke and Beatley 1995). Environmental education holds much promise as a strategy for expanding a political constituency supportive of sustainable development. Such educational programs are beginning to take hold in some parts of the Caribbean and are very worthy of expansion. Part of the education and objective is to promote a greater sense of causal connection between environmental destruction (e.g., deforestation) and the long-term negative results of such destruction (e.g., increased flooding).

Generally, keeping development away from wetlands, beaches, and other environmentally sensitive locations will satisfy important environmental management and protection goals (e.g., wildlife conservation and ecotourism) as well as reduce future losses from natural disasters.

Increased Understanding of Natural Hazards

One major obstacle to achieving safer, more sustainable land use patterns is the limited understanding of the location and nature of hazards. Many Caribbean nations have done little (if any) mapping of hazard zones, such as the hundred-year floodplain. Only recently, for instance, has Jamaica undertaken detailed floodplain mapping. The development of ecologically sensible floodplains cannot take place without detailed mapping. Similarly, few Caribbean nations have had their coastlines modeled to understand likely inundation levels under different hurricane landfall scenarios. Puerto Rico is a positive model and has had the SLOSH model (Sea Lake and Overland Surge from Hurricanes) applied to its coastline. This information will serve as an important basis for understanding the amount and types of property at risk, the number of people and communities at risk, likely future evacuation needs, and so on. Understanding the potential long-term effects of future sea levels is another example of important information lacking in most Caribbean nations.

Many Caribbean nations lack the funding and expertise to undertake such studies, of course. Development agencies can help in this regard. The cost of such studies should be viewed as essential investments in long-term, sustainable land use.

A Need for Indicators of Sustainability and Monitoring

While sustainable land use and development patterns can be monitored in conventional, quantitative terms (e.g., number of homes structurally strengthened or number of people relocated away from high-hazard areas), there is also a need for a new set of methods. While quantitative dimensions of sustainability and disaster recovery can be captured by some basic risk index, it is much more difficult to quantify the more qualitative dimensions of sustainability (e.g., local organizational capacity and environmental quality changes from predisaster to postdisaster stages). Rigorous investigations of such indexes have yet to be made for assessing the linkage between disaster recovery and sustainable development, but attempts in the direction of environmental quality, economic development (rather than growth), and equity have begun (Daly and Cobb 1989; Holmberg 1992; and UNDP 1991).

A parallel concern relates to the tradeoffs among natural hazard risk reduction, economic development, and the social equity dimensions of sustainability. Such tradeoffs can in practice be very difficult to make. For example, how many resources should be invested to obtain an acceptable level of future risk? Who benefits? And who should pay?

Thus far, the tools for helping to make the decisions about such tradeoffs are underdeveloped. Environmental economics, for instance, is attempting to seek a common system of measurement by ascribing values across dimensions, costs, and benefits, but this line of research is not without controversy. In particular, the dilemma arises in the tradeoffs between conflicting goals during disaster recovery. In the debates on the need for mitigation and long-term development, local people and government representatives often face major challenges over the distribution of aid that could be used by various groups (the landless poor, small businesses, upper-income residents) and for varying purposes (the protection of the natural mitigation functions of the environment, structural strengthening, building relocation).

Thus, there is room for research to make sustainabilty during disaster recovery as unambiguously measurable as conventional measures of development, like those related to economic growth (e.g., per capita income, per capita consumption). However, such measures must be accompanied by qualitative tools for making decisions. These tools should reflect ethical principles of sustainability, like intergenerational equity, recognizing ecological limits, and eradicating poverty, as discussed in chapter 1.

A key concern is to ensure that these tools can be used by local people who are most familiar with local damage patterns, local rebuilding skills, and culturally defined building materials and housing construction. Unlike central government agencies or external donor organizations, local people do not have to invest additional time and effort in monitoring. The Jamaican case, especially, revealed that local monitoring is a natural, low-cost by-product of local peoples' strong motivation to ensure that households receive their fare share of assistance. By not incorporating the knowledge of those close to the situation about aid infractions, many programs remained flawed. Indeed, it is local people struggling to recover from a disaster who most want to deter cheaters. More for some may mean less for others.

A FINAL NOTE

Any effective long-term reduction in vulnerability to natural disasters will occur through the broad, holistic framework of sustainable development. While the vision of a sustainable future remains ambiguous and in need of definition, it clearly seeks to direct people and social investments away from high-hazard areas, to protect and sustain the ecology, and to balance short-term needs and long-term goals. Ideally, each Caribbean nation would develop a strategy for sustainable development, which would include strategies for economic development, the location and timing of public investments, taxation policy, and natural resource conservation.

A sustainable development plan for Montserrat, for example, would consider a much longer time frame than a conventional development plan or land use plan—perhaps as far as five hundred years into the future. Where will people live? How will people earn their livelihoods? What will the condition of the environment be? How much risk and exposure to natural events such as hurricanes and earthquakes will be acceptable? Such a plan could pull together the many disparate national plans and policies—from tourism plans to infrastructure plans to plans laying out economic policy—that are frequently developed and implemented (if they are at all) separately.

For some Caribbean nations, there is a considerable planning foundation to build upon in developing such an integrated strategy. Jamaica, for instance, has developed a national environmental inventory and a physical development plan. Such plans would be useful in guiding the distribution of development funds and disaster assistance by development agencies like USAID and international disaster assistance organizations like the Red Cross (and such agencies could make the funding of such national sustainable development plans a priority). While merely attaching the label *sustainable* to such a national planning effort does little, a serious attempt at applying the theory and principles of sustainable development at such a level would do much to advance the long-term goal of reducing exposure to natural hazards in the Caribbean.

REFERENCES

Advisory Committee on the International Decade for Natural Disaster Reduction. 1989. *Reducing Disasters' Toll: The United States Decade for Natural Disaster Reduction.* Washington, D.C.: National Academy Press.

Anderson, Mary, and Peter Woodrow. 1989. *Rising from the Ashes: Development Strategies in Times of Disaster.* Boulder, Colo.: Westview.

Anonymous. 1989. "An Appeal to the People of the World Bank and the International Monetary Fund by Non-Governmental and Citizens Organizations on the Occasion of the 1989 World Bank/IMF Annual Meeting," September 27–28.

Antigua Red Cross. 1989. *Red Cross Report Immediately after Hurricane Hugo, 20 September 1989.* St. Johns: Antigua Disaster Relief Committee.

Ascher, William, and Robert Healy. 1990. *Natural Resource Policymaking in Developing Countries: Environment, Economic Growth, and Income Distribution.* Durham: Duke University Press.

Barker, David, and D. M. F. McGregor. 1988. "Land Degradation in the Yallas Basin, Jamaica: Historical Notes and Contemporary Observation." *Geography* 73.

Barker, David, and D. Miller. 1990. "Hurricane Gilbert: Anthropromorphising a Natural Disaster." *Area* 22.

Bates, Frederic. 1982. *Recovery, Change, and Development: A Longitudinal Study of the 1976 Guatemalan Earthquake.* Vols. 1–3. Athens: Department of Sociology, University of Georgia.

Berke, Philip, and Timothy Beatley. 1992. *Planning for Earthquakes: Risk, Policy, and Politics.* Baltimore: Johns Hopkins University Press.

Berke, Philip, and Timothy Beatley. 1995. "Sustaining Jamaica's Forest: The Protected Area Resource Conservation Program." *Environmental Management* 19.

Berke, Philip, Timothy Beatley, and Clarence Feagin. 1991. "Household Recovery following Hurricane Gilbert: St. James and St. Thomas Parishes, Jamaica." Hazard Reduction and Recovery Center, Texas A&M University.

Berke, Philip, Timothy Beatley, and Clarence Feagin. 1993. "Hurricane Gilbert

Strikes Jamaica: Linking Disaster Recovery to Development." *Coastal Management* 21.

Berke, Philip, Jack Kartez, and Dennis Wenger. 1993. "Recovery after Disaster: Achieving Sustainable Development, Mitigation, and Equity." *Disasters* 17.

Bolin, Robert. 1982. *Long-Term Family Recovery from Disaster*. Monograph 36. Boulder: Institute of Behavioral Sciences, University of Colorado.

Bolin, Robert, and Patricia Bolton. 1983. "Recovery in Nicaragua and the U.S.A." *International Journal of Mass Emergencies and Disasters* 1.

————. 1986. *Race, Religion, and Ethnicity in Disaster Recovery*. Monograph 42. Boulder: Institute of Behavioral Sciences, University of Colorado.

Brownell, Jennifer, and Arnie Paul. 1989. *Wild Gilbert and Development NGOs*. Kingston, Jamaica: Association of Development Agencies.

Buffong, Vernon L. R. 1989, "Considerations after Hurricane Hugo—Health Sector, Montserrat, West Indies." Plymouth, Montserrat.

Burby, Raymond, Beverly Cigler, Steven French, Ed Kaiser, Jack Kartez, Dale Roenigk, D. Weist, and Dale Whittington. 1991. *Sharing Environmental Risks: How to Control Government Losses in Natural Disasters*. Boulder, Colo.: Westview.

Caribbean Environmental Programme. 1989. "Assessment of the Economic Impacts of Hurricane Gilbert on Coastal and Marine Resources of Jamaica." United Nations Environmental Programme, Kingston.

Cernea, Michael, ed. 1991. *Putting People First: Sociological Variables in Rural Development*. New York: Oxford University Press.

Chang, S. 1983. "Disasters and Federal Policy." *Urban Affairs Quarterly* 14.

Chin, N. W., and W. H. Suite. 1989. *Hurricane Hugo: A Survey of Damage in Montserrat and Antigua*. Port-of-Spain, Trinidad: National Emergency Management Agency.

Clark, Colin. 1989. "Jamaica." In *Urbanization, Planning, and Development in the Caribbean*, ed. Robert Potter. London: Mansell.

Consulting Engineers Partnership. 1989. *Hurricane Hugo in Montserrat: Reconnaissance Report on the Structural Damage*. New York: United Nations Development Programme.

CRDC (Construction and Resource Development Centre). 1990. *Evaluation of Reconstruction Efforts in the Housing Stock*. Kingston, Jamaica.

Cuffe, O'Niel. 1989. *Impact of Hurricane Gilbert on Selected Informal Settlements and Their Effects on Rebuilding*. Kingston, Jamaica: Regional Housing and Urban Development Office, USAID.

Cuny, Frederick. 1983. *Disasters and Development*. Oxford: Oxford University Press.

Daly, Herman, and John Cobb. 1989. *For the Common Good*. Boston: Beacon.

Davies, Omar, and Michael Witter. 1989. "The Development of the Jamaican Economy since Independence." In *Jamaica in Independence: Essays on Early Years*, ed. Rex Nettleford. Kingston: Heinemann Caribbean.

Drabek, Thomas. 1986. *Human System Responses to Disasters: An Inventory of Sociological Findings*. New York: Springer-Verlag.

Drabek, Thomas, and W. Key. 1984. *Conquering Disaster: Family Recovery and Long-Term Consequences.* New York: Irvington.

Dynes, Russell R. 1970. *Organized Behavior in Disaster.* Lexington, Mass.: Heath Lexington.

Dynes, Russell, E. L. Quarantelli, and Dennis Wenger. 1990. "The Organizational and Public Response to the September 1985 Earthquake in Mexico City, Mexico." Disaster Research Center, University of Delaware.

Elster, John. 1989. *The Cement Society: A Study of Social Order.* Cambridge: Cambridge University Press.

ESCAP (Economic and Social Commission for Asia and the Pacific). 1983. "Damage Trends in the ESCAP Region." *Water Resources Journal* (June).

Friesema, H. P., et al. 1979. *Aftermath: Communities after Natural Disasters.* Beverly Hills, Calif.: Sage.

Geipel, R. 1982. *Disaster and Reconstruction: The Friuli (Italy) Earthquakes of 1976.* London: Allen and Unwin.

Gibbs, Tony. 1989. *Hurricane Hugo in Antigua: Reconnaissance Report on the Structural Damage.* Bridgetown, Barbados: United Nations Development Programme.

Gibbs, Tony, and Herbert Brown. 1989. *Hurricane Hugo in Montserrat: Reconnaissance Report on the Structural Damage.* Bridgetown, Barbados: United Nations Development Programme.

Glickman, Theodore, and Dominic Golding. 1992. "Recent Trends in Major Natural Disasters and Industrial Accidents." *Resources* (Summer).

Godschalk, David, David Brower, and Timothy Beatley. 1989. *Catastrophic Coastal Storms: Hazard Mitigation and Development Management.* Durham: Duke University Press.

Gran, Guy. 1983. *Development by People: A Citizen Construction of a Just World.* New York: Praeger.

Haas, Eugene, Robert Kates, and M. Bowden. 1977. *Reconstruction following Disaster.* Cambridge: MIT Press.

Hagman, Gunnar, et al. 1984. *Prevention Better than Cure: Report on Human and Environmental Disasters in the Third World.* Stockholm: Swedish Red Cross.

Hamilton, Robert. 1992. "In Planning for Sustainable Development and Environmental Protection, Don't Overlook the Threat of Natural Hazards." *Natural Hazards Observer* (July).

Harrell-Bond, E. 1986. *Imposing Aid.* Oxford: Oxford University Press.

Havlick, Spencer. 1986. "Third World at Risk: Building for Calamity." *Environment* 28.

Holmberg, Johan, ed. 1992. *Making Development Sustainable.* Washinton, D.C.: Island.

Houghton. G., G. J. Jenkins, and J. J. Ephram, eds. 1990. *Climate Change: The IPCC Scientific Assessment.* New York: Cambridge University Press.

IMPERU, Ltd. 1989. *Preliminary Technical Assessments and Impacts Evaluation of Hurricane Gilbert.* Kingston, Jamaica.

International Federation of Red Cross and Red Crescent Societies. 1993. *World Disasters Report.* Geneva.

International Institute for Environmental Development. 1987. *Jamaica: Country Environmental Profile.* Kingston: Ministry of Agriculture, Natural Resources Conservation Division, and Ralph Field Associates.

Jamaica Planning Institute. 1991. "People." *Newsletter of the Population Policy Coordinating Committe* (May).

Karadawi, A. A. 1983. "Constraints on Assistance to Refugees: Some Observations from the Sudan." *World Development* 11.

Kartez, Jack. 1984. "Crisis Response Planning." *Journal of the American Planning Association* 50.

————. 1991. "Problems and Alternatives in the Disaster Assistance System." In *Draft Study on Improving Earthquake Mitigation.* Washington, D.C.: Federal Emergency Management Agency.

Kingdon, John. 1986. *Agendas, Alternatives, and Public Policies.* Boston: Little, Brown.

Korten, David. 1980. "Community Organization and Rural Development: A Learning Process Approach." *Public Administration Review* (September–October).

Kreimer, Alcira, and M. Munasinghe, eds. 1991. *Managing Natural Disasters and the Environment.* Washington, D.C.: World Bank.

Kunreuther, Howard. 1973. *Recovery from Natural Disasters: Insurance or Federal Aid?* Washington, D.C.: American Enterprise Institute for Public Policy.

Levi, M. 1988. *Of Rule and Revenue.* Berkeley: University of California Press.

Lim, Gill-Chim. 1987. "Housing Policies for the Urban Poor in Developing Countries." *Journal of the American Planning Association* 53.

Lissner, J. 1977. *The Politics of Altruism: A Study of the Political Behavior of Development Agencies.* Geneva: Lutheran World Federation.

McCarthy, Lloyd, D. 1991. "Land Development Control: A Comparative Study of American and Jamaican Planning." Senior thesis, University of Virginia.

Mader, George. 1980. *Land Use Planning after Earthquakes.* Portola Valley, Calif.: William Spangle and Associates.

Markum, E. A., and Howard Fergus. 1989. *Hugo versus Montserrat.* London: New Beacon.

Mitchell, James K. 1989. "Where Might the International Decade for Natural Disaster Reduction Concentrate Its Activities? A Comparative Analysis of Disaster Data Sets." IDNDR 2. Natural Hazards Research and Applications Information Center, University of Colorado.

————. 1992. "Natural Hazards and Sustainable Development." Paper presented at the Natural Hazards Research and Applications Workshop, Boulder, Colorado.

Molina, Medardo. 1989. "The Process of Flood Hazard Mapping in Jamaica." In *Proceedings: Meeting of Experts on Hazard Mapping in the Caribbean,* ed. David Barker. Kingston: Pan Caribbean Disaster Preparedness and Prevention Project.

Nanjira, Daniel. 1991. "Disasters and Development in East Africa." In Kreimer and Munasinghe.

National Disaster Emergency Committee Office of St. Kitts and Nevis. 1989. "Field Notes on Hurricane Hugo." Basseterre, St. Kitts.

NOAA (National Oceanic and Atmospheric Administration). 1989. *Natural Disaster Survey Report: Hurricane Hugo, September 10–22, 1989.* Washington, D.C.: U.S. Department of Commerce.

OAS (Organization of American States). 1990. *Disasters, Planning, and Development: Managing Natural Hazards to Reduce Loss.* Washington, D.C.

Oliver-Smith, Anthony. 1990. "Post-Disaster Housing Reconstruction and Social Inequality: A Challenge to Policy and Practice." *Disasters* 14.

Oliver-Smith, Anthony, and Robert Goldman. 1988. "Planning Goals and Urban Realities: Post-Disaster Reconstruction in a Third World City." *City and Society* 2.

Ostrom, Elinor. 1990. *Governing the Commons: The Evolution of Institutions for Collective Action.* Cambridge: Cambridge University Press.

Pan Caribbean Disaster Prevention and Preparedness Project. 1989. "Briefing of Interested Delegations following Hurricane Hugo." Office of the United Nations Disaster Relief Coordinator, New York.

Pantelic, J. 1991. "The Link between Reconstruction and Development." In Kreimer and Munasinghe.

Paudey, G. 1990. "Development and Disasters: Tasks during the International Decade of Natural Disaster Reduction." *Disaster Management* 3.

Pereau, Jena. 1990. "First/Third World and Disasters in Context: A Study of the Saragosa and Wichita Falls, Texas, Tornadoes." Hazard Reduction and Recovery Center, Texas A&M University.

Perry, Ronald, and H. Hirose. 1983. "Volcanic Eruptions and Functional Change: Parallels in Japan and the United States." *International Journal of Mass Emergencies and Disasters* 1.

Petak, William, and Arthur Atkisson. 1982. *Natural Hazard Risk Assessment and Public Policy: Anticipating the Unexpected.* New York: Springer-Verlag.

Potter, Robert B., ed. 1989. *Urbanization, Planning, and Development in the Caribbean.* London: Mansel.

Quarentelli, E. L. 1989. "A Review of the Literature in Disaster Recovery Research." Disaster Research Center, University of Delaware.

Quarentelli, E. L., Russell Dynes, and Dennis Wenger. 1992. "The Organizational and Public Response to the September 1989 Earthquake in Mexico City, Mexico." Disaster Research Center, University of Delaware.

Redclift, M. 1987. *Sustainable Development: Exploring the Contradictions.* New York: Methuen.

Rodriguez, M. L. 1990a. *Antigua National Disaster Plan.* St. Johns: Pan Caribbean Disaster Preparedness and Prevention Project, .

———. 1990b. *Emergency Management Assistance to Antigua.* St. Johns: Pan Caribbean Disaster Preparedness and Prevention Project.

Royal Academy of Engineering. 1993. *Opportunities for British Involvement in the International Decade for Natural Disaster Reduction.* London.

Rubin, Claire. 1991. "Recovery from Disaster." In *Emergency Management: Principles and Practices for Local Governments,* ed. Thomas Drabek and G. Hoetmer. Washington, D.C.: International City Managers Association.

Rubin, Claire, M. Saperstein, and Daniel Barbee. 1985. *Community Recovery from a Major Disaster.* Monograph 41. Boulder: Institute of Behavioral Sciences, University of Colorado.

Salm, R. J., and J. R. Clark. 1984. *Marine and Coastal Protected Areas: A Guide for Planners and Managers.* Gland, Switzerland: IUCN.

Sewell, John. 1989. "No Longer a Tradeoff." *Foundation News* (September–October).

Shepard, John B. 1988. "Is the Risk of a Major Earthquake in Kinston Increasing?" *Journal of the Geographic Society of Jamaica* 24.

Sitarz, Daniel, ed. 1993. *Agenda 21: The Earth Summit Strategy to Save Our Planet.* Covelo, Calif.: Island.

Slovic, Paul, Howard Kunreuther, and Gilbert White. 1974. "Decision Processes, Rationality, and Adjustment to Natural Hazards." In *Natural Hazards: Local, National, Global,* ed. Gilbert White. New York: Oxford University Press.

Smelser, N. 1962. *Theory of Collective Behavior.* New York: Free Press.

Solo, T-M. 1991. "Rebuilding the Tenements: Issues in El Salvador's Earthquake Reconstruction Program." *Journal of the American Planning Association* 57.

St. Kitts and Nevis National Disaster Preparedness and Prevention Committee. 1989a. *St. Kitts and Nevis National Disaster Plan.* Basseterre, Office of the Prime Minister.

———. 1989b. *St. Kitts Volcanic Emergency Plan, Annex 2.* Basseterre, Office of the Prime Minister.

Sutphen, Sandra. 1983. "Lake Elisnore Disaster: The Slings and Arrows of Outrageous Fortune." *Disasters* 3.

Stone, Carl. 1989. "Power, Policy, and Politics in Independent Jamaica." In *Jamaica in Independence: Essays on Early Years,* ed. Rex Nettleford. Kingston: Heinemann Caribbean.

Sustainable Challenge Foundation. 1994. *Management of Sustainability: The Report on the First International Programme.* Breukelen, Netherlands: Nijenrode University.

Tomblin, John. 1982. "Social and Sociological Aspects." *Disaster Prevention and Mitigation: A Compendium of Current Knowledge* 12.

UNCHS (United Nations Commission for Human Settlements). 1990. "Post-Hugo Assessment of Rehabilitation Programme Proposals for Human Settlements Approach to Housing and Shelter in Montserrat." New York.

UNDRO (Office of the United Nations Disaster Relief Coordinator). 1989a. "Briefing of Interested Delegations following Hurricane Hugo." New York.

———. 1989b. *Case Report: Hurricane Hugo in the Caribbean.* Geneva.

———. 1991. *Mitigating Natural Disasters: Phenomena, Effects, and Options.* New York.

United Nations Development Programme. 1991. *Human Development Report 1991*. Oxford. Oxford University Press.

United Way (of Santa Cruz County). 1991. *Greater Bay Disaster Preparedness Planning Project*. Capitola, Calif.

Uphoff, Norman. 1986. *Local Institutional Development: An Analytical Sourcebook with Cases*. West Hartford, Conn.: Kumarian.

———. 1991. "Fitting Projects to People." In Cernea.

USAID (United States Agency for International Development). 1989. *Shelter Sector Assistance for Disasters: Lessons Learned from Hurricane Gilbert*. Kingston.

U.S. Office of Technology Assessment. 1993. *Planning for an Uncertain Climate*. Washington, D.C.: Government Printing Office.

Wenger, Dennis. 1978. "Community Response to Disaster: Functional and Structural Alterations." *Disaster Theory and Research*, ed. E. L. Quarentelli. Beverly Hills, Calif.: Sage.

Wilson, R. 1991. *Rebuilding after the Loma Prieta Earthquake in Santa Cruz*. Washington, D.C.: International City Management Association.

Wint, Elinor, and A. Piersenne. 1984." A Socioeconomic Profile of Jamaica." In *Culture, Race, and Class in the Commonwealth*. Kingston, Jamaica: Department of Intramural Studies, University of West Indies–Mona.

WCED (World Commission on Environment and Development). 1987. *Our Common Future*. Oxford: Oxford University Press.

World Bank. 1990. *The World Bank and the Environment*. Washington, D.C.

———. 1993. *Jamaica: Economic Issues for Environmental Management*. Washington, D.C.

Yin, Robert. 1984. *Case Study Research: Design and Methods*. Beverly Hills, Calif.: Sage.

Young, John. 1990. *Sustaining the Earth: The Story of the Environmental Movement, Its Past Efforts and Future Challenges*. Cambridge: Harvard University Press.

INDEX

Adaptive learning, 31–32

Agenda 21, 8, 9, 12, 13, 37

Aid delivery system: prevailing approach of, 2; sustainable development excluded from, 15–20. *See also* Disaster recovery process

Antigua, xii, 2, 6, 152, 171–74; and case studies, 20, 22; impact of Hurricane Hugo on, 152, 154–57, 160; leadership on, 167–68; linkage on, 160–61, 170–71, 173; monitoring and compliance on, 164–66, 169; organizational coordination on, 161–64; prestorm institutional context on, 153–54; recognition of local rights on, 166–67; recovery process stages on, 157–61; and resources fit, 169–70

Asian Pacific Rim countries, losses from natural disasters in, 3–4

Balancing needs and limits, principle of, 9

Barbados, research and information center on, 21–22

Barber, Martin, 18

Black market, 46; on Antigua, 166

Bottom-up recovery, 37, 185–86

Brundtland Commission report, 7, 184

Building and development control, 181

Building materials: and Antigua recovery, 163, 164, 165, 169–70; and Jamaica rebuilding, 64, 68, 69, 73; and Jamaica rebuilding (zinc sheeting), 75–78, 178–79, 180; monitoring distribution of, 40–41; and Montserrat recovery, 110; and St. Kitts and Nevis recovery, 141, 144, 146

Building Stamp Programme, Jamaica, 45, 56, 58n. 3, 60–67, 68, 70, 79, 81, 178–79, 180, 187, 188, 190

Business interests, and Peru recovery process, 29, 38–39

California, Loma Prieta earthquake in, 27, 35

Canada, national conservation strategies of, 8

Canadian University Students Organization (CUSO), 93, 97–98, 99–100, 106, 107, 109, 112–13

Caribbean Conference of Churches. *See* CCC

Caribbean hurricanes, xi, 5–6. *See also* Hurricane; *and under various hurricanes*

Caribbean region, 5–6; Eastern, 6, 21; natural hazards losses and risks in, 1, 4, 175–77; and sustainable development, 194–95

Natural hazards *(continued)*
park design, 192; understanding of, 190, 192–93
Nepal, national conservation strategies of, 8
Nevis. *See* St. Kitts and Nevis
New Orleans, and flooding, 14
New Zealand, national conservation strategies of, 8
NGOs (nongovernmental organizations): as advocates for underrepresented, 44; agenda statement of, 8; and Antigua damage assessment, 157, 163; and Antigua Disaster Relief Committee, 163, 164, 167; and Antigua National Disaster Committee, 153; and Antigua recovery, 159, 160, 166, 167, 169, 170, 171, 173; community-based, 62, 131, 185, 186, 191; and equity, 188; and interorganizational coordination, 37–38; and Jamaica damage assessment, 63; and Jamaica zinc distribution, 76, 79; and Montserrat collaboration, 97–101, 104; and Montserrat coordinating committee, 93; and Montserrat disaster plan, 83, 92, 96, 113; and Montserrat monitoring, 106–7; and Montserrat recovery, 108, 110, 114–15; and St. Kitts and Nevis monitoring and enforcement, 142; and St. Kitts and Nevis recovery, 118, 126, 127, 130, 131–34, 137, 138, 140, 143–44, 145, 147–50; and sustainable development, 7; and top-down approach, 178, 179. *See also* CCC; CCF; CUSO; External donor organizations; Red Cross
Nicaragua, 6

Organization of American States, 8
Organizational coordination. *See* Coordination, interorganizational

Pan Caribbean Disaster Preparedness and Prevention Project, 21; and Antigua, 153, 155, 167, 168, 171–72, 174; and Montserrat, 107–8, 112, 115; and St. Kitts and Nevis, 136, 147, 150, 151

Parks and protected areas, 191–92
Participation principle, 11. *See also* Equity
Peace Corps, U.S.: in Montserrat recovery, 100–101, 104, 105, 109, 111, 112–13, 114, 115; and top-down approach, 178
Peru, earthquake disaster in, 29, 32, 38–39
Philippines, economic losses from natural disasters in, 4
Planning. *See* Disaster planning; Recovery planning
Political factors: and Antigua recovery, 168; and Jamaica recovery, 23, 49, 60–61, 74–77, 79, 80, 177–78, 187; need to overcome, 186–87; and St. Kitts and Nevis recovery, 126, 132, 143, 144, 146; and top-down approach, 179
Polluter (or culpable) pays principle, 10
Population pressures in Caribbean basin, 176
Postdisaster recovery process. *See* Disaster recovery process
Poverty: disaster vulnerability from, 15, 51, 189, 190; and environmental preservation, 8; reduction of as principle, 10; top-down management as ignoring, 180; and vulnerability to natural disaster, 1, 6
Precautionary action principle, 9
Precedents, importance of, 44

Quasi-voluntary compliance, 40

Rebuilding: on Jamaica, 67–68, 69; and sustainable-development principles, 9–11
Recovery planning, 26–32; on St. Kitts and Nevis, 150, 151. *See also* disaster planning
Recovery process. *See* Disaster recovery process
Recovery strategies, on Jamaica, 60–68
Redclift, Mitchell, 7
Red Cross, 15; on Antigua, 153, 157, 159, 162, 163, 164, 165, 168, 169, 170, 171,

ABOUT THE AUTHORS

TIMOTHY BEATLEY is associate professor and former chair of the Department of Urban and Environmental Planning in the School of Architecture at the University of Virginia. He holds a Ph.D. in city and regional planning from the University of North Carolina at Chapel Hill. His primary teaching and research interests include environmental ethics, coastal management, sustainable communities, wildlife habitat conservation, and natural hazard mitigation. He is currently undertaking studies on ethics and planning focusing on natural hazards under grants from the National Science Foundation.

PHILIP R. BERKE is associate professor of land use and environmental policy in the Department of City and Regional Planning at the University of North Carolina at Chapel Hill. He has a Ph.D. from the Department of Urban and Regional Planning at Texas A&M University. His teaching and research focus on development impact assessment, land use policy, sustainable communities, and natural hazard mitigation. He is currently conducting studies on planning for hazard mitigation and sustainable communities under grants from the National Science Foundation and Lincoln Institute of Land Policy.

Other Johns Hopkins Books of Related Interest

The Energy Crisis: Unresolved Issues and Enduring Legacies
edited by David Lewis Feldman

Ethical Land Use: Principles of Policy and Planning
Timothy Beatley

Getting the Word Out in the Fight to Save the Earth
Richard Beamish

Losing Asia: Modernization and the Culture of Development
Bret Wallach

*Making Governments Plan: State Experiments in Managing
Land Use*
Raymond J. Burby, Peter J. May, *et alia*

Planning for Earthquakes: Risk, Politics, and Policy
Philip R. Berke and Timothy Beatley

*Planting Trees in the Developing World: A Sociology of
International Organizations*
Steven R. Brechin

*The Promise of Paradise: Recreational and Retirement
Communities in the United States since 1950*
Hubert B. Stroud

*Saving America's Countryside: A Guide to Rural Conservation,
Second Edition*
Samuel N. Stokes, A. Elizabeth Watson, Shelley S. Mastren

Soil Conservation in the United States: Policy and Planning
Frederick R. Steiner

Superfund: The Political Economy of Environmental Risk
John A. Hird

Water Resources Management: In Search of an Environmental Ethic
David Lewis Feldman

LIBRARY OF CONGRESS CATALOGING-IN-PUBLICATION DATA

Berke, Philip, 1951–
    After the hurricane : linking recovery to sustainable development
in the Caribbean / Philip R. Berke and Timothy Beatley.
      p.   cm.
    Includes bibliographical references and index.
    ISBN 0–8018–5624–8 (hc : alk. paper)
    1. Hurricanes—Caribbean Area. 2. Disaster relief—Caribbean
Area. 3. Sustainable development—Caribbean Area. 4. Caribbean
Area—Social conditions. 5. Caribbean Area—Economic conditions.
I. Beatley, Timothy, 1951– . II. Title.
HV635.5.B47 1997   97–115
363.34'9228'09729—dc21   CIP